TEACHING BIBLIOGRAPHY, TEXTUAL CRITICISM, AND BOOK HISTORY

TEACHING BIBLIOGRAPHY, TEXTUAL CRITICISM, AND BOOK HISTORY

Edited by
Ann R. Hawkins

LONDON
PICKERING & CHATTO
2006

Published by Pickering & Chatto (Publishers) Limited
21 Bloomsbury Way, London, WC1A 2TH

2252 Ridge Road, Brookfield, Vermont 05036, USA
www.pickeringchatto.com

BRITISH LIBRARY CATALOGUING IN PUBLICATION DATA
Teaching bibliography, textual criticism, and book history
1.Bibliography – Study and teaching   2.Criticism, Textual – Study
and teaching   3.Books – History – Study and teaching
I.Hawkins, Ann R.
010.7'1

ISBN-10: 1851968342

This publication is printed on acid-free paper that conforms to the American
National Standard for Permanence of Paper in Printed Library Materials.

New material typeset by P&C

Printed in the United Kingdom
at the University Press, Cambridge

Contents

Notes on Contributors

Martin Antonetti

Martin Antonetti is the curator of rare books in the Mortimer Rare Book Room at Smith College, where he also teaches courses in the history of the book and in contemporary artists books for the Smith College Art Department. Antonetti has written and lectured on many aspects of these fields including fine printing, the evolution of letterforms, bookbinding and book collecting. Before coming to Smith College, Antonetti was director and librarian of the Grolier Club in New York City. On the faculty of the University of Virginia's Rare Book School, Antonetti is currently president of the American Printing History Association. He took his library degree from Columbia University where he specialized in analytical bibliography and special collections librarianship.

Susanna Ashton

Susanna Ashton is an Associate Professor of English at Clemson University. She has published essays on authorship, nineteenth-century realism, library history, African American print culture, and book studies. She is author of *Collaborators in Literary America, 1870–1920* (Palgrave 2003), and her latest work, *Bound: Black Men as Book Men 1820–1920*, is forthcoming from Pennsylvania State University Press's History of the Book series. She has been a William Dean Howells Fellow at the Houghton Library, a Mark Twain Scholar in residence for the Mark Twain Society, and a Fulbright Professor of American Literature at the University College Cork, Ireland.

Timothy Barrett

Timothy Barrett is the author of two books, six videotapes and over twenty articles on the history, technique and aesthetics of hand papermaking. He has delivered more than 200 lectures nationally and internationally. Barrett joined the University of Iowa Center for the Book as its paper specialist in 1986 and served as director of the Center between 1996 and 2002. His primary research interest is in early European papermaking technology and the role of gelatin in paper permanence. He currently serves as research scientist and adjunct professor at the UICB where he oversees papermaking production, research and curriculum.

Terry Belanger

A 2005 MacArthur Foundation Fellow, Terry Belanger is University Professor and Honorary Curator of Special Collections and also Director of Rare Book School (RBS) at the University of Virginia. He has been influential in shaping the Rare Books and Manuscripts Section of the Association of College and Research Libraries, and his RBS has educated thousands of practicing librarians, booksellers, collectors, archivists, and others since its founding in 1983. He is the founder of RBS, an independent, nonprofit organization supporting the study of the history of books and printing and related subjects. Each year, RBS offers some forty five-day non-credit courses for adults on topics concerning old and rare books, manuscripts, and special collections.

Lisa Berglund

Lisa Berglund is an associate professor of English at State University of New York – Buffalo State College. She has published critical essays on Johnson's *Rambler*, Boswell's *Life of Johnson*, Tennyson's *Maud*, and Etherege's *The Man of Mode*; 'Hester Lynch Piozzi: An Annotated Bibliography'; and a review essay surveying seventeen eighteenth-century studies anthologies. She won the American Society of Eighteenth Century Studies teaching award in 1999 for her course 'Samuel Johnson and the Eighteenth-Century Reader'. Since 1988 Berglund has served as an associate editor of *The Drood Review of Mystery*, and a collection of her reviews is forthcoming from Crum Creek Press.

John Buchtel

John Buchtel was appointed Curator of Rare Books in The Johns Hopkins University's Sheridan Libraries in 2004, before which he served as Curator of Collections at Rare Book School, where he continues annually to co-teach, with Mark Dimunation, an introductory survey course, 'The History of the Book, 200-2000'. He co-curated, with Barbara Heritage, the Rare Book School exhibition 'Eyre Apparent: An Exhibition Celebrating Charlotte Brontë's Classic Novel' (7 November 2005 – 1 May 2006). In 2004, he completed his University of Virginia doctoral dissertation, 'Book Dedications in Early Modern England and the Literary Patronage of Henry, Prince of Wales (1594-1612)'.

Tatjana Takseva Chorney

Tatjana Chorney is an Assistant Professor at the English Department at Saint Mary's University in Halifax, Canada, teaching courses primarily in sixteenth- and seventeenth-century literature. Her publications include essays on Donne, satire and reading in manuscript; Milton's *Paradise Lost* and global culture; the commonplace tradition of reading in the Renaissance and in hypertext and their implications for post-secondary education in the 21st century.

Jean Lee Cole

Jean Lee Cole is an assistant professor in the Department of English at Loyola College in Baltimore, Maryland. She is author of *The Literary Voices of Winnifred Eaton: Redefining Ethnicity and Authenticity* (Rutgers, 2002); co-editor, with Maureen Honey, of *Madame Butterfly by John Luther Long and A Japanese Nightingale by Winnifred Eaton: Two Orientalist Texts* (Rutgers 2002); and compiler and editor of the *Winnifred Eaton Digital Archive* (etext.virginia. edu/eaton). She is co-editing a forthcoming collection of plays by Zora Neale Hurston. She teaches courses in American literature and gender studies.

Erik Delfino

Erik Delfino is an adjunct faculty member at the School of Library and Information Science at the Catholic University of America, where he teaches 'History of the Book' and library technology courses. He received his MLS and BA from Rutgers University. Assistant to the Director for Technology Policy (Library Services) at the Library of Congress, Delfino advises the Director on digital library developments and policy, and assists with coordination of digital projects throughout Library Services.

Mirjam M. Foot

Mirjam Foot is Emeritus Professor of Library and Archive Studies at University College, London. She is an honourary senior research fellow at the School of Advanced Study, where she currently teaches. She is the author of many books and articles on the history of bookbinding, including *Studies in the History of Bookbinding* (1993); *The History of Decorated Bookbinding in England* (with Howard Nixon, 1992); *The History of Bookbinding as a Mirror of Society* (1998), *Eloquent Witnesses* (2004), and *Bookbinders at Work: their Roles and Methods* (2006).

Ian Gadd

Lecturer in English Literature at Bath Spa University, Ian Gadd earned his D.Phil. from University of Oxford in 1999. He was Munby Fellow in Bibliography at the University of Cambridge for 1999–2000 and a Research Editor at the *Oxford Dictionary of National Biography* between 2000 and 2002. Since 2000, he has also been *DNB*'s Associate Editor for entries on the book trade between 1500-1640. He was co-editor of *Guilds, Society and Economy in London, 1450–1800* (2002) and of *John Stow (1525–1605) and the Making of the English Past (2004)*. He acted as the textual editor for Jonathan Swift's Political Writings 1711-14.

Sean C. Grass

Sean Grass is an Associate Professor of Victorian literature at Texas Tech University with special interests in the nineteenth-century novel and the Victorian literary market. He has published *The Self in the Cell: Narrating the Victorian Prisoner* (Routledge, 2003) and essays on Dickens, Wilkie Collins, Christina Rossetti, and other writers. His current work, entitled *'Portable property': Theft and the Commodification of Identity in Victorian Narrative*, studies autobiography, the mid-century literary market, and the rise of sensation fiction.

R. Carter Hailey

Carter Hailey received his PhD at the University of Virginia and teaches Medieval and Early Modern literature at the College of William and Mary; he is working on a book *On Paper: The Description and Analysis of Watermarks from the Hand-Press Period.*

Ann R. Hawkins

Ann R. Hawkins has published scholarly editions of Benjamin Disraeli's *Henrietta Temple* (1836) and *Venetia* (1837) and Marguerite Gardiner, Countess of Blessington's *Victims of Society* (1837) as well as articles on nineteenth-century writers and the book trade. Named a 2004 New Scholar by the Bibliographical Society of America, she has held fellowships from the Bibliographical Society of America and the Folger Shakespeare Library where she will guest-curate an exhibit – "Marketing Shakespeare, 1788-1806" – in 2007. An Assistant Professor of Bibliography at Texas Tech University, she is series editor for Pickering & Chatto's Book History series.

Maura Ives

Maura Ives is Associate Professor of English at Texas A&M University. She is the editor of *George Meredith's Essay on Comedy and Other New Quarterly Magazine Publications* (1998), and has published articles on bibliography and Victorian literature in *Studies in Bibliography* and *PBSA* and the *Journal of Pre-Raphealite Studies*. She is currently working on a descriptive bibliography of Christina Rossetti and a critical edition of William Thackeray's *The History of Samuel Titmarsh and the Great Hoggarty Diamond*.

Erick Kelemen

Erick Kelemen received his PhD from the University of Delaware and has taught at Widener University, Wabash College, Columbia College, and The University of Missouri. He is at work on a textbook about textual criticism for undergraduates.

Thomas E. Kinsella

Thomas E. Kinsella is Associate Professor of British Literature at the Richard Stockton College of New Jersey. He has written on bookbinding, book cloth, and on Samuel Johnson's biographers.

Together with Willman Spawn he published *Ticketed Bookbindings From Nineteenth-Century Britain*, Bryn Mawr College and Oak Knoll Press, 1999.

Matthew G. Kirschenbaum

Matthew G. Kirschenbaum is Assistant Professor of English at the University of Maryland, where he specializes in digital studies, applied humanities computing, images and visual culture, and postmodern/experimental literature. Kirschenbaum's book *Mechanisms: New Media and the New Textuality* is forthcoming from MIT Press, Spring 2007. He is local Project Director for the nora project, a multi-institutional Mellon-funded initiative to develop advanced text mining and visualization tools for digital humanities collections. He is Articles Editor for *Digital Humanities Quarterly* and sits on the Board of Directors of the Electronic Literature Organization, as well as on the editorial boards of *Postmodern Culture* and *Text Technology*.

D. W. Krummel

D. W. Krummel has been a regular instructor at Rare Book School at the University of Virginia since 1990. Earlier he was at the Newberry Library and the Library of Congress, and for thirty-five years Professor at the library school at the University of Illinois in Urbana. His writings include *Bibliographies: Their*

Aims and Methods (Mansell, 1984) and numerous studies in music bibliography and library history.

Jennifer Phegley

Jennifer Phegley is associate professor of nineteenth-century literature at the University of Missouri-Kansas City. She is the author of *Educating the Proper Woman Reader: Victorian Family Literary Magazines and the Cultural Health of the Nation* (Ohio State University Press, 2004) and co-editor of *Reading Women: Literary Figures and Cultural Icons from the Victorian Age to the Present* (University of Toronto Press, 2005).

John T. Shawcross

John T. Shawcross is Professor Emeritus of English at the University of Kentucky. His most recent publications include *Rethinking Milton Studies: Time Present and Time Past* (2005); an edition of the first edition of 'Paradise Lost' in 1667 (2006); and a collection of essays on the significance of that publication, co-edited with Michael Lieb and to be published by Duquesne University Press. Shawcross edited *The Complete Poetry of John Milton* (1970), *The Complete Poetry of Donne* (1970) and *John Milton, 1732-1801, The Critical Heritage* (1970-72). His *Milton Bibliography 1624-1799* is forthcoming from Iter/University of Toronto.

Sydney J. Shep

Dr Sydney J. Shep is Senior Lecturer in Print & Book Culture at Victoria University of Wellington, New Zealand and The Printer at Wai-te-ata Press, a letterpress and bookmaking teaching and research laboratory founded in 1962 by the late D.F. McKenzie. She teaches book history at the undergraduate and graduate level, in both the media studies and library and information studies programmes. Her innovation in combining hands-on and digital technologies was recognised with a National Tertiary Teaching Award of Excellence in 2003.

Steven Escar Smith

Dr Steven Escar Smith is Associate Dean for Advancement for the Texas A&M University Libraries and Director of the Cushing Memorial Library and Archives. He holds the C. Clifford Wendler Cushing Library Professorship and adjunct appointments on the Graduate Faculty of the English Department at Texas A&M and in the School of Library and Information Science at the University of North Texas. Author of two books and more than 30 essays and articles on bibliography and other book history topics, Smith is founder and director of the Book History at A&M Workshop, now in its fifth year, which provides students with hands-on experience in printing and its allied technologies prior to 1800.

Willman Spawn

Willman Spawn's thirty-seven-year career as conservator at the American Philosophical Society has been followed by twenty years as Honorary Curator of Bookbindings at Bryn Mawr College. He has been researching and writing on colonial American bookbinding for more than half a century.

Together with Thomas Kinsella he published *Ticketed Bookbindings From Nineteenth-Century Britain*, Bryn Mawr College and Oak Knoll Press, 1999.

Deirdre C. Stam

Deirdre C. Stam directs the Rare Book and Special Collections concentration of the MSLIS program at the Palmer School of Library Science, Long Island University. She also serves as Executive Director of the New York Center for the Book. Educated at Harvard University, Johns Hopkins University, New York University, Catholic University, and Columbia University, Dr. Stam has held numerous posts in museums, libraries, professional societies, and schools of library and information science. Her current research interests centre on education for rare book curatorship, nineteenth-century New York State book culture, and polar literature.

Daniel Traister

Daniel Traister is Curator of Research Services, at the Rare Book and Manuscript Library as well as English-language Literature Bibliographer for the Van Pelt-Dietrich Library, and Faculty in the Department of English, University of Pennsylvania. He has published many articles in bibliography, sixteenth-century literature and in rare books and special collections librarianship. With Terry Belanger, he teaches the RBS course in 'Teaching History of the Book.'

Foreword

Terry Belanger

I began to teach book history courses at Columbia University's School of Library Service (SLS) in 1971, when Dean Richard L. Darling gave me a brief to develop a master's program in rare book and special collections librarianship and antiquarian bookselling at the school.

After more than a decade of rapid expansion, new college and university teaching jobs in the humanities rapidly disappeared in the United States in the early 1970s, with the result that a number of first-rate students (caught in the PhD pipeline) devolved into our new SLS rare book program with doctorates in hand; nearly half of the other students in the early days of the Columbia rare book program came in with at least a subject master's degree. Assisted by a succession of excellent students, I set up a bibliographical laboratory to support SLS's courses in historical and descriptive bibliography, borrowing iron printing presses, foundry type, printing-house furniture, papermaking and binding equipment, and a name – the Book Arts Press – from a defunct Columbia University Libraries venture established in the 1930s by Alice Bonnell, Helmut Lehmann-Haupt, and other Columbia rare book librarians. Over the next two decades, I more or less learned how to determine format and establish a collation; make, marble, and decorate paper; set type, impose, and print on a hand press; identify and date type faces, illustration processes, and binding styles; and etch, engrave, and cut relief blocks – all in service to laboratory sessions that everyone in the rare book program was required to take.

In class, I taught book history. A recently released 30-minute black-and-white 16mm film, *The Making of a Renaissance Book* (1969) was very useful. The challenge was to find adequate readings for students to look at *outside* class. A number of grim old reliables were readily available in 1971: surveys like Lawrence Wroth's *Colonial Printer* (1931 and 1938), Lehmann-Haupt's *Book in America* (1939 and 1951), and S. H. Steinberg's *Five Hundred Years of Printing* (1951 and 1961); books on specialist topics such as Daniel Berkeley Updike's *Printing Types* (1922 and 1937); Dard Hunter's *Papermaking* (1943 and 1947);

and Edith Diehl's *Bookbinding: Its Background and Technique* (1946). There were long periodical runs of *The Library, The Papers of the Bibliographical Society of America, Studies in Bibliography,* and *The Book Collector* in the neighborhood, and G. Thomas Tanselle's indispensable articles had begun to appear in them. Some newer books had recently come along: Norma Levarie's *Art and History of Books* (1968); Harry Carter's *View of Early Typography up to about 1600* (1969); and Warren Chappell's *Short History of the Printed Word* (1970). The annual Toronto Editorial Conference, begun in 1965, had published several volumes of its proceedings, and there was even an anthology of relevant articles, *Bibliography and Textual Criticism,* edited by O M Brack, Jr and Warner Barnes (1969). Alexander Lawson's *Printing Types: An Introduction* (1971) had just been published, as had Tanselle's two-volume *Guide to the Study of United States Imprints.*

Still, it was a tough go. Among the books that were *not* yet available in 1971 were Philip Gaskell's *New Introduction to Bibliography* (1972); the Lucien Febvre/Henri-Jean Martin *Coming of the Book* (1976 in English translation); and Bamber Gascoigne's *How to Identify Prints* (1986). When it did appear, Gaskell's *New Introduction to Bibliography* was a lifesaver. *BiN: The Bibliography Newsletter* put out its first issue in 1973, establishing what the late Robert Nikirk used to call the bibliographical gutter press. Under the impetus of J. Ben Lieberman, the American Printing History Association (APHA) was founded in 1974 and held its first annual conference two years later. The monthly *Rare Book Review* (under various titles) began its long career in 1975, the year in which both Sandra Kirshenbaum's quarterly *Fine Print* and Ellen McCrady's *Abbey Newsletter* made their debuts. Robert Fleck established Oak Knoll Books in 1976; in 1977, the Library of Congress established a Center for the Book under the direction of John Y. Cole.

Elizabeth Eisenstein's *Printing Press As an Agent of Change* and Robert Darnton's *The Business of Enlightenment: A Publishing History of the Encyclopédie, 1775-1800,* both published in 1979, encouraged meat-and-potato historians to take an interest in historical bibliography; the same year saw the first issue of the APHA journal, *Printing History,* edited by Susan Otis Thompson. John Randle began publishing *Matrix* in 1981, the year in which both the Society for Textual Scholarship and the Friends of Dard Hunter were established. Rare Book School started in 1983. The long Robin Myers/Michael Harris Publishing Pathways series began in 1985 as a supplement to Michael Turner's journal, *Publishing History,* which itself had begun in 1977. *Rare Book and Manuscript Librarianship* (later *Rare Books & Manuscripts*) debuted under the editorship of Alice Schreyer in 1986, the year when the British Library published D. F. McKenzie's inaugural Panizzi Lecture. Peter Graham founded the electronic bulletin board ExLibris in 1989. Jonathan Rose's SHARP (the Society for the

History of Authorship, Reading, and Publishing) arrived in 1991, as did the videotape *Anatomy of a Book: I: Format in the Hand-Press Period.*

Columbia closed SLS, the oldest library school in the world, in 1992, and RBS moved to the University of Virginia (UVa). Walter Henry established Conservation OnLine (CoOL) in 1993. Fredson T. Bowers's *Principles of Bibliographical Description* (1949), out of print by the late 1970s, came back as a paperback edition in 1994. The Institute of English Studies at the University of London established a master's program in the history of the book in 1995, and Peter Verheyen started his Book Arts Web. Anirvan Chatterjee set up www. bookfinder.com in 1996. Consuelo W. Dutschke's Digital Scriptorium made its first appearance on the web in 1997. SHARP's first annual volume of *Book History* was published in 1998. Volume 3 (1400-1557), the first volume of *The Cambridge History of the Book in Britain* to be published, came out in 1999, edited by Lotte Hellinga and J. B. Trapp; the first volume of its American equivalent, *A History of the Book in America: The Colonial Book in the Atlantic World*, edited by Hugh Amory and David D. Hall, appeared a year later. In 2003, under the direction of Deirdre C. Stam, the Palmer School of Library and Information Science of Long Island University inaugurated a master's concentration in rare books and special collections.

Along the way, we learned about OCLC and the ESTC and OPACs, and Apples and PCs and DOS, and Telnet and Kermit and Gopher, and email and Mosaic and the World Wide Web, and video cassettes and CD-ROMs and DVDs. Thus I fumbled my pedagogical way through the final decades of the 20th century. As a teacher of book history, I had one advantage: I taught the same courses over and over again. Between 1971 and 1992 (when Columbia closed its library school and I moved self and RBS to UVa), I taught the first-semester SLS descriptive bibliography course forty-one times and the second-semester course twenty-six times. Between 1983 and 2005, I taught the RBS course on book illustration processes twenty-seven times and co-taught the introduction to descriptive bibliography course twenty-one times. At UVa, I have taught the same undergraduate book history course eighteen times since 1995. If I cannot yet claim to know what I am doing in the bibliographical classroom, at least I have an arresting record of pedagogical failure.

What I desperately needed along the way was a book like the one in your hands. Give me credit for realizing this: in 2003, Daniel Traister and I co-taught an RBS course called "Teaching the History of the Book." Among the twelve students in this course was a ball of fire from Texas named Ann Hawkins; her classmates included Lisa Berglund, John Buchtel, Jean Lee Cole, Erik Delfino, and Deirdre Stam – all of whom are contributors to *Teaching Bibliography, Textual Criticism, and Book History*. (While I am pointing with pride, I also mention that of the other contributors to this book, Martin Antonetti, Timothy Barrett, Mirjam Foot, D. W. Krummel, and Willman Spawn have all taught RBS courses (most of them many times), and that Ian Gadd will begin to do so in 2006.

I have read the essays in this book with pleasure and profit, and I commend them to you. My own teaching would have been greatly improved if I had had access to a resource like this one available to me in 1971, when I first began offering courses in the field.

Introduction: Towards a Pedagogy of Bibliography

Ann R. Hawkins

> Case Studies aspire to science. Stories of teaching
> and learning aspire to poetry.[1]

I'd like to start by considering this volume's unwieldy title: teaching bibli-ography, textual criticism, and book history. I fumbled about for a shorter, hipper, sexier title, something pithy and smart. But in describing our field, I was thwarted by 'interdisciplinarity run riot' (to co-opt a phrase from Robert Darnton[2]) – by history of books, history of the book, print culture, manu-script circulation, readers and reading, textuality, materiality, textual studies, textual editing, documentary editing, descriptive or analytical bibliography, authorship, etc. – in other words, by the diversity of terms practitioners use to describe their courses and course contents. Would a teacher wanting ideas for using textual criticism know to look at a book whose title only included book history? Would a teacher wanting ideas about print culture (who would look for book history in a title) know that bibliography included her interests? and so forth.

The most elegant solution would likely have been to call the volume simply *Teaching Bibliography*, alluding to D. F. McKenzie's term in his 1985 Panizzi lectures, the 'sociology of the book' which includes not only its history but its making and its continuing reception.[3] (In fact, I'll use that term throughout this introduction, not as a disciplinary marker – though it might be – but as a con-venient short-hand for the field in all its facets, then shift to specific terms when talking about particular courses.) But as Jerome McGann indicates, McKenzie's 'watershed' essay remains 'scarcely known to most humanists'.[4] Furthermore, whether one teaches 'bibliography' or 'book history' depends on disciplinary preferences.[5] For example, history, library science and art departments prefer 'history of the book'; library science programs use 'bibliography' as a descriptor for descriptive or analytical bibliography, but English departments use the term to also cover research methods. Historians favor 'documentary editing,' while English departments use 'textual criticism' or 'scholarly editing.' Thus, though unwieldy, our title chooses practical over pithy, simply indicating the sites of instruction for a body of knowledge variously called by these (and other) terms and the groups most likely to find this volume helpful.

At the same time, the fact that practitioners (or departments) use a variety of terms to describe their practice has interesting theoretical implications for our understanding of the field as a whole. For example, one could ask what are the distinctions between 'history of the book' and 'book history'? Are print culture, visual culture, even manuscript studies, part of book history or are they something else? Does the term *bibliography* really cover all these areas or is that term too broad, too open to misprision? These are important questions, and a vital part of our pedagogy involves, as Maura Ives puts it, 'engaging the question of what is bibliography, what "fits" or "doesn't fit" the definition, what is included or excluded': 'the goal is not, and never will be, to definitively settle or resolve questions of terminology, but to somehow map the constellation of related areas of inquiry in ways that are helpful to us.'[6]

When we talk about pedagogy, then, what matters is what works, or appears to work in specific moments and situations. And, answers to pedagogical questions are almost always determined by local context: the individual goals of the class, its target audience (including student skills and backgrounds), the place it fills in a curriculum overall, and the practices and purposes of individual teachers. Those teachers are the audience to whom this book is directed, specifically to two groups: those already teaching the field, for whom this book will be a resource and supplement to their current pedagogical practices; and those new to the field, wishing to find ideas about how to incorporate bibliography into their classrooms.

Why Teach Bibliography?

Having identified both the who, what, and where of our book, I'd like to look briefly at the whys. Why should we devote a book to the teaching of this field, or this related set of fields? For justification, I offer Jerome McGann's sobering prophecy:

> In the next fifty years the entirety of our inherited archive of cultural works will have to be reedited within a network of digital storage, access, and dissemination. This system, which is already under development is transnational and transcultural. Let's say this prophecy is true. Now ask yourself these questions: who is carrying out this work, who will do it, and who should do it? These turn to sobering questions when we reflect on the recent history of higher education in the United States. Just when we will be needing young people well-trained in the histories of textual transmission and the theory and practice of scholarly method and editing, our universities are seriously unprepared to educate such persons. Electronic scholarship and editing necessarily draw their primary models from long-standing philological practices in language study, textual scholarship, and bibliography. As we know, these

three core disciplines preserve but a ghostly presence in most of our PhD programs.[7]

For McGann, the lack of required bibliographic training is tied to a disciplinary rift, a 'corrupt[ing]' 'apartheid' between 'literary and cultural studies,' wherein 'editing and textual studies' is 'regarded as menial if somehow also necessary' by 'theory and interpretation.'[8] That rift led to 'some seriously misguided academic/institutional decisions of the past 30 or 40 years, when the requirement of textual studies and bibliography was gradually dropped from most PhD programs in English language and literature.'[9] Nor has McGann been the lone voice to notice this deficiency in training and its resulting 'degree of ignorance about information technology and its critical relevance to humanities education and scholarship.'[10] In1996 Philip Cohen pointed to the same rift:

> [d]uring much of the present century, the profession of literary studies has aggressively marginalized textual scholarship, the study of the genesis, transmission, and editing of texts. While the New Criticism and its formalist descendants paid little attention to the discipline that had previously been central to literary studies, traditional textual scholarship's insistence on authorial intention and the single-stable text as the embodiment of a literary work has also helped to maintain the rift between the two disciplines. Although contemporary textual scholarship has become more theoretically literate, literature professors generally remain ignorant of textual scholarship, missing the contribution that textual scholarship, both traditional and contemporary, can make to literary studies.'[11]

And Cohen offered the same explanation: faculty 'ignor[ance]' results from required courses on critical theory' taking the place of the 'required research methods and bibliography classes.'[12] For both, disciplinary rift has led to devaluation, to pedagogical change which deepens the rift, and to increased devaluation. It is against this disciplinary background that David Leon Higden concludes that rather than being an 'ancient madness,' 'outdated and irrelevant,' bibliographic training 'can be and still should be at the heart of a graduate program.'[13] This mirrors McGann's repeated call for bibliography to be repositioned 'at the center of scholarly work.'[14]

The Center of Scholarly Work: Bibliography and Curricular Change

The future of the book, then, isn't so much a theoretical problem as much as a pedagogical one: whose decisions will shape our textual landscape? and how have these people been trained to make those decisions? On that front, I would argue, however, that the situation for bibliographic training *overall* is less dire than it has been in the past, a shift likely due to the repeated warnings of

McGann and others.[15] For example, of the fifty-six graduate programs accredited by the American Library Association, thirty-six offer at least one course in book history each year. This course is typically called either 'History of the Book' (thirteen programs); 'History of the Book and Printing' (eleven programs); or 'History of Books and Libraries' (twelve programs). Fifteen Library Science Masters or PhD programs supplement this introductory course with at least one other course, either a second book history course or 'Bibliography,' whether historical, descriptive, and/or analytical.

Additionally a number of library science programs also provide expanded offerings in either book history or bibliography. As I mentioned, fifteen Library Science graduate programs have deepened their course offerings to two or more courses beyond the introductory, but some – including Dalhousie, University of California at Los Angeles (UCLA), University of Toronto, and University of Texas at Austin – offer as many as four advanced courses. Catholic University, University of Iowa, and University of Alabama offer specialized programs in Book Arts, which builds on their courses in bibliography and book history. A number, such as Indiana University and Long Island University, offer specializations in Rare Books or Special Collections Librarianship, that include courses in bibliography such as Indiana's three courses: 'Descriptive bibliography,' 'History of the Book to 1450,' and 'History of the Book from 1450.'

In contrast, the status of bibliography in English departments is more difficult to trace, largely because of the diversity of terms used to identify bibliographic training. Certainly, the teaching of bibliography declined in the years leading to the height of literary theory, but there appears to have been significant renewal of interest in such training. One indicator could be the website of the Society for the History of Authorship, Readership, and Publishing (SHARP) which collects syllabi: offering around twenty syllabi in 2003, in two years the collection has grown to forty-two. To assess the state of bibliographic instruction, I analyzed the program offerings of fifty graduate programs in literature across the United States; in each instance I examined actual course descriptions, both in university catalogs and in the semesterly blurbs provided on departmental websites, to ensure a particular course focused on or included bibliography or textual criticism. From the list below, only two programs use the traditional term 'Bibliography' in their titles, but all include bibliographic training:

- 'Introduction to Graduate Studies': University of Alabama, Bucknell University, University of Kansas, Loyola University of Chicago, Ohio State University, Washington University at St. Louis
- 'Introduction to Bibliography': University of Texas, University of South Carolina
- 'Introduction to PhD Research and Professional Development': University of Colorado

- 'Introduction to Critical Methods': Boston University
- 'Introduction to English Studies': Purdue University
- 'Introduction to Literary Research': University of Virginia
- 'Introduction to Professional Study': University of Rhode Island
- 'Introduction to Graduate Literary Study': Rutgers University
- 'Introduction to Scholarly Methods': SUNY-Buffalo
- 'Approaches to Literary Research': UCLA
- 'Problems in the Study of Literature': University of California at Berkeley
- 'Methods of Literary Study': Brandeis University
- 'Theory and Practice of Literary Scholarship': City University of New York
- 'Methods of Research': University of Delaware
- 'Bibliography and Methods of Research': Louisiana State University (LSU)
- 'Bibliography and Methodology': University of North Carolina
- 'Methods of Graduate Studies': University of Oklahoma
- 'Materials and Methods of Research': Penn State University

The lack of consistency in these course titles (for courses that really *do* teach bibliography) suggests that changes in content may well have occurred over the past several years. The important point being, however, that though literary theory does account for a significant portion of graduate program curricula (often with more than a single course devoted to it), bibliography is *still* being taught – and its proportion of the graduate curriculum in the US is growing. This change appears to result from the focus on the social or cultural construction of texts, which places skills in bibliography at the forefront of scholarship.[16]

In addition, as bibliography has gained status and importance in literary studies, a number of graduate programs have begun offering bibliography or book history as a research focus. In the US, University of South Carolina, LSU, University of Texas, UCLA, University of Virginia, Penn State University, and Ohio State University all offer graduate students the option of a concentration or specialization in bibliography or textual studies. At LSU, that focus is called 'Analytical Bibliography and Editing'; at Virginia, 'Textual Criticism'; at University of Wisconsin at Madison, 'Print Culture.' Furthermore, several US universities have begun degree programs in the field, such as Drew University's MA in Book History or the University of Washington's PhD in Textual Studies. University of Iowa Center for the Book offers a graduate certificate, as well a graduate emphasis for MAs and PhDs in a variety of departments. We see this movement in Britain and Europe as well, with programs of study at the University of London, the University of Reading (in Printing and Book Design History), the University of Edinburgh (Book History), the University of Leiden (Book Studies Program), and the University of Erlangen. In Canada, the University of Toronto offers an MA in book history as well a PhD concentration.

Other institutions without a specific degree program or certificate support research in book history, such as the University of Minnesota's Book History and Literacies group. Some institutions, like the Hampshire College's Center for the Book, even focus on undergraduate pedagogy. This data suggests that although we may have far to go, we have come to see the swing of the pendulum back towards bibliographic instruction, including a rise in the numbers of classes engaging in bibliographic training (whether under the diverse names in the title of this book, or under different ones).

The Practice of Teaching

Given this increase in the teaching of bibliography, we should begin to discuss more formally how to teach the subject. But this conversation is complicated by the isolation many teaching the subject feel. Most of us teach in departments which have a variety of constituents. My own department, for example, houses literature studies (American, British and comparative), linguistics, technical communication, creative writing, composition and rhetoric, and bibliography. Though bibliographers and textual critics have long held positions in literature departments, we have always been a minority group (the situation is little different for teachers of book history in library science programs). As a result, we often find ourselves 'making do' (in Michel de Certeau's terms), negotiating for our programmatic needs alongside the claims of other, usually larger, interest groups.[17] This book traces the efforts of teachers to develop resources where resources are limited or nonexistant. It outlines how to scavenge for useful tools and materials (when one needs to), and how to work with colleagues in other departments. For me, in an English department, I have learned that librarians – both in special collections and in the general library – are the best friends my courses could have. This book offers, then, 'tactics' for developing courses or programs, and the questions it attempts to answer are practical and essential:

- How does one develop a course from scratch?
- What resources can one use when resources are limited?
- What available technologies support teaching bibliography?
- What strategies (and materials) do teachers use to bring bibliography or textual criticism into the classroom?
- What values does teaching bibliography bring to the classroom?
- What purposes do teachers hope to fulfill by raising such issues in their courses?
- Does teaching bibliography require teachers to reconceptualize existing courses or can it be added into existing classes effectively?
- What purpose does teaching bibliography in the undergraduate curriculum serve?
- What purpose does teaching bibliography in the graduate curriculum serve?

In addressing these questions, our essays present a broad spectrum of approaches taught under a variety of terms, and investigate how these approaches can be explored in the classroom. But just as this book hopes to offer collegial advice about how to develop, structure and teach courses in our broad field, so too can we learn from those outside our field who have thought long and deeply about the practice and theory of teaching. In bibliography, we haven't had that focused conversation on pedagogy, and as a result, we haven't yet considered how a pedagogy of bibliography might differ from (or be similar to) other pedagogical inquiries. I hope this book begins that conversation, leading us to consider not just how we teach, but why, and eventually how well.

To that end, the essays in this book first offer lore: what Stephen North defines as 'the accumulated body of traditions, practices, and beliefs' within which practitioners learn and teach.'[18] The value of lore is its emphasis on the practical: what has worked in the past for one teacher and what might work in the future for another. Though often dismissed in the past as interesting but unverifiable context-dependant stories (the pedagogical equivalent of anecdotal information in medicine), lore has recently received higher valuation, from the popular 'Approaches to Teaching' literature series published by the Modern Language Association to the Duke University Press-sponsored journal *Pedagogy*. This shift in the place of lore – from the substance of conversations between colleagues to published records of reflective, thoughtful or provocative teaching – has raised the status of pedagogical discussion, as has the movement towards pedagogical research, encouraged by such organizations as the Carnegie Foundation.

As bibliographers, we have very little transmitted lore, and our lore-based conversations have been limited to those at Rare Book School (RBS) where Terry Belanger and Dan Traister have co-taught the 'teaching history of the book' course in 1999 and 2003, and to occasional presentations and panels on bibliography at professional meetings, such as the SHARP, the Rare Books and Manuscripts Section of the American Library Association, the Association for Documentary Editing, or the national meeting of the College English Association where RBS has sponsored book history panels since 2004. Lore offers 'rich and powerful bodies of knowledge' which are 'concerned with what has worked, is working, or might work in teaching, doing, or learning,'[19] and these presentations have been important in establishing an interest in the pedagogy of bibliography. But the influence of these presentations has been limited to the practitioners who hear (or hear about) the presentations and to their classrooms.

This volume, then, collects existing lore (acknowledged whenever possible) and presents it – tested and sometimes refined – through the experience of the essayist-teacher (or through the experience of more than one teacher as with Terry Belanger's popular reading-by-candlelight assignment). In addition, for some of the writers, their experiences as teachers has asked them to reframe their expectations of their pedagogical task, to think against or outside their own training, and to discover practices to suit a new community of learners or to address unexpected challenges. In that sense, these essays offer the results of 'practice as inquiry,' [20] the activities of teachers in the classroom developing pedagogical methods and activities that work in uncertain or unexpected circumstances. These essays offer a variety of methods and methodologies; for as Marshall Gregory argues, 'no one teaching method can meet all the demands of learning. Sometimes lecture will work best, sometimes collegiality and fellow-learning, sometimes Socratic needling, and so on. Every *good* teacher should be able to vary pedagogical practice to meet the needs of student learning ... according to the demands of the material and the needs of students on any given day.' [21] Further, we must ask ourselves, 'what kinds of student development do we want, and what kinds of teaching promote those kinds [of learning]?' [22] Collecting lore, discussions of practitioner inquiry, and effective teaching methods are vital to beginning our discussion of pedagogical practice in our field. For the beginning teacher (or the teacher new to teaching bibliography), these essays offer something to do in class today or next week, practical help in imagining a classroom. Similarly the experienced teacher will find here many ideas for practical pedagogy.

But the experienced teacher will find that the benefit of these essays extends beyond lore to offer opportunity for reflection. The reflective model of teaching draws on Aristotle's *techne* – 'an intellectual or rational state that was concerned with making' – and *theorein* – the activity of studying the making of something, two conditions that lead to *praxis*, or theory-informed practice. [23] Thus, reflective practitioners must both recognize 'the theories behind [their] practice and tak[e] time to observe and reflect upon the practice of those theories.' [24] Given this model, the experienced teacher's response to these essays will be shaped by existing classroom knowledge. By reading, the experienced teacher can 'listen' to others facing similar questions and problems and can critique their solutions, successes, and failures. This is particularly useful when the reader and essayist faced the same problem but used different solutions, or when both used similar solutions but garnered different results. This reflective interaction allows for self-assessment, where the reflective teacher determines which practices or approaches have been productive and which need reframing or revision.

Reflective practitioners, according to Donald Schön, recognize new situations (a classroom of new students, a new curriculum, etc.) as unique, but can see that situation both as unique *and* as 'something already present in his repertoire' 'of examples, images, descriptions' etc. [25] That recognition allows the reflective practitioner to 'fram[e] the present, unique situation' in such a way that neither simply applies experience from the past, nor 'invent[s]' anew 'without any reference to what he already knows'[26] Such reflection ultimately enables teachers to be more flexible in future pedagogical situations, gaining, as Robert Yagelski puts it, 'the ability to think critically about what they are doing as they face unfamiliar or difficult situations in their practice as teachers.'[27] This reflection, or critical thinking about one's practice, leads to a capacity for 'reflection-in-action', an artistry in the classroom whereby the teacher is able to improvise when faced with unexpected situations.[28] Lee Shulman calls this artistry 'the wisdom of practice', and Murphy describes it as a 'subtle understanding that grows out of teacher practice ...[and] enables [teachers] to respond to the complex, specific, and dynamic demands of particular teaching situations.'[29] As a result of reflection, 'content knowledge, pedagogical experience and 'the wisdom of practice,' combine to create 'teacher knowledge,'[30] a flexible and artful poise in the face of shifting circumstances.

Given that reflection leads to 'reflection-in-action,' which leads ultimately to 'teacher knowledge,' Once we begin to discuss what it means to teach bibliography and its associated fields, we'll also begin to examine what it means to teach bibliography well. What artful moments does our teaching evoke? What do we learn about our field in general by teaching our specific classes?

Divisions of the Book

Part I – Rationales – offers some broad perspectives on our field, its definitions, and its pedagogical practices. Part II – Resources – offers advice that could be applied more generally to the development of specific courses or on how to develop and manage resources. Part III – Methods – offers practical advice for approaching courses or course components in book history, bibliography and textual criticism. Part III is subdivided according to these sections whether that material is taught in a full course or just as a course component. At the same time, these divisions into parts and subdivisions are slippery: Dierdre Stam's essay on history of the book contains excellent activities useful to teachers of bibliography more generally or even textual criticism; Matthew Kirschenbaum's essay though focused on literature students raises questions important for library science students working with digital resources, even if only in evaluating which ones to provide for patrons.

Overall, the essays suggest recursively that bibliography is a way of making things clear, of making things accessible, even obvious, that were hidden or obscure before.[31] Is one of the characteristics of bibliographic pedagogy, then, a making clear of complicated issues?

In his preface, Terry Belanger, Founder of RBS, examines his own history as a teacher of bibliography and book history in the context of the books and resources available in the course of his long career. He then charts the development, not just of bibliographical pedagogy, but of our field as well.

Part I: Rationales

Part I offers generalized advice, about how to approach the field of book history overall (Antonetti), about how curricula have been structured (Foot), and how do laboratories (Smith) or a book arts approach (Shep) aid instruction. Martin Antonetti nicely overviews the history of the field, providing a rich analogy (architecture v archeology) to distinguish between the French and Anglo-American schools. Though directed at practitioners, Antonetti's clear contextualization and accessible prose makes a good introductory reading for teachers and students alike. Mirjam Foot also surveys the field, examining how bibliographic training developed in British universities from the early twentieth-century to the present curricula at the University of Aberystwyth (Wales) and at London University. Foot's essay will be especially helpful for those wishing to establish a specialization or graduate emphasis in history of the book or bibliography. Steven Smith examines pedagogical trends, focusing on historical approaches to technical instruction; Smith's descriptions of what the laboratory model offers (and requires) will be helpful to teachers thinking about including technical instructions in courses. Sydney Shep offers a pendant to Smith, overviewing specific assignments her students complete in a course integrating book history, descriptive bibliography, and book arts. Shep's students gain technical skill in what she calls, 'artefactual apprenticeships' where students design, handset and print postcards letterpress.

Part II: Creating and Using Resources

Part II, 'Creating and Using Resources' offers several models of how to organize courses when access to physical books is limited. In discussing how to start a book history course from scratch, Lisa Berglund includes practical information, such as how to manage costs on excursions, but she also carefully explains the pedagogical rationale that undergirds her choices. Jean Lee Cole offers advice in how to organize a course around limited resources, explaining how to go about buying materials, what not to buy, and more importantly, how to use the materials she gathered. Cole provides specific assignment instructions for using contemporary magazines to contextualize and clarify materials in student anthologies. John Buchtel shows how much more one can do with a slice of publishing history than we frequently imagine. Even for teachers not interested in developing their own 'teaching collection' using online auction houses, Buchtel's overview of the kinds of topics students can develop will help teachers reassess local holdings or imagine what kinds of materials students would need for exciting projects. Ian Gadd traces the development of a history of the renaissance book course, from proposal through teaching and assessment. In particular, he offers helpful advice on using local or regional library collections as well as online resources like Early English Books Online (EEBO) and course-management tools like Blackboard.

Part III, Section I, Teaching 'History of the Book'

The first two essays in this section focus on teaching book history to graduate students in library science programs, while the last three focus on the undergraduate literature classroom. Teachers looking for practical exercises and activities shouldn't overlook Stam's essay's *many* practical teaching tips which would work in classrooms at many levels and in many departments. Also writing for the graduate classroom, Erik Delfino offers a pedagogy based in current events to teach book history: drawing on library fires, power-outages, the Harry Potter craze, Delfino reveals that book history happens all the time, all around us; his is a powerful argument for encouraging students to read the world with a critical eye. Teaching undergraduates to value difference is one of the problems that Sean Grass, Jennifer Phegley, and Susanna Ashton tackle in their essays. Grass provides a broad vision of how to contextualize nineteenth-century concerns using book history, a discussion that librarians preparing to teach a class in support of nineteenth-century literature faculty will find helpful. Likewise, Phegley outlines an assignment requiring students to read part of a novel in its original periodical context, including clear advice on how to manage both assignment and student queries. Ashton shows how incorporating publishing context (in one instance, the craze for sentimental giftbooks) helps students approach poets like Emily Dickinson whose values appear strange otherwise.

Part III, Section 2, Teaching Bibliography and Research Methods

John T. Shawcross and Maura Ives take two approaches to the bibliography and research methods course, though both make use of the same set of skills and theories. Shawcross helps students see the broad outlines of the field (and what's necessary for writing theses and dissertations), by using short skills-building assignments that build to papers and presentations integrating bibliographic work. Maura Ives offers a more holistic approach, focusing all work on a single author and text for which students write a comprehensive research guide, including descriptive bibliography. Don Krummel opines entertainingly on the challenges of teaching research skill, while describing sample research assignments that require students to use the print tools they (so often) slight in favor of online resources. Thomas Kinsella and Wilman Spawn explain how to use print resources and archival materials to answer literary, historical, or cultural questions. Fascinating reading, Kinsella and Spawn's essay will help students understand the thrill of literary detective work and of finding answers where one least expects them. Timothy Barrett's essay on papermaking condenses and clarifies the much larger body of literature on papermaking , just as his instructions on making paper with students (on our companion website) simplify an otherwise daunting task. Barrett makes one think about paper, perhaps even seeing it for the first time, while Carter Hailey explains how to analyze the paper that makes up early modern books. Hailey's method traces conjugate leaves, by analyzing watermarks, chainline spacing, and mould spacing.

Part Three, Section 3: Teaching Textual Criticism

Matthew Kirschenbaum encourages students to think about how technology changes texts by having them produce digital editions. His assignment requires students to face important theoretical questions about the nature of textuality, the social formation of texts, etc., helping them understand the ways that digitization is transforming their literary landscape. Erick Keleman takes the low-tech approach to teaching editing: students create a 'scholarly' edition, then examine their editorial choices and assumptions. For Keleman's students, the work of the editor becomes visible in interesting, but disturbing ways, and they learn that editorial choices are not always divinely inspired. Tatjana Chorney doesn't ask students to edit a text, but she does use the apparatus of several texts, particularly the list of variants, to raise questions about editorial practice and ultimately about literary interpretation. I offer a series of assignments using the skills of textual criticism, such as annotating, editing, and collating, to teach students in an undergraduate general-education classroom how to improve analytical skill and to become more focused readers.

Finally, in the afterword, Daniel Traister takes our book beyond practical pedagogy to address more theoretical questions about materiality, and ultimately to pose questions about the nature of our field itself.

Companion Website

In addition to the essays in this volume, we offer a companion website at http://www.pickeringchatto.com/bookhistory.htm. The website supplements these essays, providing course syllabi and assignment descriptions as well as other resources useful for the teaching of bibliography.

Notes

1. Richard J. Murphy, Jr., 'On Stories and Scholarship', *College Composition and Communication*, 40:4 (Dec. 1989), p. 466-72.
2. Robert Darnton, 'What is the History of Books?' in Finkelstein and McCleery (eds), *Book History Reader* (London: Routledge), p. 10.
3. D. F. McKenzie, 'The Book as an Expressive Form' in *Bibliography and the Sociology of Texts* (Cambridge: Cambridge University Press, 1999), p. 15.
4. Jerome McGann, 'Literary Scholarship in the Digital Future,' *Chronicle of Higher Education*, 49:16 (13 December 2002), p.B7.

5. While this diversity of departments teaching bibliography may cause some consternation for job seekers or for program directors, this volume is written to those already teaching, those who hold appointments in a variety of departments and who are able to incorporate those materials into their courses, whether already existing or proposed.

6. Maura Ives. Personal Communication. 11 January 2006.

7. McGann, 'A Note on the Current State of Humanities Scholarhip,' *Critical Inquiry*, 30 (Winter 2004), p. 410. This essay is an expanded and heavily revised version of the 2002 'Literary Scholarship'. McGann has been calling for reform in graduate training since his 1985 volume, *The Beauty of Inflections*, where he noted the problematic absence of required courses in bibliography and textual criticism in literature department. Since then, he has reiterated the consequences of the dearth of bibliographic instruction in several publications, including the above and the 'Gutenberg Variations' *RBM: A Journal of Rare Books, Manuscripts, and Cultural Heritage*, (2002), pp. 15-31; 'Culture and Technology: the Way We Live Now, What is to be Done?' *New Literary History*, 36:1 (2005), pp. 71-82; and throughout *The Scholar's Art. Literary Studies in a Managed World* (Chicago, University of Chicago Press, 2006). While McGann directs his comments particularly to the humanities, his concern with the processes of textual transmission and archiving (particularly digital storage) is a salient one for librarians and library science training as well. In fact, in 'Literary Scholarship,' McGann also criticises library science programs for not requiring history of the book courses.

8. McGann, 'A Note', p. 409. I would like to thank Maura Ives for calling my attention to McGann's heavy repetition in 'Literary Scholarship' and 'A Note.' Her observation sent me back to McGann's articles to trace the arch of his arguments.

9. McGann, 'Gutenberg,' p. 18.

10. McGann, 'Culture,' p. 71.

11. Philip Cohen, 'Is There a Text in this Discipline? Textual Scholarship and American Literary Studies,' *American Literary History*, 8:4 (Winter 1996), p. 728.

12. Cohen, 'Is,' p. 742, fn 1. The complaint of disciplinary rift and the decline of bibliographic instruction – particularly in textual editing – appears repeatedly, most recently, at the 2005 meeting of the Association for Documentary Editing, in the presentations of Joel Myerson and Ronald Bosco who during their careers have watched bibliographic training lose ground to theory.

13. David Leon Higdon, 'Ancient Madness or Contemporary Wisdom? A New Literary Research Methods Course', *Profession* (2002), p. 143.

14. McGann, 'Gutenberg ,' p.17.

15. My research based as it is in the ephemera of departmental websites and university catalogs can only indicate how the courses are currently being taught, not what content they included even five years ago. Though in January of 2005 I reexamined the MLS programs, my research for English departments dates to 2003.

16. 1990 saw both the founding of the Society for Textual Scholarship and SHARP.

17. Michel de Certeau, *The Practice of Everyday Life*, trans. Steven Rendell (Berkeley, University of California Press, 1984), p. 660.

18. Stephen M. North, *The Making of Knowledge in Composition: Portrait of an Emerging Field* (New Jersey, Boynton/Cook Publishers, 1987), p. 22.

19. North, ibid, p. 27, 23.

20. North, ibid, p. 33.

21. Marshall Gregory, 'Curriculum, Pedagogy and Teacherly Ethos,' *Pedagogy* 1:1 (2001), p. 75.

22. Gregory, ibid.

23. James Dubinsky, 'Becoming User-Centered, Reflective Practitioners' in James Dubinsky (ed.), *Teaching Technical Communication: Critical Issues in the Classroom* (Boston, Bedford/St Martins, 2004), pp. 4-5. Dubinsky's essay nicely overviews other influences on the reflective model, including John Dewey, Isocrates, Plato and Zen Buddhism.

24. Dubinsky, ibid, p. 4.

25. Donald Schön, *The Reflective Practitioner*, p. 66.
26. Schön, pp. 68 and 66
27. Robert P. Yagelski 'Portfolios as a Way to Encourage Reflective Practice Among Pre-service English Teachers,' in Kathleen Blake Yancey and Irwin Weiser, (eds.), *Situating Portfolios: Four Perspectives* (Logan, Utah State University Press, 1997), p. 226.
28. Schön, p. 67.
29. Lee S. Shulman, 'Knowledge and Teaching: Foundations of the New Reform', *Harvard Educational Review*, 57:1 (1987), p. 11; Murphy, 'On Stories,' p. 468.
30. Murphy, 'On Stories,' p. 468.
31. I would like to thank Deirdre Stam for graciously reading the whole volume and for making this observation.

Exploring the Archaeology of the Book in the Liberal Arts Curriculum

Martin Antonetti

You might think of your next visit to the college's rare book room this way: handling an old book may be the closest you will ever come to physically holding hands with your intellectual predecessors.[1] This is why rare book reading rooms are for me numinous spaces: when they are interpreted by an energetic curator the physical objects contained in them may be catalysts for deep intellectual and emotional connections and insights unavailable elsewhere or by any other means. At the same time, those of us who work in rare book rooms tend not to think of them as temples or shrines or (even worse) mausoleums of the book. Nor do we consider them any longer as 'Treasure Rooms', although the notion of rare books may conjure something elitist, rarefied, clubby, and a reminder of the pretensions of earlier generations of college benefactors. On the other hand, whereas at many colleges the rare book room may be the pride of the development office, it may also be an embarrassing burden to the library administration and a puzzle to everyone else on campus. In fact, many rare book curators in liberal arts colleges these days may be faced with a lack of enthusiasm or even apathy from the faculties they seek to serve. The following remarks are an attempt to explain how a small college's rare book collection may be relevant and useful to all constituents of its home institution.

As many of today's curators approach it, the rare books program in a liberal arts college has three separate but inter-related emphases or foci. The first is about presenting the book as a physical, an archaeological, object, about uncovering patterns in its physical fabric. In other words, we curators attempt to teach students how to look at a book – and, by extension, any artifact from the past – and to discover information about the features, the intent and the implications of its type, paper, printing, illustration and binding. Harold Brodkey, in the eloquent memoir of his dying, wrote about his own similar experience of visual discovery:

> At one time I was interested in bird-watching, and I noticed that when I saw a
> bird for the first time I couldn't really see it, because I had no formal arrange-
> ment, no sense of pattern for it. I couldn't remember it clearly, either. But
> once I identified the bird, the drawings in bird books and my own sense of
> order arranged the image and made it clearer to me, and I never forgot it.[2]

We are involved in exactly the same process in our reading rooms – all of
our deconstruction, classification and examination of the minutiae of books,
paradoxically, provides us with a broader as well as deeper understanding of
their role in history and a richer, more complete, appreciation of the objects
themselves.

Our second focus is the impact of the book on society. Here we are concerned with the book not only as a commercial commodity or as vehicle for
the transmission of ideas, but as an expression of the *mentalité* of all those who
came in contact with it: author, printer, binder, illustrator, publisher, seller,
reader, and censor. And our third focus is the mutability and transience of the
text, the sometimes fragile and tenuous transmission of any given text from
edition to edition, century to century, culture to culture. In exploring this we
are mainly concerned with the question of how the reception of any given text
is conditioned or mediated by the physical form and the physical appearance
of its presentation.

Today, the history of the book is a relatively new field, rich with possibility, interdisciplinary in the widest possible sense as it constitutes a nexus
between literature, bibliography, social history, intellectual history, mechanical
arts, graphic arts, the history of science, and many others. The following brief
observations on the intellectual undergirding or foundation of history of the
book a field of inquiry are relevant because the conventions of the field as they
exist at any given moment in time determine the shape of operations like college special collections departments as well as the types of goods and services
librarians and conservators make available to faculty and students.

Until the mid 1980s the history of the book had been approached by means
of two separate and distinct methodologies: the French school, which examines the effects of the impact of the book on society, and the Anglo-American
school, which is primarily bibliographical, and concerned with the book as a
physical object. Of course, each of these two methodologies has its own view-
points, means, and ends.

Even in this country we refer to the French approach to the history of the
book by its French name, *l'histoire du livre*. The *fons et origo* of the discipline
is Henri-Jean Martin's and Lucien Febvre's magisterial *L'Apparition du Livre*
(1958), one of the most important products of the *Annales* school of historiography founded by Febvre and Marc Bloch in the late 1920s. In general *Annales*
addresses the social and cultural aspects of historical events, and attempts to
interpret these events and their effects from the point of view of ordinary peo-

ple. *Annales* historiography is primarily based on the analysis of archival materials – in this case of documents such as library inventories and borrowing records and booksellers' and collectors' catalogues.

Certainly *L'Apparition du Livre* (translated into English in 1976 as *The Coming of the Book)* revolutionized the way American scholars thought about the book. Before this book history was construed mostly as the documentation of developments in the technique of printing and related crafts and, to a lesser extent, the dissemination of texts. Instead, *L'Apparition du Livre* attempted to describe the role and function of the printed book in society in order to demonstrate 'that the printed book was one of the most effective means of mastery over the whole world'.[3] Febvre and Martin's arguments were so startling, so compelling that in the decades since their work appeared, a long line of historians, mostly French, but notably including Elizabeth Eisenstein and Robert Darnton in the US, has explored the social and economic consequences of the presence of books in society.

To help students understand the French approach, I propose the following exercise: imagine a book as if it were a building, as if it were architecture and, concomitantly, book history as if it were architectural history. If you wished to study a cathedral in a European town, for example, you might analyze it in terms of style (gothic or romanesque or baroque or renaissance) or materials (marble, granite, stucco etc). But the *Annales* historian would be primarily interested in the significance that this cathedral held for the inhabitants of the town, and would ask questions related to the way they used it. How did the building itself condition the religious life of the townspeople? Were they even allowed inside? How often? What did they do there? How did the building contribute to the way the citizens thought of themselves, especially in contradistinction to citizens of neighboring towns. Public buildings like cathedrals were municipal projects that often took centuries and enormous human and capital resources to complete; they were complex human endeavors involving the collaboration of many sectors of the society. How was all of this collaborative activity coordinated, and what social, intellectual, financial and emotional results did it produce? These would be some of the questions that the *Annales* historians would ask – about buildings and about books.

On the other hand, the Anglo-American practice of book history was originally bibliographical, concerned with type, paper, printing and publishing. In addition, up until the rise of deconstruction, the Anglo-American approach had been considered a necessary adjunct to textual analysis. It was the study of early English literary works, especially Renaissance drama, by such scholars as R. B. McKerrow and W. W. Greg in the early twentieth century that provided the context for the development of 'analytical bibliography' (defined by G. Thomas Tanselle in his 1981 Hanes Lecture as 'the elucidation of the printing history of a particular book by analysis of the physical evidence of its typography and paper'[4]). These scholars noticed that the texts they were working on might differ from copy to copy, even in the same edition. In an attempt to understand how that could happen they undertook the first detailed studies of what actually went on in English Renaissance printing shops. How did what transpired in the crowded and chaotic atmosphere of the shop affect the ways that the text was set up in type and printed? This question preoccupied English and American literary scholars, who were primarily concerned with textual analysis, and the evidence they uncovered fueled the engine of bibliographical scholarship for many decades.

To help my students grasp the Anglo-American approach, I propose another exercise: think about a book as if it were an archaeological artifact and book history as if it were archaeology. You have unearthed a small potsherd from a dig at a Neolithic site. From an observation of the artifact's curvature and thickness you may be able to infer the size and shape of the original vessel. From this you make conjectures as to its function: was it used for storage, or transportation, or cooking? You might then go a step further and deduce the particular foodstuff that was stored, transported, or cooked in it. This may suggest the agricultural level of the people who made it and perhaps even the climate and meteorological conditions that prevailed. Perhaps most importantly, knowledge of all of the above will certainly help you assign a date range to your little shard. And so it is with bibliography: an analysis of the physical evidence in books allows us to make statements about how they were produced and how they were used.

Analytical bibliography is fascinating work, of course, but we realize now that dependence upon this strictly archaeological method is not sufficient. Indeed, in recent years English and American historians and bibliographers are finally venturing a comprehensive description of the workings of the book trade, something not previously considered as part of the practice of bibliography, which has, as I mentioned, focused for the most part on the production of books. We now see that such an approach does not possess the critical means to grapple with questions of the significance and implication of books in the lives of individuals of various classes and of society as a whole. Yet this is precisely something about which we've discovered we know much less than we need to know. And something, obviously, that is at the root of our understanding of our own intellectual history.

In the last decade or so an international group of semioticians and structural sociologists has also turned its attention to the history of the book. These scholars, following the lead of Gerard Genette, W.J.T. Mitchell, and others, analyze signs and visual communication – or rather, the *form* of a given sign, the *form* of a mode of visual communication – and interpret how that form conditions our understanding of the meaning of the sign. For the history of the book the key insight deriving from this new approach has been Genette's theory of paratexts.[5] Paratexts are liminal devices and conventions, both inside and outside of the book, that form part of the complex mediation between book, author, publisher, and reader. These conventions are found in most books – title pages, forewords, tables of contents, subscribers' pages, indices, epigraphs and publishers' jacket copy – and make up all of the things that are *not* the text but that surround and contextualize it. Along with Derrida, these scholars limit the value of the text in its traditional static sense (as an author's 'creation'); instead, they understand it as something more dynamic and fluid, reaching completion only after being 'encorporated' as it were by a publisher and then ultimately consumed by a reader. Thus publishers, readers, and authors form a dynamic triad responsible for the realization of the text. 'Text' is here defined as a relationship or as process.

Earlier, I said that up until the mid 1980s the history of the book had been approached by means of separate and distinct methodologies. Since then, many scholars and teaching curators in college special collections have attempted to reconcile or harmonize the separate methodologies, to forge something new. If we American scholars and curators can also adopt and adapt the socio-economic approach of the French historians and the theoretical insights of the international semioticians, blending them with our own techniques of bibliographical analysis and description, we will not only broaden the definition of the history of the book, we will also deepen its scholarly significance and intellectual excitement as well.

So, I propose the merits of this new amalgam, and urge you to consider its value to your own teaching and scholarship. Let's move toward a fusion of these seemingly disparate methodologies. Let's move toward an understanding of rare book collections as something with resonance for a wide variety of subjects and with a variety of access points. And we curators are committed to catalyzing this fusion of methodologies in the field since it is bound to result in the more sophisticated use of special collections materials in your classrooms. In fact, the entire program of the pedagogical curator could be said to rest upon this new way of interpreting the book and its history.

Finally, the nineteenth-century historian and literary critic, Francis Underwood, wrote that 'the life of every community is made up of infinite details'.[6] How should we keep ourselves warm? What do we eat for breakfast? Where do we empty our chamber pots? How do we see well enough to work when the sun goes down? What do we keep in our pockets? The lives of the printers and publishers, the writers, readers and censors, the lives of all whom students encounter in the rare book room were filled, dominated, conditioned by these ' infinite details' – just as ours are today. But, when we think about history and the history of the book we tend to overlook these everyday details in favor of grand themes and big books which characterized each age and genre. Special collections librarianship used to be practiced as the quest for the big books, the important collections. Instead, we now train students to focus on the 'infinite details' of people's literary lives (if and what and how they read) as well as of the 'infinite details' of life in the pressroom and bookshop. This is no trivial pursuit but rather, as social historian Jack Larkin describes it, the fertile and rewarding investigation into *what has been taken for granted*. We curators now recognize that the study of things not recorded, not commented upon – the mundane and arcane routines of daily work, the archaeological clues left behind in the fabric of material culture, the skein of little facts and details that make up the stuff of people's lives – this is a gold mine for those of us who attempt to enliven with flesh and blood the bare bones of the past.

With all of the above in mind, the history of the book then can be understood as a crucible in which social history, bibliographical analysis, material culture, and semiotic theory is compounded. Indeed, the special collections curator oversees a laboratory that employs books as raw materials for scholarship in a discipline that at the same time impacts upon, and draws from, all others.

Notes

1. This essay is a version of a lecture presented to a faculty forum at Smith College in September 2001.
2. Harold Brodkey, *This Wild Darkness: the Story of My Death* (New York: Metropolitan Books, 1996), p. 109.
3. Lucien Febvre and Henri-Jean Martin, David Gerard tr., *The Coming of the Book* (London, Verso, 1976), pp. 10, 11.
4. G. Thomas Tanselle, *The History of Books as a Field of Study* (Chapel Hill, NC, Hanes Foundation, 1981), p. 2.
5. See Gerard Genette, *Seuils* (Paris: Editions du Seuils, 1987); this appeared in English as Jane E. Lewin tr., *Paratexts: Thresholds of Interpretation* (Cambridge, Cambridge University Press, 1997).
6. Francis Underwood, *Quabbin; the Story of a Small Town, with Outlooks upon Puritan Life* (Boston, Northeastern University Press, 1986) reprint of the London 1893 edition, p. 29.

Historical Bibliography for Rare-Book Librarians

Mirjam M. Foot

In 1912 W.W. Greg in a lecture to the Bibliographical Society described 'a dream of my own. It is of a course of lectures on English bibliography which may one day be delivered at one of our so-called seats of learning'.[1] Although Greg's dream was not fulfilled as he envisaged, beginning in 1919 with Arundel Esdaile and extending through the present in what seems like an unbroken tradition, bibliographers – including Greg himself; Theodore Besterman of *World Bibliography of Bibliographies* fame; Frank (later Sir Frank) Francis; and Howard Nixon (the latter two rare-book experts at the British Museum) – have lectured in bibliography at University College, London. Over the decades the course has developed from one focused on English textual bibliography and textual criticism into a more rounded history of the book.

However, the provision for teaching bibliography in all its aspects, or for teaching the history of the book in Great Britain, is too slight, particularly for future rare book librarians. Some descriptive, analytical and textual bibliography is taught (but on the whole not to future librarians), and there are occasional one-off courses in printing history, descriptive bibliography, or, specifically, in rare books cataloguing. But as most Library Studies departments at British universities do not include anything like rare books studies or historical bibliography, much of what is needed to acquire, catalogue, preserve and give access to rare book collections, has to be learnt on the job. The fallacy that rare books cataloguing can be taught without also providing sufficient knowledge of analytical and descriptive bibliography, unfortunately means that, in Fredson Bowers's words: 'books cannot be recorded accurately in libraries'.[2] The future rare book librarian who wants to be trained in Britain has the choice between three main educational opportunities: one in Wales and two in London.

The University of Aberystwyth (Wales) offers two modules: 'Introduction to rare book librarianship' and 'Advanced rare book librarianship'. They are distance-learning courses mainly aimed at library staff in need of further education or at those who want to develop rare books skills. The more basic course provides a general introduction to the development of the printed book in the hand-press period and aims to enable students to identify materials in a rare books collection, to give them the appropriate curatorial care, to give help and advice to the general public about materials in a rare books collection, and to deal with bibliographical queries. The more advanced course goes into more detail and greater depth, looking at the development of the printed book in continental Europe, considering all aspects of the book as a physical object, and teaches descriptive bibliography and specialised rare books cataloguing.[3] The course materials and the aims of the courses are sound, and they provide useful extra education for prospective rare book librarians. The disadvantages of this kind of distance teaching are the lack of personal contact with the students and, more importantly, the lack of supervised hands-on experience, something from which the London courses also suffer, but to a far lesser extent, as the presence of some of the best and most extensive rare book collections brings hands-on teaching material within easy reach. The collections at the British Library, the National Art Library (Victoria & Albert Museum) and St Bride Printing Library are all used and so are the rare book collections of University College Library and of the main London University Library at Senate House. A number of smaller special collections also open their doors to students; learned society libraries, ecclesiastical libraries and even the better club libraries provide excellent teaching material. Although the amount of time spent on using actual books in the teaching programmes is limited, there is some opportunity to visit these collections and to show examples of early printing, illustrative processes, bindings, printed ephemera, and such like.

At London University there are two possible ways of developing rare books knowledge and skills: one at the School of Advanced Studies, where an MA in the History of the Book is taught, the other at University College London, where in the School of Library, Archive and Information Studies (also as part of an MA-degree programme) the most popular option is 'Historical Bibliography', and where the eighty-six-year-old tradition is strong. Over the decades the course, as well as the whole subject field, has changed,[4] and although analytical and descriptive bibliography remain important components, the course as a whole tries to achieve a balance between the history of printing, papermaking and bookbinding, with some excursions into the history of publishing, the book trade and collecting. As the course only covers one university term (or ten three-hour sessions), the great difficulty is, to paraphrase Greg, to know where to stop.

Of course there is more to educating rare book librarians than teaching them a smattering of historical bibliography, and at UCL the Library MA students take cataloguing and classification, collection development and collection management, preservation, general library management, information technology, web design, and information sources, all providing a good basic grounding, as well as a range of optional courses. For rare book librarians there are, as well as historical bibliography, optional courses in manuscript studies, children's books, the modern book trade, further cataloguing and classification, and advanced preservation (some even take database design or electronic publishing).

Moreover, before students are accepted they have to have worked for at least a year in a library. Given few job opportunities for rare book librarians in the UK, this education tries to fit them for a more general post (e.g. in a College library with a rare books collection, but with more general main duties).

Over the past seven years the historical bibliography course at UCL has developed and changed in terms of weight given to and time spent on different subjects. The coverage of the history of bookbinding has suffered: the three sessions in 1998/9 have been reduced gradually to one, or in a good year one and a half. The question of 'what is bibliography?' now takes up the whole first session, giving an overview of how the subject developed from the late nineteenth century onwards, and how it changed from what A.W. Pollard called 'a big umbrella',[5] covering all aspects of 'book-making and of the manufacture of the materials of which books are made,… a knowledge of the conditions of transcription and reproduction, of the methods of printing and binding, of the practices of publication and bookselling –…the whole of typography and the whole of palaeography',[6] to the narrower and more focused creation of a 'detailed, analytical record of the physical characteristics of a book…as a trustworthy source of identification'[7] of the late 1940s and 1950s, with its overriding emphasis on the concept of 'ideal copy', to the more liberal and wider approach, inspired by the French proponents of *l'histoire du livre*.

This is then followed by a session at St Bride Printing Library, including discussion of the workings of various kinds of hand presses, and demonstrations of how to cast type, how to set it, and how to work a printing press. The next few sessions deal with the history of printing. The first covers the period from the earliest developments until the middle of the sixteeenth century; this is followed by a session on the period of consolidation and further change up to the late eighteenth century; the third session deals with the developments of gradual mechanisation during the nineteenth century, finishing with the private press movement. The same historical pattern is followed for the history of papermaking, which starts with a short session on the production of parchment or vellum, and for the history of bookbinding, which begins with the development from scroll to codex. In all three subjects the nineteenth century gets the shortest shrift. Mainly through lack of time, but also because there is a great deal of literature on the early mechanisation processes and on the impact of the expansion of literacy, learning, the development of leisure time devoted to reading, and the need for more information of all kinds on the various book-making processes and on the publishing and printing trades. Publishing and book trade history is slipped in to the sessions on printing, as is the history of typography; and collecting is included in the session on bookbinding. We only scratch at the surface, hoping to awaken interest and offering pointers for future self study.

The last sessions of the term are devoted to descriptive and analytical bibliography – the only subject expanded over the past seven years from one to three sessions, largely as a result of student need. Usually there is the opportunity for an extra, unscheduled visit to some rare books library or another. Voluntary attendance, late in the afternoon or in early evening, has proved to be remarkably high. All full-time students do two weeks' practical work at the beginning of the second term, and all attempts are made to place those interested in historical bibliography in one of the many rare book libraries or rare book departments in or near London, including Oxford and Cambridge, but also in various National Trust Libraries and places further afield, if near a student's home town.

Students are deemed to be fit for employment, or at least for the award of an academic degree, provided they have passed all core courses and two optional courses with satisfactory marks and have produced a dissertation. Most courses are judged on written work. For historical bibliography, the students write an essay of about 4000 words about a subject, chosen from a list of about ten or twelve topics. Three years ago, written exams for individual courses were abolished; therefore the students need to produce a second piece of coursework on which they are assessed. This has varied considerably, from being given an early book (usually dating from the seventeenth or eighteenth century) for which they have to compile a full bibliographical description, to being asked to explain eight collational formulae and being given a title-page, of which to make a quasi-facsimile transcription.

For those who are really interested in any of the more historical subjects, the MA dissertation on a subject chosen by the student, albeit in consultation with whoever is going to supervise it, gives the opportunity of going into a particular topic in some more depth. This is guided by individual teaching sessions as well as a great deal of email contact all through the summer months, often resulting in a considerable piece of work, sometimes of publishable quality.

However, this remains a typical university assessment, and whether it satisfies future employers remains an open question. One general problem is that university teachers are not fully aware what employers need, unless they have been recent employers themselves – something that is very rarely the case – while employers have no opportunity to influence the teaching. The Chartered Institute of Library and Information Professionals ratifies taught library courses on a five-yearly cycle, and its Rare Books Group is active in providing guidance and training for those who deal with rare books. But, considering the enormous variety of libraries (even of rare book collections within libraries), how can all employment needs be met? Perhaps employers may have to accept that their new recruits will come with a wide variety of elementary skills, and only some with slightly better developed or more focused knowledge in a particular area. Perhaps universities ought to encourage more employers' involvement in the design of the syllabus.

Where higher degrees and original research are concerned, the rare books specialists do better than most, as there is more interest in and scope for MPhil and PhD dissertation topics of historical and book-historical interest. There is no scarcity of applications. The scarcity is in supervisors.

As employers' needs change, and libraries develop and change their emphasis, academic education cannot stay the same. Over the years the library education curriculum has increased its emphasis on information technology and web design for rare book and general librarians, but there still seems to be the need for knowledge of book production, for an understanding of books as physical objects, for an understanding of the transmission of texts and the implications this may have for the transmission of ideas. Therefore an historical bibliography course or a history of the book course, with an element of descriptive and analytical bibliography, remains a crucial component in the education of those in whose care these physical objects will be. Existing provision is slight and expanding it may remain a pipe dream. At UCL in the immediate future, it may be possible to organise more library visits, always tremendously popular. Ideally some of the binding history that was axed should be restored, and, most important of all, there is the need to go into more depth for almost every topic that is discussed; illustration is a good example of a popular topic that gets only minimal coverage. It is also desirable that some attention be paid to the cultural and social circumstances in which books are produced and received. All this would need a year instead of a term, unlikely as long as funding remains insufficient, librarians have to know a smattering of everything, and as long as the emphasis on information provision gets stronger, while the realisation that this information had somewhere a physical shape gets weaker.

Interestingly, students from the History of the Book MA (at the Institute of English Studies, School of Advanced Studies), have 'historical bibliography' as one of their options, but have to come to UCL for this. Their own MA is entirely in the 'History of the Book' and they therefore should get a more rounded education, as well as a more detailed one. Like most university degrees, this programme is not aimed at educating professional librarians. It is aimed at anyone with an interest in the history of books, their production and reception. Having said that, future or mid-career rare book librarians could do a lot worse than studying in this programme which ranges widely, covering the relationship between authors, publishers, booksellers and readers; discussing all sorts of texts in all forms and formats, placing special emphasis on books as physical objects that are multiplied and distributed; and including library history and the history of reading. As it is considered an historical discipline, books, their production and reception are always considered in their historical context. Moreover, this is not a purely theoretical academic programme, but one in which students are encouraged to handle all kinds of books and manuscripts, set type, print, attempt some binding and generally get the feel of what book production might have been like. Nor is it limited to the scriptorium or the hand press; the electronic book also figures.

This course has its defects. Its coverage depends on who is available for teaching and, although teachers are drawn from a wide variety of institutions, they by no means cover the full span. Apart from a core course on general book history (again not more than scratching the surface) and a short course in research methodology, the programme consists of a series of options, four of which are chosen, covering such diverse topics as the medieval book, the Italian book, authors, publishers and textual theory, western book structures, the look of the book, the historical reader, the serial and the book, and the electronic book. Wide ranging indeed, but leaving large gaps.

Ideally the two London programmes – currently less than a mile apart – should be combined. Together they would be more attractive, as well as covering a wider and more coherent field. But university politics and inter-college rivalry seem to prevail over common sense.

If, like Greg, I too may have a dream, it is of a two-year full-time course, combining the best elements of the two London courses, with much more emphasis on hands-on experience in London's many rare book collections. It is for smaller classes (at UCL the average number is thirty students), but a viable number (at the Institute for English Studies the numbers are smaller); it is for greater practical input from rare book professionals (the History of the Book MA scores over UCL); for closer contacts with employing institutions. It is for a series of summer schools, taking one topic per school and going into much greater depth, a part of the dream that may well come true before long. It is of more time for supervision of PhD candidates (now many are turned away, a waste of talent and a potential undermining of future professionals), but it is also, and most importantly, of a change of attitude of the professional senior library administrators: an acceptance, maybe even an understanding, of the value of the book as a physical object with all that implies.

Notes

1   W. W. Greg, 'What is Bibliography?', *Transactions of the Bibliographical Society*, XII (1912), pp. 39-53 (for quotation see p. 50).

2   Quoted in G. T. Tanselle, 'The Achievement of Fredson Bowers' in *Fredson Bowers at eighty* (New York, Bibliographical Society of America, 1985), p. 7.

3. Archived information about these courses is available at http://www.aber.ac.uk/modules/2005/ DS36210.html and http://www.aber.ac.uk/modules/2005/DS36310.html (accessed 7 May 2006).

4 For a more detailed discussion how the concept of bibliography as an academic subject has changed and developed see M. M. Foot, 'The study of books', *Aslib Proceedings*, 58:1/2 (2006), pp. 20–33.

5 A. W. Pollard, 'Note' at the end of S. Gaselee, 'The aims of bibliography', *The Library*, 4th series, XIII:3 (December, 1932), p. 258.

6 W. W. Greg, 'What is Bibliography?', pp. 44-6.

7 F. Bowers, *Principles of bibliographical description* (Princeton, Princeton University Press, 1949), reprinted with an introduction by G. T. Tanselle, (Winchester, St Paul's Bibliographies, 1994), p. xv.

'A Clear and Lively Comprehension': the History and Influence of the Bibliographical Laboratory

Steven Escar Smith

Understanding the practical details of printing and its related processes is essential for researchers working in the field of bibliography and textual studies. As early as 1913, R. B. McKerrow advocated that all students gain a 'mechanical' knowledge of printing processes:

> It would, I think, be an excellent thing if all who propose to edit an Elizabethan work from contemporary printed texts could be set to compose a sheet or two in as exact a facsimile as possible of some Elizabethan octavo or quarto, and to print it on a press constructed on the Elizabethan model. Elementary instruction in the mechanical details of book-production need occupy but a very few hours of a University course of literature, and it would, I believe, if the course were intended to turn out scholars capable of serious work, be time well spent.[1]

What McKerrow regarded as necessary for bibliographical understanding was a 'clear and lively comprehension', allowing researchers to see the book 'not only from the point of view of the reader interested in it as literature, but also from the points of view of those who composed, corrected, printed, folded, and bound it'.[2] Gaining such knowledge has never been easy, and it has become less so over the last century as the industry has evolved away from hot and cold metal technology.

Over the years, many teachers and scholars have followed McKerrow's recommendation in their quest to provide themselves and their students with a better grounding in the mechanics of book production. Their efforts have often taken the form of teaching presses or collections, sometimes also known as bibliographical laboratories, usually as part of a graduate program in English or library science and sometimes in connection with an academic library. In 1963, Philip Gaskell defined a bibliographical press as 'a workshop or laboratory which is carried on chiefly for the purpose of demonstrating and investigating the printing techniques of the past by means of setting type by hand, and of printing from it on a simple press'. At that time he found twenty-five operations that met this definition and characterized their collective establishment and growth as a 'movement'.[3] There are many advantages to the bibliographical laboratory as well as challenges, some more apparent than others. Such undertakings also exist in a broader pedagogical paradigm, though we rarely stop to consider their educational context or precedents, nor their theoretical underpinnings. The impulse to inform pedagogy with experiential learning is not unique to bibliography. The re-enactment movement, for example, grows out of the study of warfare, and perhaps represents the most committed effort yet to learn by experiencing history, some of its proponents even going so far as to live on the kind of rations (or the lack thereof) appropriate to the battle in question. I know of many great and innovative efforts among book historians to use practical exercises in their teaching, but I am not aware of anyone going so far as to forego artificial light, impose a hand press period work week (about seventy hours in the eighteenth century), or use urine-soaked pelts on classroom ink balls!

Moreover and less dramatically, almost every vocational and professional course of study seeks to balance classroom instruction with so-called 'real world' projects. However, we are not training printers or other craft workers, though some of our students may go on to pursue these activities and even achieve a high degree of skill in them, and many of us have undertaken craft training to improve our knowledge of the processes and technologies of book manufacturing. We often also borrow exercises from the studio to enhance our teaching. Furthermore, many of our students are preparing themselves for professional careers, namely in library or information science. But despite these similarities, our aims are not those of the trade school. The difference lies primarily in that ours is a critical and historical pursuit. We use 'hands on' exercises to teach the technical processes that give birth to texts so that we might better understand how these processes bear on textual form, meaning, transmission, and reception.

Historically, teachers of bibliography and related subjects have taken two approaches to technical instruction: either integrating it into a course or, as mentioned above, teaching these skills via a laboratory or workshop setting. Representative of those who have incorporated practical exercises into a class or two over the course of a term is William A. Jackson's famous bibliography course at Harvard, which ran from the late 1930s to the early 1960s. Jackson's course offered practical training, integrating lectures, physical books, and secondary literature:

> The bibliography course at Harvard absorbed much of Jackson's thought and effort. Its format and syllabus were entirely of his own devising. Composed mainly of graduate students in the English Department, it met once a week

through both terms of the academic year in a two-hour session with a short break for a tea and cigarette. Enrollment was limited to ten or twelve at most, and some years was much smaller.

The baptism of fire was immediate: Jackson's customary inaugural lecture, 'Linked and Unlinked Books', was sufficiently different from anything the class had ever heard to bring them to a pitch of attention that never slackened throughout the year. All students were expected to master McKerrow's *Introduction to Bibliography* as rapidly as possible. With that as a common background, Jackson launched into the bibliographical stratosphere in all directions. Each session revolved about a special topic: signatures, cancels, collation, provenance, type identification, and the like. Jackson's remarks were generally informal, based partly on outline notes but mostly on actual examples chosen from Harvard collections. He demonstrated each book in turn, then passed it about the table for the students to see at close range. Few could forget this experience of examining a procession of fascinating books with perhaps the best guide in the world standing by to explain and illuminate.

Each member also had to take part in composing and printing a short text edited by the class. Producing this pamphlet provided an actual printing experience that was more valuable than reading any textbook, and their copies were greatly treasured by those who had worked on them. A high point of each year was an invitation from the Jacksons to cocktails and a buffet supper, after which all hands set about the dining-room table to stitch the pamphlets into their covers.[4]

Although a press and type were located in the library, the students carried out their project at the Harvard Printing Office.[5]

On a larger scale are the efforts to form teaching presses or collections, usually as part of a graduate program in English or library science and sometimes in connection with an academic library. The first person known to have followed McKerrow's injunction was Carl Rollins, who set up a bibliographical press at Yale in 1927. In the United Kingdom, Kenneth Povey established a press at Durham University in 1928. Hugh Smith did the same at University College, London, in 1933.[6] In the early 1950s, Philip Gaskell, whose *New Introduction to Bibliography* (1972) built on and extended McKerrow's work, founded the Walter Lane Press at Cambridge 'to provide graduate students of English with a little printing office that would enable scholars to solve the textual puzzles due to accidents of the press, following the model recommended by English bibliographers like R. B. McKerrow'.[7] James Mosley, Librarian at the St Bride Printing Library from 1958 to 1999, has described working at the Walter Lane Press as an undergraduate in the early 1950s:

> Gaskell wanted to do serious work, and his major project was to print an edition in octavo. The apprentices were allowed to set long takes of copy,

which Gaskell put through the stick again to bring them up to his standard of setting. I came back to Cambridge during a vacation to act as puller to his beater (Gaskell didn't trust anyone else to do the inking, but the pressman could provide muscle and could do relatively little damage). We printed on reams of paper that had been properly damped in the traditional way. There were a thousand sheets to print – so two thousand impressions to make. It would have been a day's work in the 18th century, but it took us three days, painfully acquiring the technique of printing a full octavo forme and backing it up. It was only on the third day that the job quite suddenly began to acquire its own natural rhythm. We found that we were coordinating the two tasks of pulling and beating more easily. I was no longer pulling the bar of the press like a rower but letting my body-weight do the work. (Just how effective this technique was I found out when, becoming just a bit too relaxed, I failed to grab the bar in time and shot myself backwards across the pressroom).[8]

Mosley described this experience as a 'revelation . . . between slow and painstaking reconstruction and reliving the experience'.[9]

The typical laboratory program consists of a printing press (usually an iron hand press of late nineteenth or early twentieth century vintage), enough type for simple projects, and related tools – composing sticks, furniture, galley trays, a chase or two, and other necessities. The larger programs have often included equipment for bookbinding, papermaking, and type founding, and sometimes even a reference library and a combination of original texts and facsimiles illustrating various genres (novels, pamphlets, periodicals, etc), and features (chained books, fore-edge paintings, vellum bindings, etc).

The scarcity and age of surviving tools and equipment, especially in regard to the hand press period, makes them too precious for student use. A few surviving wooden presses may be capable of being put into working order, but the idea of using one in a classroom is untenable. There are many replica wooden presses around, and a good set of plans for building them was published in 1978.[10] But a replica is still a replica, and regardless of how carefully constructed we can never really know to what extent it may vary from an original in operation, and thus to what degree we are removed from a truly authentic experience. A far more serious obstacle exists in regard to type. The few antique founts that remain have long since been taken out of use. Students may be able to study them as artifacts, but they will never be able to use them. For classroom printing we rely on Monotype, usually in modern faces and with a far smaller character set than a hand press font.

The scarcity of surviving tools, our reliance on replicas, and the use materials from a later period to illustrate the processes of an earlier one all point to the necessity of resourcefulness and improvisation. The teacher of bibliographical printing must use the tools available in ways that are instructive and effective. The teacher must also be clear about the objectives of the course and honest as to the compromises necessary to achieve them. William A. Jackson, for example, was careful to tell his students that his course would 'not make them bibliographers – that would only be possible by looking at, really looking at, thousands of books, many thousands of books, and making themselves familiar with what is normal and what is phenomenal in at least one period of printing history'.[11]

We should be equally clear in what students should expect from our efforts. Our courses and workshops cannot on their own make bibliographers and book historians. We offer printing exercises as a means of moving students toward this goal. We are not training craft practitioners; at the most, we are providing students with tactile learning experiences to promote a 'clear and lively comprehension' of the processes behind textual production.

As to the compromises, we should deal with these openly, for in doing so we are not only honest about our methods but we also create teaching opportunities. For example, if one is using an iron hand press to teach printing before 1800, an effective way of highlighting the difference between a wooden and an iron press is by pointing out that one of the intended improvements of the latter was the ability to print an entire forme with a single pull of the bar. An iron hand press also provides an opportunity to talk about changes to the screw in the quest for more pressure on the platen and the need these changes created for a stronger and more durable frame.

While Gaskell wanted to create an immersion experience, most teaching programs are not so ambitious. Mosley's account of his time at the Walter Lane Press underscores both the value of such training and its challenges. Significant time and labor are required to print a work of any length in numbers approaching even the low end of the average hand press print run. It is telling that not until the third day did Gaskell's team begin to achieve a rhythm similar in feeling to that of historical pressmen, and still to complete the project the run for the second sheet had to be cut to five hundred, and the third sheet had to be printed by the University Press. Moreover, to take part in the project, Mosley came back to school during vacation. An exercise on this scale is impossible to complete on a standard class schedule.

But no matter the size of the project, the more time – and the more flexible the time – the better. Gaskell's workshop model required many hours over a few days. Jackson's classroom model extended those hours out over the length of an entire academic year, though students completed the setting and printing as well the binding or stitching of the pamphlets outside of class.

Jackson's example also indicates the importance of having help. While not essential, an assistant is useful for managing all the elements of an effective printing exercise. Someone, after all, has to stay late to clean and distribute the forms of type. Students can help, but if one hopes to use the type again someone must follow behind. In most cases this job will fall to the instructor, but an assistant can speed the work – and help avoid burnout.

The difficulty of replicating an historic process and the impossibility of avoiding compromise are challenges that all teachers face when incorporating practical work into the classroom. Taken together, all of these collections, presses, and classes have provided thousands of students with the chance to set type, pull on the bar of a printing press, or some other activity as part of their bibliographical education. The extent and the influence of these initiatives are unrecognized aspects of McKerrow's legacy. Though Gaskell's *New Introduction* was a great advance and remains an indispensable aid, it has alleviated neither the need nor the desire for learning by doing, in large part because it has proven so useful in conjunction with hands-on experience. As David McKitterick has written, 'Many a student has come to understand the principles of bibliographical practice by the joint lessons offered on the one hand by McKerrow, and on the other by a hand-press and its associated equipment'.[12]

Generations of students have benefited from hands-on training, and those students have included some of the most influential individuals in the field. The theoretical changes we have experienced have not decreased the need for or interest in practical training. Rather, these changes have arisen in large part because of such training, which in turn has only increased its importance and prevalence.

Notes

1. R. B. McKerrow, 'Notes on Bibliographical Evidence for Literary Students and Editors', *Transactions of the Bibliographical Society*, 12 (April 1913), p. 220.

2. McKerrow, *Introduction to Bibliography for Literary Students* (Oxford, Oxford University Press, 1927); reprinted, (New Castle, Delaware: Oak Knoll Press, 1994), p. 4.

3. Philip Gaskell, 'The Bibliographical Press Movement', *Journal of the Printing Historical Society*, 1 (1965), p. 1.

4. William H. Bond, 'Introduction', in William A. Jackson, *Records of a Bibliographer: Selected Papers of William Alexander Jackson* (Cambridge MA, Belknap Press of Harvard University Press, 1967), p. 23.

5. Bond, 'Introduction', p. 14.

6. Gaskell, 'The Bibliographical Press Movement', pp. 7–13. For background information in Albert Hugh Smith, *A Description of the Hand-press in the English Department at University College, London* (privately printed, Department of English, University College, London, 1933). For a list of laboratory programs, please see Resources, p. 185.

7. James Mosley, Acceptance Remarks for APHA's 2003 Individual Award, Annual Meeting of the American Printing History Association, New York, New York, 25 January 2003, http://printinghistory.org/htm/misc/awards/2003-james-mosley.htm (accessed 7 May 2006).

8. Mosley, acceptance remarks.

9. Mosley, acceptance remarks.

10. Elizabeth Harris and Clinton Sisson, *The Common Press: Being a Record, Description, & Delineation of the Early Eighteenth-century Handpress in the Smithsonian Institution* (Boston, D. R. Godine, 1978).

11. Jackson, *Records of a Bibliographer*, pp. 211–12.

12. David McKitterick, 'Introduction' in McKerrow, *Introduction to Bibliography*, pp. xiii-xxiv.

Bookends: Towards a Poetics of Material Form

Sydney J. Shep

Anyone involved with the teaching of book history, bibliography, or textual criticism must, at some point, address both the definition of and our relationship to the book.[1] Guglielmo Cavallo and Roger Chartier have commented that 'no text exists outside of the physical support that offers it for reading (or hearing) or outside the circumstance in which it is read (or heard). Authors do not write books; they write texts that become written objects'.[2] Yet paradoxically, as Robert Escarpit suggests, 'when we hold it in our hands, all we hold is the paper: the *book* is elsewhere'.[3] *That* book is the sum of its textual incarnation, its modes of communication, and its legacy of preservation: that is, the entire constellation of documents and voices which surround and penetrate the permeable membrane of the material form as it moves through time and space. As such, the book is not elsewhere, but everywhere, manifestly present as a reading machine, remaining both transparent and opaque, the vehicle for intellectual content at the same time as inseparable from the individuated and historicized experience of that content. To understand *this* book, to see the object in its material form, to describe it, and to embed it in a multiplicity of interpretive contexts is paramount.

The book that is here but not here informs the ways we frame our research and talk about books. Cataloguing conventionally separates the carrier from the content, even in the new FRBR system (Function Requirements of the Bibliographic Record).[4] Descriptive bibliography is built on the rationale of the ideal copy – a kind of transcendental sign – that is used as the yardstick to interpret copy-specific evidence. Textual editing wrestles with authorial intent. The re-purposing or multi-purposing of content across a myriad of media formats in the digital age problematises the relationship between expressive forms and sociologies, between texts and contexts, and, in the process, dematerializes one object to create a new type of object record. It is timely to re-examine that fundamental unit of our research – the book object – and think about whether our methods and discourses have sufficiently addressed 'the mutual entailment of the lexical and non-lexical dimensions of the physical artifact'.[5]

Many of the bibliographical breakthroughs and explanations of textual cruces in the twentieth century were dependent upon the reconstruction of practice – imaginatively or tangibly – predicated on an intimate knowledge of process recovered through the intensive reading of trade manuals and practical experiments. McKenzie's legacy was not only a recognition of the importance of printing house archives in the investigation of the physical remains of those houses – the books themselves – but also the need to understand the processes which created those artefacts, often through simulations in the research laboratory of the bibliographic press with its array of printing presses, type, and industrial realia. But what is the evidential relationship between the interpretation of books and the notional recreation of printing house practice? What authority does a first-hand, working knowledge of historic practice have for our understanding of technology's social, economic, and political formations, for our mapping of textual transmission, and for our historically-situated textual interpretations? Does such knowledge furnish 'privileged paths of access'[6] to culture, especially cultures not our own? Or is it simply one of a larger repertoire of historiographical techniques which is as fallible and contestable as any other?

Historical reconstructions or simulations mediated by the bibliographic press have enabled some book historians to engage with artifacts on a deeper level. Philip Gaskell has noted that 'For most people, a few moments in which printing equipment is actually seen in use is worth more than hours of reading textbooks about it'.[7] I would argue, however, that this kind of passive looking is not enough; students need to consolidate and apply their visual understanding by acts of doing and making. Take a book from the handpress or machine printing era, for instance. It is easy to point to where a letter at the end of a line has slipped below the baseline, where a piece of spacing matter has forced its way up to type height and been printed, or where the edge of a stereotype plate has started to wear away. It is another experience to demonstrate how this could happen using a locked-up forme as an exemplar. It is quite a different experience for students to discover and rectify the problem when it occurs in the process of handsetting and proofing their own work. To put it another way, students have moved through the educational taxonomy from simple remembering and understanding, through application and analysis to the highest order of information processing and cognitive complexity, that of evaluation and creation.[8]

A problem-based or inquiry-led approach to bibliographic understanding is central to another domain of artifactual apprenticeship currently untapped by the book history community: the field of creative practice known as book arts. By applying technical knowledge to the creation of works which challenge the relationship between structure and meaning, form and function, sequentiality and process, text and reader, students achieve not only a profound understanding of the nature and behaviour of the materials they are handling, but an awareness of the interrelationship of book production methods and their interpretive consequences. It is well documented in the pedagogical literature that students learn better and retain more information when the classroom experience includes an active engagement with multiple senses. One only has to refer to developmental psychology and physiology to note that childhood acquisition of motor skills is achieved through the interactive encounter of eye and hand which stimulates and trains the motor neuron cortex. Gary Frost, conservation and bookbinding specialist at the University of Iowa, refers to this dialogue between hand and mind as 'haptic' learning, evoking Marshall McLuhan's writings on the five sense sensorium,[9] but also drawing on the new area of scientific research dealing with virtual reality, psychophysics, intelligent mechanical systems, and the tangible-tactile universe of the new electronic media. As Frost remarks, 'the hands prompt the mind in an ergonomic of comprehension … We always recall read precepts in their physical location on the page of a specific booke. Other fingerings of page turning and manipulations of booke structure work as prompts to our progression through content'.[10] By extension, the practice of marginalia performs a comparable mnemonic function, despite its reputation in the public sphere as institutional trespass.[11]

Tactile reading interactions with the material object are heightened in the book arts world of tangible making. The book artist takes as given McKenzie's notion of the book as an expressive form,[12] or Johanna Drucker's 'idea of the book as a performative space for the production of reading'.[13] They regard the book as a specimen of three-dimensional paper engineering and typographic architecture, and are well equipped to assess the relationship between its mechanical and conceptual parts. Students who bring to the bibliographic press and descriptive bibliography a background in artist printmaking immediately recognise how ink behaves, have an intimate knowledge of paper, display an affinity with metal and wood, and can identify the printed evidence of mechanical image-making processes with precision and insight. The professional or amateur bookbinder who is asked to analyse a binding will see more varieties of evidence, interpret what is visually present, and extrapolate what is absent more often than his/her untrained peer. The artist papermaker is adept in reading the blank or printed sheet and is hypersensitised to the sound, smell, touch, and taste of paper, as well as its visual characteristics. Book artists who combine all these skills can make an invaluable contribution to the study of book history and enrich our language of bibliographic description, particularly as we face the challenge of new media forms and the problematic of the virtual codex.

The haptic philosophy of teaching and learning which supports the integration of descriptive bibliography, book history and the book arts is exemplified in the work done at Victoria University of Wellington's Wai-te-ata Press, founded by D.F. McKenzie in 1962, and re-established in 1995. The Press today is a living laboratory of technical experimentation, both in the reconstruction of historical practice, and through the active engagement with materials in an environment of creative research. Undergraduate and graduate students collaborate in self-generated rather than facsimile projects in a setting of research-led learning and teaching.[14] They hone their technological skill-set, build their bibliographic language library, and activate their manually-acquired knowledge along with archival and field research to analyse and evaluate the role of print in historic and contemporary cultural milieux. Furthermore, by introducing print as a part of a mutually entangled continuum of oral, manuscript, print and electronic communication media, the initially unfamiliar experience of the print shop is given contemporary relevance and meaning through the creative processes of making.

One successful example is a major assignment in a twelve-week, second-year undergraduate course entitled 'Print, Communication, & Culture'. Students working in small groups of three or four design, handset, and letterpress print a postcard. Research includes identification of a client (real or imagined), a robust and integrated promotion and distribution campaign, the creation of a suitable text for printing on the card (maximum fifteen words, no graphics, one colour), the formulation of a budget for an edition of 100 cards, and the printing of 10 specimens for marking, archiving, and personal record. The group's paper trail in portfolio form accompanies the specimens as do confidential peer evaluations which are used for moderation. All students in the group receive the same grade. Because this assignment is about synthesizing and applying knowledge in a creative and collaborative space, students are taught about effective group collaboration from the outset. Course learning tools such as BlackBoard are harnessed to facilitate communication and collaboration outside of the studio environment. This assignment occurs three-quarters of the way through the course, after the completion of a series of letterpress labs. In week one, the analysis of freely available, commercially produced postcards helps students develop and hone their interpretive vocabulary. The mechanics of handsetting and printing are taught in the context of expressive typography in week three, with research on specific type fonts one of the course's compulsory short exercises. Historic examples of advertising and ephemera are consulted and discussed in week five. The design of the entire course ensures that the necessary conceptual and practical building blocks are built from the ground up, reinforced through lecture-discussion sessions, short exercises, and weekly assigned readings. Comments from students about this piece of assessment are overwhelmingly positive. They are surprised to find such a project occurs at a university and that it can be so much fun. They are motivated to devote quality time to the project and in company with peers who often become good friends. Word-of-mouth about this particular project has contributed to student enrolments; requests for more time in the print shop are a constant refrain in the course evaluations.

Despite this success, it is no easy task in the current academic environment to bring together the two bookends on the book studies bookshelf – bibliography and book arts – through such artifactual apprenticeships. For Prown the problem is one of methodological training: 'we have been inculcated with a mode of hierarchical ordering in the way in which we evaluate human activities and experiences, privileging that which is cerebral and abstract over that which is manual and material'.[15] Put another way and in the context of creative research, Paul Carter finds that because of 'the lack of credibility given to the vital processes of design and creativity … scholarship and research in these fields, where it does occur, is "about" them, rather than "of" them'.[16]

Roger Chartier characterizes book studies as an amalgam of textual criticism, bibliography and cultural history. Such interdisciplinarity continually energises the field, but how can we adequately equip students to enter and thrive in such a complex discourse arena? It is time for book history to confront its alter-ego, the book, and teach the next generation of scholars the importance of learning from things. We must reassess the book as material form, evaluate whether our current descriptive practices are adequate, discuss how to develop a requisite skills base within the teaching/learning environment, and provide the appropriate building blocks to advance the material thinking of our field. Bridging the gap between bibliography and book arts through artifactual apprenticeships is one way of achieving both an informed understanding of the visible evidence resident in print objects, and a deep knowing of their processes of creation. As Corn advises, 'In the context of the debate over when and how scholars learn from things, it behoves us to spell out more precisely our debts to objects and to think about how those artifactual apprenticeships, however minor, have shaped our historical questions and interpretations'.[17]

Notes

1. 'book' is used as a shorthand term for what Adams and Barker term the more comprehensive, though admittedly awkward, 'bibliographical document'. 'Book history' is also used here as a shorthand term intended to embrace print culture as well as book studies and book culture, even though I acknowledge that the semantic differences are increasingly regarded to be theoretical and methodological ones.
2. Guglielmo Cavallo and Roger Chartier, tr. Lydia G. Cochrane, 'Introduction', *A History of Reading in the West* (Oxford, Polity Press, 1995), p. 5.
3. Robert Escarpit, 'Historical Survey', in *The Book Revolution. Books and the World Today* (London and Paris, Harrap and UNESCO, 1966), p. 17.

4. International Federation of Library Associations and Institutions. Cataloging Section of the FRBR Review Group. Final Report. http://www.ifla.org/VII/s13/frbr/frbr (accessed 7 May 2006)

5. Abhijit Gupta and Swapan Chakravorty (eds), *Print Areas. Book History in India,* (Delhi, Permanent Black, 2004), p. 7.

6. Jules D. Prown, 'Material/Culture. Can the Farmer and the Cowman still be Friends?' in W. David Kingery, (ed.), *Learning from Things: Method and Theory in Material Culture Studies* (Washington, Smithsonian University Press, 1996), p. 24.

7. Philip Gaskell, 'The Bibliographic Press Movement', *Journal of the Printing History Society,* 1 (1965), p. 6.

8. See L.W. Anderson and D.R. Krathwohl (eds), *A Taxonomy for Learning, Teaching, and Assessing: A Revision of Bloom's Taxonomy of Educational Objectives* (New York, Longman, 2001).

9. Marshall McLuhan, 'Inside the Five Sense Sensorium', in David Howes (ed.), *The Empire of the Senses. The Sensual Culture Reader* (Oxford & New York, Berg, 2005), pp. 43-52.

10. Gary Frost, 'Future of the Booke', for Craft, Culture, Critique symposium, April 2004, and found at http://www.futureofthebook.com/storiestoc/booke (accessed 7 May 2006) and reprinted in *SHARP News*, 13:2 (Spring 2004), pp. 3-4. Frost's spelling of 'booke' is intentional.

11. See H. J. Jackson's discussion of the psychology of marginalia in *Marginalia. Readers Writing in Books* (New Haven and London: Yale University Press, 2001), chapter 3.

12. D.F. McKenzie, 'Typography and Meaning: The Case of William Congreve', in *Making Meaning: 'Printers of the Mind' and Other Essays*, Peter McDonald and Michael Suarez (eds), p. 210; also the title of McKenzie's first Panizzi Lecture "The book as an expressive form," in *Bibliography and the Sociology of Texts*, 1986; reprint (Cambridge, Cambridge University Press, 1999).

13. Johanna Drucker, 'The Virtual Codex from Page Space to E-Space', (2003) at http://www.philobiblon.com/drucker/ (accessed 7 May 2006).

14. A term used by Professor Tom Angelo and Dr. Christine Asmar of Victoria University of Wellington to describe a student-centred model which connects research-led teaching, inquiry-based learning, and the scholarship of teaching and learning.

15. Prown, p. 19.

16. Paul Carter, *Material Thinking. The Theory and Practice of Creative Research* (Melbourne, Melbourne University Press, 2004), pp. 7-8.

17. Joseph J. Corn, 'Object Lessons / Object Myth? What Historians of Technology Learn from Things', in W. David Kingery, (ed.) *Learning from Things. Method and Theory of Material Culture Studies* (Washington & London: Smithsonian Institution Press, 1996), p. 49.

Book History on the Road: Finding and Organizing Resources outside the Classroom

Lisa Berglund

I first taught the history of the book while a faculty member at a New England liberal arts college. My syllabus centered on the figure of Samuel Johnson, and our class met in the Rare Book Room where we examined treasures from its underutilized collection of eighteenth-century materials. My ten students examined a first edition of Fanny Burney's *Evelina*, a second edition of Johnson's *Dictionary*, Johnson's *Plan for a Dictionary*, volumes of the Harleian Miscellany, a second edition of Christopher Anstey's *New Bath Guide*, and local newspapers from the 1790s. My determinedly contemporary students enjoyed the atmosphere of the Rare Book Room: its white gloves, pencil-only policy, and leather and wood interior, gave them the thrill of visiting a dignified time capsule. They also enjoyed a strong sense of privilege, as they entered a room not normally used for classes. Studying the history of the book made students feel like academic insiders.[1]

When I joined the faculty at Buffalo State College, I couldn't imagine how to teach my seminar in its old format. Buffalo State College, with an enrollment of 11,000 students, offers a standard liberal arts curriculum, but specializes in teacher training and technical studies. The library has no Rare Book Room, and its collection in areas like eighteenth-century studies has not been consistently maintained, though its electronic resources are excellent. The English Department's standard enrollment in upper-level courses is thirty-five students, with most courses oversubscribed. Even if I brought some of my own hand-press era books to class, what would be the point of asking thirty-five English majors to crane their necks for a glimpse of a small octavo volume of Hester Thrale Piozzi's *Anecdotes of Dr. Johnson*? I certainly could not pass rare books around a large lecture hall. Yet I also could not expect a substantial reduction in class size or funds for buying old and rare books.

As I searched for a way to teach book history in this new setting, I realized that neither Buffalo State nor the City of Buffalo, New York, lack resources.

Rather, my challenge was learning to recognize resources as such, and to look beyond the bibliographer's haven of the Rare Book Room. Once I began thinking outside that space, I discovered an equally vital setting for a course on the history of the book.[2] To my surprise, I also realized that my students at Buffalo State found the world outside the Rare Book Room just as unfamiliar as the inner sanctum had been to my students at the liberal arts college. In this essay, I offer ideas that may be useful to faculty in similar situations, particularly those who are attempting to start a book history course or program without the assistance of a Rare Book Room librarian. I'll first summarize the topics covered in my course, then outline practical ways to adapt to the lack of conventional resources, including ways of turning unlikely library materials to good account as well as ideas for inexpensive classroom materials. I will discuss field trips to local libraries, bookstores and other venues. Finally, I will describe specific logistical arrangements that can allow an instructor to organize field trips without conflicting with students' other courses or exceeding the time commitment of an ordinary class.

Problem Solving through Special Topics courses. For most literature and history professors, a book history course will offer new challenges, particularly if you plan to take the class 'on the road'. Whatever your resources, if you are introducing a book history course, first pilot the course through your department's Special Topics or Senior Seminar class (or whatever flexible format is available). This will allow you to iron out kinks before you argue for its addition to your department's regular curriculum. In my case, I used the Senior Seminar slot (a one-time option), which offered a limited enrollment of fifteen English majors. I was thus able to solve logistical problems before addressing the challenges of teaching a large class.[3]

Scavenging in the library and the hallway. Where my earlier course concentrated on the eighteenth century, at Buffalo State, resources are broad rather than deep. Consequently I now teach a survey, covering 1) Construction of the Printed Book; 2) Introduction to Descriptive Bibliography; 3) History of Print Technology; 4) History and Theories of Readership and Authorship; 5) Issues in Textual Editing; and 6) The Future of the Book. We use *The Book History Reader*, supplemented by other readings.[4]

Since I wanted students to work with books from the hand-press era, the college archivist found eighteen books printed before 1800 (yes, *eighteen* – though two are three-volume sets). Of these, one book was printed in the sixteenth century, one in the seventeenth, and the remaining sixteen books in the last quarter of the eighteenth century. The books included a number of dull but respectable histories, grammar texts (Latin, German, Russian), a religious tract, and a book of familiar essays. One poem, no fiction. None were in folio format. The most intriguing find was a joke book bound together with a scrapbook of clippings from newspapers, advertisements for the theater, and broadside ballads.

During our three library sessions, each student chose a book to examine and describe in detail for the class. Ironically, the fact that the texts were not terribly interesting motivated closer study of book construction and paratexts. One student discovered that in her Russian book (which she couldn't read), the signatures were in Greek. The student examining the German/Latin grammar discovered evidence of bookworms. The second volume of *A History of Wales* proved to have several unopened bolts. Deteriorating bindings made it easy to see how the books were put together. Thus, the fact that these books were *not* Johnson's *Dictionary* or *Evelina* ensured that my students, possibly for the first time, looked at, rather than read, the books before them.[5] The fact that the books, though old, were not particularly valuable meant that students could examine them without extraordinary precautions.

In the classroom, I conduct paper-folding exercises using both ordinary sheets of newspaper (scavenged from the hallway) and photocopier paper decorated with fake chainlines and watermarks. I distribute cheap candles and send my students home to read by candlelight for fifteen minutes.[6] A quick raid on departmental offices turned up a variety of abandoned early editions of the Norton *Anthology*. To supplement our discussion of the English literature canon, I distributed photocopies of the tables of contents of these anthologies and asked students to draw conclusions about the political and social changes reflected therein. I also asked them to compare the physical construction of the second edition (the oldest anthology I found) and the current seventh edition, in its optional six-volume paperback format.

Field trips. None of my students had ever entered Buffalo & Erie County's Central Library. This startling revelation confirmed that one outcome of my course must be to introduce my students, through the medium of the book, to their own city. Yes, students had patronized branch libraries; most of them live in the suburbs or residential sections of Buffalo. But they didn't know that Buffalo owns a nationally renowned collection of Mark Twain material, including Twain's revisions to *Huckleberry Finn*. Nor that the library has a Shakespeare First Folio, John James Audubon's *Birds of North America,* a Copernicus, and a collection of other rare books acquired during the Gilded Age. The Lockwood Collection at the University at Buffalo has impressive holdings of incunabula and original manuscripts donated by wealthy Buffalo residents of the late nineteenth and early twentieth centuries. Both libraries generously arranged tours and presentations for my students, and expressed a willingness to host similar gatherings when the course becomes a regular part of the curriculum. In the future I hope to arrange trips to the Buffalo Historical Society and to libraries at other area colleges. But to avoid imposing too much on the generosity of the librarians and archivists who are donating their time and expertise to my students, I plan to identify at least a half-dozen sites where students can view rare books, and to visit two of them whenever I teach the course.

While most colleges and universities will be within reasonable distance of a decent collection of old books, finding a moveable-type press is not as easy. Luckily, Western New York is the home of Roycroft, the Arts & Crafts community founded by the eccentric disciple of William Morris, Elbert Hubbard. The Roycroft campus and its press closes for the winter; however, keen to spread the Hubbard gospel, the director opened the main building and prepared a special lecture and tour. She also allowed me to show my class the parts of the press, as well as type and composing sticks, which they had only seen in illustrations.[7] To give students background for our visit, I added a lecture on Morris and the Arts and Crafts movement.

The final field trip was a visit to the Old Editions Book Shop in downtown Buffalo. Surprisingly only two students had ever visited a used book store before. Along with the tour, the owner talked about how he got into book dealing and the rare book business. The store has a huge selection of used books but specializes in modern first editions and Buffaloiana; my students were delighted to see books they were reading in their other courses and shocked by the prices. This was probably the single most successful field trip of the semester, and several of my students reported subsequent visits and purchases.

To ensure that my students were active participants in these trips, I required 300-500 word informal essays after each field trip, describing what they saw and what they learned; these essays and participation in the field trips counted for twenty percent of the class grade. Many essays turned into reflective journal-style entries, in which the students expressed their growing astonishment as they learned more about the world of the book outside the classroom.

Independent expeditions. In addition to group field trips, I required my students to go on the road individually. Five students visited both a chain bookstore (Barnes & Noble, Borders, etc.) and any other venue in which books were sold. I supplied a list of questions, such as 'Based on the arrangement of the store, what are its priorities?' or 'What aspects of the reading experience does the store want to sell?' Presenting the results of their research in oral reports, most students understood how chain stores relegate books to almost secondary status, and they were increasingly sensitive to the different ways books signify in the marketplace. For their second bookshop, two students visited a popular independent bookstore, one visited a small used book store, and one a comic book store. Perhaps the most creative student reported on the bin of discards for sale at her local branch library, where she had taken her daughter for an afternoon story group. This assignment was supported by short readings exploring the commodification and consumption of books, Janice Radway's *Reading the Romance*, and essays on readership studies in *The Book History Reader*.[8]

Another group did their independent field trip online, finding and comparing electronic versions of works they were reading in their other classes to the texts assigned by their professors.[9] The students' outrage over the liberties taken by with various online 'editors' signaled a real end of innocence; they now approach the Internet with a skeptical eye. Finally, as a make-up assignment for one of the group field trips, several students visited the Karpeles Manuscript Museum. In the future, I may shift visiting the Mark Twain Room at the Central Library to an individual, rather than a group field trip.

Logistics. At a largely commuter college such as Buffalo State, most students have family and job obligations and extra-mural activities can be extremely hard to coordinate. Indeed, the practical difficulties of teaching 'on the road' represent the greatest challenge of designing this course: it's easy to talk about visiting a local printing plant or Rare Book Room, but very difficult to get one's students to that venue. Even at a residential college, it can be impossible to coordinate trips during the day, when both students and faculty have competing obligations, yet most Rare Book Rooms and other institutions are not open during the evenings. The following solution may not work at all colleges, but I hope it will provide a model that can be adjusted to fit your particular circumstances.

I could not sign up for a regular three-hour 'seminar' timeslot, because the earliest available at Buffalo State is at 4:30 p.m. By then, most Rare Book Rooms are closed. I needed a time that: 1) fell between 10 a.m. and 4 p.m., when libraries and museums are open; 2) was long enough to accommodate a 45-60 minute visit and at least an hour of round-trip transport; and 3) would not conflict with students' other courses or with my own departmental obligations. Moreover, I could not ask students to spend more than three hours per week in meetings for the class, whether on or off campus. Finally, I needed to ensure that no student would enroll in the course without being able to participate in the field trips.

Therefore, I requested the MWF 2:00-2:50 p.m. time slot. At Buffalo State, courses are scheduled on Mondays and Wednesdays until 10 p.m., but there are no courses after 3 p.m. on Fridays; thus our class could meet for an extra hour on Friday afternoons without conflicting with another class. Next, through the college's online course registration program, I required instructor permission for registration. When students sought my permission, I explained that the course would include required field trips on some Friday afternoons, from 2-4 p.m; if they could not be available for those trips, they could not enroll in the class.

I offered librarians and other potential field trip hosts a choice of Friday afternoons, and I ultimately spread the trips out over three months (putting two in April when the weather was better). I scheduled the presentations to begin at 2:30 or 2:45 p.m. (depending on the distance of the venue from the campus) and to conclude around 3:30 p.m. Once our schedule was established, I cancelled four other Friday classes, ensuring that students were not obliged to meet for more than three hours per week overall. Three students and myself did the driving (carpooling was necessary since parking is tight downtown and impossible on the UB campus). I secured parking passes and paid for parking as necessary. Before assigning students to individual off-campus trips (e.g., to bookstores) I learned which students owned cars; those who did not completed the online investigation, which could be carried out on campus.

Realizing that most of my students drive to Buffalo State on the freeway, bypassing downtown Buffalo (and the Central Library) altogether, I deliberately drove students through the spectacular residential area north of the commercial downtown, so they could see the old mansions once owned by the same rich families who built up the Central Library's rare book collection. The history of the book had become a way to introduce my students to their own home town.

Teaching book history from within a Rare Book Room is like teaching at a liberal arts college; in either case, you nestle comfortably within a restricted sanctum from which all but the richest and rarest are excluded. And teaching book history on the road reflects the atmosphere of a large commuter university. My students at Buffalo State learn about print culture as they absorb the rest of their education, in a sprawling array of classrooms and other sites, in lectures and presentations slotted between job shifts and childcare obligations and complicated by parking problems. Yet ironically, my students in both academic settings began at much the same place. Just as none of my students had visited Buffalo's Central Library, none of my earlier students had ever set foot in the college's Rare Book Room. Along with a deepened awareness of print culture, perhaps the most important lesson students taking our courses may acquire is an enlightened citizenship, whether their world of the moment is a privileged city on a hill or an aging metropolis on the shore of Lake Erie.

Notes

1. For a fuller description of this course and its assignments, see my article 'Samuel Johnson and the Eighteenth-Century Reader', *Teaching the Eighteenth Century*, 7 (1999), pp. 45-58.
2. Credit for stimulating my thinking in this new, fruitful direction goes to my fellow students in 'Teaching the History of the Book' at the Rare Book School at the University of Virginia, June 2003.
3. To solve the enrolment problem I've requested an enrolment cap of twenty-five, as with our writing-intensive courses. Since most Rare Book Rooms limit visitors to fifteen, I break the class into two groups, taking half the students to one venue and half to another. Ideally, I find pairs of comparable venues – two rare book rooms, two presses, etc. – so students have similar experiences.
4. David Finkelstein and Alistair McCleery ed., *The Book History Reader* (New York, Routledge, 2001). Syllabi of the pilot version of 'The History of the Printed Book' (Spring 2004) and the

version proposed for permanent inclusion in the Buffalo State English Department curriculum appear at our companion website.

5. Books – not just old books – are alien to many English majors. Though long resigned to my students' inability to figure out the 'long s,' I was thunderstruck when fifteen senior English literature majors claimed never to have seen a bookplate.

6. See note 1.

7. Roycroft, which charged student-rate admission, was the only trip that cost students money, apart from travel expenses.

8. Janice A. Radway, *Reading the Romance: Women, Patriarchy, and Popular Literature* (Chapel Hill, University of North Carolina Press, 1991).

9. This assignment was supported by readings from Geoffrey Nunberg, ed. *The Future of the Book* (Berkeley, University of California Press, 1996).

Jane Eyre on eBay: Building a Teaching Collection

John A. Buchtel

Book history presupposes that the physical artifacts in which texts appear fundamentally shape the experience, reception, and meaning of those texts. A book history approach, then, engages students with texts-as-artifacts. In teaching a novel, that engagement might take two shapes: first, an encounter with contextualizing materials that illuminate the content of the novel; and second, an examination of materials that reveal what happens when a novel becomes a cultural icon. With modern editions of *Jane Eyre*, for example, students will not realize that the novel's original form – as a three-decker – influenced the way the work took shape. If apprised of this original structure, students can trace the cliff-hanger-like endings of the first two volumes, contemplate how this structure affected Charlotte Brontë's compositional strategies, and imagine what the experience of reading the novel was like for members of subscription libraries as they checked out one volume at a time.[1] Nothing can replace the experience of *seeing* a three-decker novel, or of examining at first hand the kinds of contextualizing materials that can help bring a novel like *Jane Eyre* to life, such as a marriage license on parchment, examples of the sort of 'Hindustanee' glossaries St John Rivers gives Jane Eyre to study, or illustrations from books Jane Eyre describes, such as the potent wood engravings in Bewick's *British Birds*.

Examining such contextualizing materials has typically been possible only in a special collections library. But this essay is not about 'What Special Collections Can Do for You' – but rather about what instructors can do for themselves, with just a few hours surfing eBay and BookFinder.com and browsing in secondhand bookshops. A collection of meaningful artifacts for use as a teaching laboratory can be assembled inexpensively and quickly, using non-traditional collecting strategies, as has recently been done at Rare Book School (RBS) at the University of Virginia. The RBS *Jane Eyre* collection was formed to answer the question, 'What happens when a novel becomes a classic?' While bypassing first and private press editions, the collection encompasses a universe of other materials, from nineteenth-century popular editions to comic books to other novels that allude to *Jane Eyre* to a wide range of ephemera. The collection's rich array of teaching examples also serves as a rewarding primary source research laboratory. The comparison of objects in the collection provides powerful evidence of cultural change, from the development of the high school English curriculum, to the introduction of various theoretical perspectives, to shifts in publishing practices and consumer culture, to the changing tastes of the reading public.

The search will uncover numerous relevant and surprising artifacts. One such item in the RBS collection – a pamphlet-sized object with the familiar black-and-yellow striped pattern of Cliffs Notes – is an audio study guide: 'Because', the box cover slogan insists, 'books are long, and life is short'.[2] Another pamphlet sporting the same black-and-yellow color scheme, with a 'Study Guide' label on its back cover, is in fact a heavily reduced reprint of a 1940s Classics Illustrated comic book.[3] In isolation, such items could be relied upon for little more than a few chuckles. But when presented in the context of a body of related materials, such objects form powerful pedagogical tools. With little trouble and less expense, one can bring together more than two dozen different *Jane Eyre* study guides, covering a span of 50 years. Some, like the Cliffs Notes, appear in up to four editions, each reflecting the theoretical concerns of its time.

We often dismiss mass market paperbacks as cheap and disposable, but they can do much to reveal the history of a novel's cultural status and readership. How many printings has the Penguin paperback of *Jane Eyre* been through? How many cover designs has Penguin used, and how might each predispose a reader? The RBS collection will soon include a copy of every printing of the Penguin *Jane Eyre*, from the first, in orange-and-white wrappers (1953), to the classy redesign of 2003. We chose Penguin not because it is more textually significant or more interesting than the Signet Classics or Bantam or Dell: any of these could do the same job. One long row of books from the same publisher illustrates how popular a novel can become: each copy represents the thousands produced in each printing, graphically supporting Penguin's claim in a 2003 trade catalog that their *Jane Eyre* has gone through 500,000 copies. Row upon row of these books reveals the marketing genius behind mass market paperbacks – books produced for sale in uniformly sized racks in supermarket and drugstore checkout lines. Heavily read copies work best, with creases, gift inscriptions, annotations, and even highlighting: all evidence for a work's cultural pervasiveness, right down to the banal marginalia of high school students.

Of similar interest, the 1953 Cardinal paperback cover shows Jane and Rochester embracing passionately, wedding the text of a nineteenth-century gothic romance to the modern conception of a bodice-ripper (a useful object to help students broaden their definitions of 'romance'). Not surprisingly, then, eBay searches reveal that the advertising copy on the back covers of a number of modern romance novels use *Jane Eyre* as part of a marketing strategy, from Judith Bowen's Harlequin 'Superromance' *Charlotte Moore* (2001) to Amy Fetzer's *Taming the Beast* (2001) to Diana Palmer's *Lady Love* (1984), whose back cover proclaims, 'Jane Eyre, eat your heart out'. Only the most random of traditional bookstore browsing would uncover books like these, whereas dedicated eBay sellers, impractical in their keenness to gain a slight edge, type in hundreds of words from the blurbs on no-account novels. Obscure bits of information suddenly become keyword searchable. It was because an eBay seller's description of *The Quiet Stranger* (1991) included the dust jacket flap's passing reference to *Jane Eyre* that RBS discovered that *Wide Sargasso Sea* (1966) is not *Jane Eyre's* only 'prequel'.

Internet trawling can lead in very short order to dozens of sequels, retellings and derivatives, including two novels called *Mrs Rochester* (1997 and 2000); *Jane Rochester* (2000); *Jane Eyre's Daughter* (1999); *Adele: Jane Eyre's Hidden Story* (2002); *It All Began with* Jane Eyre (1980); D. M. Thomas's *Charlotte: The Final Journey of Jane Eyre* (2000); Jasper Fforde's *The Eyre Affair* (2001). With these in hand, an instructor can ask a class why so many sequels have been published in just the past decade – or offer concrete examples of young adult fiction, Australian-only editions, science fiction, transatlantic textual and cover art variants, uncorrected proofs, text-on-demand Internet publishers, vanity press, lesbian fiction, and even underground alternative press, such as the retelling of the Lowood School episode called *Disciplining Jane* (2001).

RBS now owns over fifty different hardcover and sixty paperback editions, many represented in multiple printings showing changes in price, book design, and cover art. Some editions are critical, scholarly, and authoritative; others target niche audiences from juveniles to moviegoers to the readers of romance novels. Many are illustrated, from the first illustrated edition in 1872 to the latest comic book, providing opportunities for students to think about the effects of different visual representations of the narrative. Editions by series publishers yield intriguing questions: why was Penguin's *Jane Eyre* printed as number 960 in 1953, when the novel had been number 1 in the World's Classics in 1901? Other items – a *Jane Eyre* trivia game, tea towel, thimble, commemorative plate, paper doll, and a CD by a rock group called Grace Poole – lend a carnivalesque sensibility to the novel's appeal. The collection contains dozens of children's and English-as-a-second-language adaptations – all condensed, some retaining the novel's famous first line and 'Reader, I married him', some paraphrasing or skipping even those. RBS has found an astonishing number of theatrical productions – from the 1850s through the 2000 Broadway flop – yielding masses of scripts, handbills, flyers, posters, postcards, songbooks, and t-shirts; a half-dozen film adaptations, with attendant spin-offs; and numerous audio-books.

Jane Eyre has seen a Babel of translations – Spanish, French, Russian, German, Hungarian, Japanese – and even a Greek comic book.

Collections of this kind could be developed for any of a number of works: *Hamlet, Don Quixote, Pride and Prejudice, The Scarlet Letter*, not to mention influential and frequently reprinted, translated, and condensed non-literary texts like *The Wealth of Nations* or *The Origin of Species*. The publishing history of each of these works might bring different issues to bear, but regardless, selective exhaustivity must be exercised in order to differentiate teaching from more traditional author collections. It is one thing to collect copies of every printing of just the Penguin, and quite another to attempt to do the same for every paperback edition; it is one thing to collect a few representative examples of nineteenth-century reprint editions, and quite another to try to collect them comprehensively. The materials in a teaching collection are useful only insofar as they serve as examples of points the instructor wishes to demonstrate in class.

The Mechanics of Collecting

Many curators would be eager to assist faculty in forming hands-on teaching collections. In practical terms, institutional online purchases can be difficult: at my own institution, librarians pay out of pocket for eBay purchases, and must then wait for reimbursement. One solution might be to use a departmental grant and graduate student assistance in building the collection, and then to house the materials in special collections with the proviso that they are intended for in-class use. Many special collections are increasingly open to serving as working humanities laboratories in addition to their more traditional research library roles.[4] If collecting on one's own, keeping track of items is critical, but need not be inordinately complicated. A word-processed list or spreadsheet will do just as well as an elaborate database or full item-level cataloging. The list should include details on all copies owned, and can be printed out or carried on a pocket PC for use while browsing in second-hand bookshops: this comes in handy when one needs to know, for instance, if the collection already includes the forty-sixth printing of the Penguin.

The RBS list contains several categories. The Hardbound, Paperback, Translations, Study Guides, and Other Brontës categories are arranged alphabetically by publisher. Other categories are arranged alphabetically by author or editor's last name: Abridgements and Adaptations; Prequels, Sequels, and Retellings; Anthologies and Excerpts; Criticism and Critical Biography. Several categories are arranged by date: Audio, Video, and Soundtracks; and Theater and Movie Ephemera. The Ancillaries category (which lists examples of the Bewick wood engravings, a contemporary wedding license, an anonymous three-decker novel, etc.) is arranged alphabetically by subject or genre. The list is heavily

abbreviated, recording only the information necessary to distinguish one printing or copy from another: name of editor; format (mass market paperback or
trade paperback – mmpb or tpb); publisher's codes; publication price; date and
printing; indication of redesigned covers; presence, absence, or price-clipped
status of dust jacket (dj, xdj, or dj pc); number of copies. Here are a couple
entries from the Paperback category:

> *Aerie* mmpb (nd [c.1990?]; same cover art as *Tor*, but maroon spine): 2 cop.
> Wal Mart '2 for $1' circle printed on cover (defaced in copy 1)
> *Bantam Classic* mmpb (1981- ; intro Joyce Carol Oates in 10th(?) and later
> ptgs): **$1.95** 1 cop 8th 1/86, 1 cop 10th 11/87; **$3.50** 2 cop 22nd; **$3.95** 1
> cop 25th; **$4.95** 1 cop 37th

RBS originally had only the defaced copy of the Aerie paperback; knowing that
there was missing information was useful. Without the second copy we would
have known neither the retailer nor the price: both useful in demonstrating
that middle America pays less for *Jane Eyre* than for a soft drink. The Bantam
list shows how collecting can be used to solve questions about textual history:
RBS now needs only a copy of the ninth printing to know for sure when the
Oates introduction first appeared.

The list should include desiderata, with information gathered from many
sources: lost and overpriced eBay lots; publishers' and bookdealers' catalogs;
fan Web sites; *Books in Print* and Amazon.com; exhibition catalogs and finding
aids from libraries with collections of the work in question. With *Jane Eyre*,
traditional author bibliographies do not to cover the materials needed for this
kind of collection, though Patsy Stoneman's *Brontë Transformations: The Cultural Dissemination of* Jane Eyre *and* Wuthering Heights (London: Prentice
Hall, 1996) points toward several avenues for collecting.

One quickly learns to distinguish the common from the unusual, and the
bargains from the overpriced. Classroom experience with the collection soon
teaches one to pass by things that would not play well to undergraduates: a
full-color 1970s Argentinian poster of George C. Scott as Rochester works
brilliantly; an unmarked 8 mm film canister of the same movie may not 'speak'
as articulately in the classroom. For non-book items and ephemera – and for
providing pictures of books – eBay works well – but when selling books, eBay
sellers frequently overestimate starting bids, and descriptions are not always
trustworthy. Prices and descriptions should be checked against used book
umbrella search engines like BookFinder.com or AddAll.com – or, for more
precise search capabilities, Abebooks.com, ILAB-LILA.com, or ABAA.org.
The latter three sites also permit users to save want lists for specific titles.

Teaching from the Collection

In our RBS history of the book survey course, my co-instructor and I use the full *Jane Eyre* collection as a series of case studies in industrial-era publishing and marketing practices, shifts in cultural attitudes, changes in reading habits, and so forth. In English literature courses, the collection provides an overview of how novels are transformed in the process of canonization. In pop culture or media studies courses, the collection reveals how a narrative becomes embedded within a culture even among people who will never read it. In whatever context I teach *Jane Eyre*, I start with a three-decker (whether the Special Collections copy of the first edition, or a less well-known title as a stand-in) contrasted with a late nineteenth-century cheap newspaper-like reprint,[5] and end by showing a pocket PC loaded with an e-book version side-by-side with the two-volume Tauchnitz edition (1850) from which the e-book was encoded. Form affects content! The remainder of the class period focuses on materials supporting the course's themes. For a class interested in contemporary publishing practices, I walk the students through the 'sequels' and mass market paperbacks. For a class concentrating on issues of text-and-image, I focus on sets of leaves removed from a defective copy of Bewick's *British Birds*, including the wood engravings described in *Jane Eyre*, and then move on to illustrated editions or comic book versions or examples of changes in cover art.

Teaching with a collection like this could be limited to a once-a-semester introduction to the materials and a writing assignment based on some aspect of the collection (thereby an introduction to research based on primary sources). One could gradually build up to integrating materials on a weekly basis. The course could be divided into units focusing on different works: one week on contemporary parodies of Dickens; another week on theatrical adaptations of *Jane Eyre*; a third week on sequels and popular retellings of *Pride and Prejudice*, and so forth.[6] The term papers and the primary research skills this raw material fosters will be a welcome diversion to instructor and student alike from the usual (and more plagiarism-prone) discussions of theme or image. Since many of these items will have escaped previous scholarly attention, students are more likely to produce original and perhaps even publishable essays. The collection normally needs to be constructed in advance: though affordable enough for a student to undertake, such collections usually take more time and expertise than a single semester affords. An exception might involve a book collecting project as an independent study, using an undergraduate research fellowship to fund purchases, and a small exhibition space to display the results.

The mechanics of using a teaching collection in the classroom need not be complicated. For classroom display, a few dozen items are sufficient – although for primary source research assignments, more is usually better. To permit the collection to move easily and quickly in and out of the classroom, it could be stored in boxes rather than on shelves. Acid-free boxes for books, paper or poly-ester envelopes or folders for ephemera, and polyester dust jacket protectors (see archival supplies dealers like Gaylord or University Products) mitigate the effects of repeated handlings. If the classroom lacks shelves, consider a folding bookcase. Since most items are inexpensive and few are fragile, they can safely be passed around. If a classroom's tables can be arranged in a U-shape, the instructor can walk fragile items around while discussing them.

The key is to let the physical artifacts tell their stories, and to train students to look for the nuances to be found not only in a book's contents, but also in its container. Some students may become excited enough to start collecting on their own. Others will warm to the idea of conducting primary research in special collections. All the students will be exposed graphically and tangibly to the idea that information is always mediated, and perhaps they will carry away a more sophisticated understanding of the social contexts of the novels they read, and of the media environment in which they live.[7]

Notes

1. See Anthony Rota, *Apart from the Text,* (New Castle, DE, Oak Knoll, 1998), chapter 8.
2. TimeWarner Audio Books, 1998.
3. Acclaim Classics Illustrated, 1996.
4. See Ann Schmiesing and Deborah R. Hollis, 'The Role of Special Collections Departments in Humanities Undergraduate and Graduate Teaching: A Case Study', *portal: Libraries and the Academy,* 2 (2002), 465–79.
5. The Leisure Hour Library (New York, F. M. Lupton, 1896).
6. Rota, *Apart,* provides effective reading assignments for such a course.
7. Inquiries about the RBS *Jane Eyre* collection should be directed to Rare Book School (see Resources, p. 185).

History of the Book in the American Literature Classroom: On the Fly and On the Cheap

Jean Lee Cole

I had always dreamed of teaching at a small liberal arts college. But when my dream came true, I suddenly realized something was missing: the wealth of archival and special collections materials that had surrounded me at the huge public university where I had done my graduate work. My research had become increasingly dependent on these materials, and I also (unsurprisingly) wanted to bring them into my teaching. But I discovered to my chagrin that my library did not have a special collections department, it did not have any archives, nor did it have a librarian who knew anything about rare books and manuscripts. It had a rare books room – but no one seemed to know where it was. When I finally found a librarian who had the key to the room, I discovered the reason for this ignorance. A room was all it was – a small room containing a few stacks of old books that had belonged to previous administrators, resident Jesuits, and alumni, and moldering cardboard boxes filled with textual detritus in varying stages of decay. Nothing in the room had ever been catalogued, and at first glance, little appeared to be usable. There certainly was nothing like what had graced the special collections at my graduate-school alma mater: three copies of Shakespeare's First Folio and thirty-six copies of the first edition of James Joyce's *Ulysses* (of the 1000 printed). Even if there had been, there would have been no way for my students to actually *look* at them, as there was no way to check out the books or even a desk at which to read them.

But I believed it was important to expose my students to living, breathing printed artifacts: what Terry Belanger fondly but more prosaically refers to as 'stuff'. By seeing – and even better, touching – the real stuff, students would be able to mentally repackage the texts they read in bland, homogenous anthologies and Penguin editions, seeing them instead on the pages of nineteenth-century periodicals, clothbound duodecimos, triple-deckers. They can experience texts in the forms through which they gained their original influence – or fell into obscurity. They can, in a literal sense, touch history, or at least, as Jules David Prown has argued, a metaphorical representation of it.[1]

My problem was, how to get the stuff? Obviously, there would be no First Folios (or even Poor Richard's Almanacs) in my classrooms' future. I could show students things on line – at the Library of Congress's American Memory site, Cornell's Making of America site and HEARTH home economics archive, ProQuest's American Periodical Series database, and so on.[2] But looking at artifacts on line is not the same as touching them. So I decided to collect them for myself.

I obviously could not afford the 'great books' of American book history. I couldn't even afford first editions of anything. But I *could* get everyday reading materials – items that would be representative of a particular time period or a particular kind of publication.[3] Once I started looking for materials along these lines, stuff started to pile up. I went back to the rare books room, and also scanned the regular stacks of our library, and found some gems: children's books; spiritual autobiography; books of nineteenth-century verse. I even found some first editions – including an almost complete set of Sarah Orne Jewett's Houghton Mifflin publications, complete with original covers designed by Sarah Wyman Whitman. I also started tracking on-line sources like eBay, focusing on American periodicals, which would provide a wide variety of literary output, but remained affordable. In the spirit of Henry David Thoreau, I list a few representative purchases, and use his 'excuse … that I brag for humanity rather than myself':

3 issues of *Ladies' Home Journal*, 1896-1897	$22.50
26 issues of *The Youth's Companion*, 1887-1913	10.50
6 issues of *Ladies' World*, 1890-1902	18.49
April 1904 *McClure's* (containing installments of Ida M. Tarbell's *History of the Standard Oil Trust* and Lincoln Steffens' *Enemies of the Republic*)	15.00

As the list shows, I focused my initial efforts on 1890-1910, a period I taught frequently but which was only sparsely represented in my college's library. Keeping these considerations in mind helped me get the most bang for my buck. Another key to collecting classroom materials on a budget is to find materials that are historical, but not necessarily rare. This enables one to amass a sufficient quantity of items so that each student, or at least each pair of students, can look at a single item. It also enables one to *use* the materials in class – if they are neither expensive nor rare, one does not have to worry so much about their handling. Within six months, I had collected over sixty individual issues of magazines from the 1890s for less than $150.[4]

So how did I end up using this stuff? One example is an assignment I call 'Time Capsule', which I've used both in lower- and upper-division surveys and in upper-division topics courses. Either at the beginning or the end of a unit, the class spends a day examining a collection of textual artifacts. Then students write a short report on one artifact, first describing its form, possible function, and potential audience, and then using it to test the claims made in a secondary-source reading about the period or its literature.

To expand: in an undergraduate survey of American literature, I assign a 'period overview' of the 1890s from a standard-issue anthology at the beginning of the unit, and then, in the middle of the unit, students spend a class browsing through a variety of 1890s-era magazines. This scheduling allows students to develop a basic understanding of the period before facing the cacophony of voices, perspectives, and images they will encounter in the magazines. The 'standard story' of the overview as well as the 'standard stories' represented by the major literary texts assigned for the unit familiarize students with the kinds of themes (urbanization, class stratification, alienation, shifting gender roles, for example) and literary styles (realism, naturalism, local color) considered hallmarks of the period.

Once students are grounded in the period, we look at the magazines. After passing the magazines out, I insist that students take down bibliographical information (doing this is oddly important). Then, after a brief lesson on 'dos and don'ts' of handling the magazines, I provide a list of questions for students to consider, beginning with gaining a holistic sense of the magazine they have been given. How big (page size, number of pages) is it? Of what is it composed (stories, articles, poetry, puzzles and games, advertisements) and how is that content organized? Who (men, women, adults, children, urban or rural folk, rich, middling, or poor) appear to have been its likely readers? Who wrote for it? I suggest that they jot down the names of the editor(s) and authors, especially those that seem to be considered important, as well as historical events and social issues that appear significant, so that they can look them up later. Then, students choose a single story, article, poem, illustration, or advertisement to analyze in light of the other readings for that section of the course. I suggest students choose something they found particularly striking or unexpected, or something that resonates strongly with one or more of the literary works we have read. Once students have chosen their analytical focus, the rest of the hour is spent in reading and taking careful notes. (Some students may need to look at their magazines again; if the magazines are in reasonably good shape, photocopying is an option.)

The actual report is due on the last day of the unit. The written portion consists of three parts: 1) a bibliographical citation of the artifact chosen; 2) a paragraph describing the magazine itself as well as the specific artifact; and 3) a two- to three-page analysis of the artifact in light of the ideas presented in the secondary-source overview and one or more of the literary texts assigned in the unit. In class, we basically play show-and-tell: students discuss what they chose to analyze and what they discovered. (This show-and-tell process is much aided if the artifacts can be displayed, either on-screen or through handouts.) The in-class presentation has been one of the most successful aspects of the assignment: here, the sheer variety in artifacts and approaches is made manifest, attesting both to the creativity of individual students and the productive power of the class as a whole.

The assignment can be adapted to use on-line documents and artifacts. In the same course, in a unit about depictions of slavery and freedom in antebellum America, I have students look at advertisements, reviews, illustrations, and the sales prospectus of the first edition of *The Adventures of Huckleberry Finn* (all from Stephen Railton's excellent website at the University of Virginia); in a unit about colonial Salem, I refer them to court testimony and contemporary treatises on witchcraft held at various sites, including the Essex County Court Archives, which has hundreds of page images of the actual testimony of figures depicted in Arthur Miller's *The Crucible* and Maryse Condé's *I, Tituba*.[5] One significant difference between using 'real' versus 'virtual' artifacts, it should be noted, is that while online materials allow for a wider array of artifacts from which to choose, they can also be bewildering for students to navigate. This is, I believe, the result of the lack of physical, tangible presence that would allow students to more easily distinguish between items. Take, for example, three images from Benjamin Ray and Bernard Rosenthal's *Salem Witch Trials Documentary Archive and Transcription Project*: an 1876 book illustration of the girls in court, a 2001 newspaper illustration, and an 1884 painting.[6] In one unfortunate case, a student assumed that the 1876 and 2001 illustrations were in fact contemporaneous – something that would not have happened if he had paid attention to the descriptions provided on the website (and required in the bibliographical citation portion of the written report), but almost certainly *could* not have happened if he had been examining the actual book and newspaper. The painting poses a more subtle problem: what *is* the artifact – the website image, the 1942 *Life Magazine* illustration that was scanned, or the 1884 painting? And how would you be able to discuss the painting, given that no indications of size are given?

These confusions in themselves can be pedagogically useful, in that they call to students' attention the significance of both historical context and physical presence: two of the key points of the assignment. A side benefit is that it demonstrates to students one of the limitations of on-line archives – the postmodern collapsing of time (not to mention flattening of affect) that results from the homogenization of presentation.

In happier instances, however, students make strong and often surprising connections between the artifacts and the literature. For example, one student compared the unusually spare style of a 1907 Kodak camera ad from *McClure's* to the shift in advertising and marketing strategy depicted in Stephen Millhauser's *Martin Dressler.* Another discussed how E.W. Kemble's ironic employment of conventional religious imagery in two illustrations from chapters twenty-one and twenty-two of the 1885 edition of *The Adventures of Huckleberry Finn* ('The Death of Boggs' and 'Colonel Sherman Steps Out') underscore Twain's mockery of American religiosity and individualism. A third discussed the long-winded and circumlocutory title page of John Hale's *A Modest Enquiry Into the Nature of Witchcraft* (1697) and how it reveals Arthur Miller's revisionist intent in depicting Hale's change of heart in *The Crucible.* In all three cases, as in many others, students demonstrated an understanding of how the extratextual and contextual shapes reading, and how the historical and physical environ-ment in which a text is read is a fundamental aspect of its meaning. As one student commented, the Time Capsule assignment 'adds an extra dimension to each novel by giving it a historical and cultural element aside from the obvious literary element it already contains'.[7]

On its most visceral level, of course, students simply love touching the stuff! Many of them have never seen an old magazine before, much less a nineteenth-century children's book or an eighteenth-century newspaper. Their contact with these items, especially in their original, real forms, gives them contact with a history, society, and culture that, simply through its passing, has become lost to them. Objects, in a way that textbooks cannot, can help them understand this history, if only in a metaphorical or metonymic way.[8] Susan Pearce argues that this is

> a crucial way in which material culture does not match language in a one-to-one sense, still less in a one-in-relation-to-one sense, but has an independ-ent social existence of its own which contributes to social reproduction. ... Imagine trying to describe the difference between two shirts, similar in cut and each in two different shades of blue ... We are all acutely aware how inadequate language is to encompass this kind of detailed materiality and how frustrating it is to try and make it serve the purpose. We also know that one glance at the actual object will solve the problem and create immediate understanding, because we are capable of making fine perceptual discrimina-tions between one object and another. This quality of material discrimination, presumably a combination of eye, sometimes hand, and culture stored in the memory, is immensely significant in the construction of the social world.[9]

Stated in another way, one student wrote that the assignment fostered an understanding she would never have gained from 'any textbook because it was the knowledge of the true way of life of those periods, rather than the dates and events that history books decide to remember'.[10]

With respect to developing students' understanding of literature, the act of seeing and feeling these artifacts helps them, in a way I am yet unable to fully quantify, appreciate older styles of writing that especially beginning students of American literature find archaic, if not completely inaccessible. When I tell them that Emily Dickinson and Mark Twain both published in periodicals like the *Youth's Companion,* and were published alongside ads for patent medicines, bicycles, and pianos, they see their actual writings in a different light. It makes them more human; it transforms them from monolithic cultural icons into active participants in a cultural conversation. They also begin to appreciate the true variety of American textual production in a given period, making them more sensitive to the stylistic modulations of the writers we examine. Finally, the exercise demonstrates to them key differences between primary and secondary sources; in particular, the fact that secondary sources are selective in their use of evidence and often reductive in their delineation of trends, tendencies, and 'movements'. In an upper-division seminar on gender in American literature, for example, students read articles on the cult of true woman and the emergence of the New Woman at the end of the nineteenth century, and then examined the depiction of women in 1890s-era magazines. As we discussed their findings, it became patently obvious that at this time, there was no clear-cut division between these two types of 'womanhood', despite what the historians might argue – that within one magazine, or even one article, both aspects of women's roles were in a state of ambivalence, exhibited sometimes in direct conflict, in other ways through a startlingly easy co-existence.

Daniel Boorstin has claimed that 'our democracy is based on books and reading'.[11] The two terms, books and reading, are distinct. Developing an understanding of what books *are* – the words in books, of course, but also the physical forms that house those words and present them to the reader – ultimately will enrich our students' understanding of the history and workings of this nation. In our increasingly electronic and visually oriented culture, it becomes more and more difficult, but increasingly crucial, to communicate to students the meaning and experience of print culture – a culture that is fundamental to the development of American identity. The books themselves can help make that happen.

Bibliography

1. Jules David Prown, 'The Truth of Material Culture: History or Fiction?' in Jules David Prown and Kenneth Haltman ed., *American Artifacts: Essays in Material Culture* (East Lansing, Michigan State University Press, 2000), pp. 18-19.
2. Library of Congress, American Memory site: http://memory.loc.gov/ammem/; Making of America: http://cdl.library.cornell.edu/moa/; Home Economics Archive: Research, Tradition, History: http://hearth.library.cornell.edu/ (accessed 7 May 2006). The American Periodical Service is avaiable by subscription.
3. The areas of book history I have employed in undergraduate courses are those that align themselves with material culture analysis rather than, say, with descriptive bibliography.
4. One mistake I made was in buying bound volumes of periodicals. While cost-effective (I bought four volumes, or forty-eight issues, of *St. Nicholas Magazine* [1898-1901] for about $70) they are difficult to use in classes unless you are willing to cut up the volumes into

individual issues and, in many cases, do without covers—which, despite the old saying, are a critical way books (and magazines especially) are judged.

5. Stephen Railton, *Mark Twain and His Times*, http://etext.lib.virginia.edu/railton; Essex County Court documents are available through Benjamin Ray and Bernard Rosenthal's *Salem Witch Trials Documentary Archive and Transcription Project*: http://jefferson.village.virginia.edu/salem (accessed 7 May 2006).

6. 'Witchcraft at Salem Village', illustration from *Pioneers in the Settlement of America*, Vol. I (Boston, 1876); Steve McCracken, 'Witchcraft in Colonial America: A Matter of Lies and Death', *Washington Post*, KidsPost section, Oct. 31, 2001; 'Accused of Witchcraft', 1884 painting by Douglas Volk, reproduced in *Life Magazine*, 1942; all available at *The Salem Witch Trials Documentary Archive and Transcription Project*, http://jefferson.village.virginia.edu/salem/generic.html (accessed 7 May 2006).

7. John Luksch, personal communication, 4 January 2005.

8. Prown argues that because of material culture's inherently metaphorical nature, it conveys a 'fictional' depiction of history much like that presented in literary texts, pp. 15–16.

9. Susan Pearce, *Museums, Objects and Collections: A Cultural Study* (Leicester and London, Leicester University Press, 1992), p. 22.

10. Caroline McAllister, personal communication, 3 January 2005.

11. Boorstin, quoted in Richard W. Clement, *The Book in America* (Golden CO, Fulcrum Publishing [with the Library of Congress], 1996), p. 3.

From Printing Type to Blackboard™: Teaching the History of the Early Modern Book to Literary Undergraduates in a 'New' UK University

Ian Gadd

I begin with a book and a blindfold. A volunteer – blindfolded – handles a modern book, perhaps a paperback novel or a cookery book. The student is asked to describe the book out loud: to feel it, heft it, listen to it and even smell it. I ask questions: what *kind* of book do you think it is? what might it be *used* for? does it feel *expensive*? is it *portable*? might it have *illustrations*? would the type be *densely set* or *spaced out*? does it feel *important*? Though deprived of sight, the student discovers with surprise that he or she can interpret the non-visual signs every book possesses. Nearly always, the student correctly identifies the genre of book with remarkable speed; occasionally, the student offers unexpected, even revealing, insights, as when a copy of the adult hardback edition of the latest *Harry Potter* was dismissed as cheaply produced.

This activity imitates D.F. McKenzie's famous teaching exercise of handing 'an utterly blank book' around his postgraduate class.[1] Through a sequence of questions, McKenzie notes how students identify the book's genre and date with impressive precision. McKenzie concludes: 'My students already knew more than they thought they did. One had only to make their knowledge conscious.'[2] These blindfold exercises help students consider what questions to ask of old books and reveal how much latent 'biblio-kinaesthetic' knowledge they already have.

The blindfold also provides an apposite metaphor for my teaching experience, particularly the compromises involved in teaching a subject demanding rich resources where those resources are unavailable. This essay has two purposes: ideological, arguing that *undergraduate* literary students can be taught history of the book, and evangelical, preaching that it can be taught with limited resources and facilities.

Contexts

Bath Spa University is a medium-sized institution of approximately 4500 students, with a creative and liberal arts focus. English academic staff teach 150-180 undergraduates annually, many defined as 'mature' or 'nontraditional'. When I joined, the department had no prior experience of teaching history of the book – nor, for that matter, had I.

Neither situation is surprising. As a taught subject, the history of the book is still finding a presence in undergraduate English programs, despite the fact that basic textual scholarship is often expected in Masters- and Doctoral-level courses. Therefore, I had no pedagogical models or case studies on which to draw in planning and teaching the course: for example, Elaine Showalter's study of literary teaching does not discuss book history; SHARP has published only occasional pedagogical articles, and Rare Book School's course for teachers began only in 1997.[3]

Preparation

In proposing a history of the early modern book course, I was motivated by two beliefs: first, that bibliography and the history of the book have an important place in literary criticism; second, reinforced by my experience of bringing the subject into regular literary classes, that 'history of the book' *can* be taught effectively to undergraduate literary students. For this latter belief I drew on my own undergraduate experiences discovering, almost by chance, that learning about the publication history of *Hamlet* significantly enhanced my literary interpretation. However, to achieve this I had to teach myself, haphazardly and not all together successfully, the key terms, processes and historical contexts. An undergraduate course on the history of the book would need to equip students with exactly that knowledge so that they could apply an informed approach to texts of their choice. At its simplest, therefore, I imagined this course as one I wished I could have taken as an undergraduate.

My departmental proposal emphasised that the course would focus on the relationship between material form and verbal content in printed books: students would be encouraged

> to think critically about how texts in this period were 'made' and 'read, how
> the material form of a text could significantly affect its meaning, and how
> literary authorship in this period was shaped by scribal and print culture.

Implicit was the expectation that students would demonstrate what educationalists term *performative* understanding: they would be able to apply their understanding to other situations.[4] The course posters ('You'll never look at a book the same way again') and handbook emphasized that students would learn a new way of reading applicable to any text.

Since my students would be literary undergraduates with little or no prior knowledge of bibliography, of book history or of Early Modern England's literature (apart from Shakespeare) or history, I presented the history of the book as a way of looking at texts in light of the material processes that shaped their construction and reception. This approach was pragmatic: the course was more likely to be successful if it explicitly linked the history of the book with familiar objects like literary texts and with familiar skills like literary interpretation. This hermeneutic use of history of the book enabled the proposal to gain departmental approval, even being described by one senior colleague as 'very original and striking'.

The course – *Authors, Books and Readers in early modern England* – divided into three sections: 'The Printed Book' (weeks 1-4) covered basic technical knowledge and terminology; 'The English Book Trade 1500-1700' surveyed the historical context (weeks 4-6); and 'Print and early modern English literature' (weeks 6-12) applied this technical and historical knowledge through themed seminars, supporting students' work on their independently-chosen final research project.[5] This structure followed B. S. Bloom's famous 'taxonomy of learning' in that students moved from knowledge reproduction and comprehension through to application and analysis (and ideally synthesis and evaluation) – a development from 'surface' to 'deep' autonomous learning.[6] Identifying appropriate readings was not easy: the few existing 'history of the book' textbooks are not aimed at undergraduates and many 'key' articles presuppose prior bibliographical or historical knowledge. In conjunction with a coursepack, D. C. Greetham's *Textual Scholarship*, the most accessible introduction to the field, served as a useful reference book.[7] The reading was cumulative, with prescribed weekly readings linked to our lectures and seminars; this represented a different reading experience for students who typically read the texts in advance and see each as an independent entity. Our coursepack also included extracts from early modern texts (from Thomas Nashe's portrayal of the loafing Stationer to Samuel Pepys' confession that he bought three books 'for the love of the binding') and the tables of contents for key reference books to reveal what topics these unfamiliar books included.[8] In addition, the library purchased a number of secondary texts and a near-full run of *The Library*.

To reveal the diversity of early modern books in terms of content and quality, we used online databases of facsimiles, such as subscription-only *Early English Books Online* (EEBO) and the more modestly-sized, high-quality and freely-available Schoenburg Center for Electronic Text and Image (SCETI). But digital facsimiles diminish and can even falsify the material reality of the book in question; at some point, students need actual old books in the classroom. I searched local collections and discovered unexpected treasures.[9] There is a moral here: not just that early modern books can prove surprisingly enduring but that what may seem to be an unpromising repository (Bath University is a largely science-focused institution only chartered in the 1960s; Bath Central Library, located above a supermarket, is the city's main public library) can prove rewarding.

Assessments

Assessments should be appropriate (assessing what the students have learnt), proportionate (establishing challenging but not impossible expectations) and useful (helping students to consolidate learning). Moreover, as educationalists stress, assessment should complement course objectives and teaching methods through a process of 'constructive alignment'. I felt that a traditional 'essay and exam' package was not appropriate and so designed three course-specific assessments, two of which involved practical skills. The first took place as part of a day-trip to the printing room at the Bodleian Library, Oxford[10]; here students learned to set type with a composing stick and type-cases and then, under supervision, set two lines of justified type within approximately forty-five minutes. The assessment was marked on a pass/fail basis and the accuracy of the setting was not assessed, but the exercise demonstrated the labour, skill and decision-making required in the early modern printing house. (All the set lines were digitally photographed and then reversed so that students could see their lines as if they had been printed.) A second assessment required students to transcribe, using the usual conventions, an early modern title page within a set time-limit. Each then examined a pre-1750 book for forty minutes: they were to identify certain features of the book (chainlines, format, age of binding, the signature of a particular page, type-size) and, over the following week, prepare a 500-word report in which they described the book bibliographically, provided some historical context, and related the book's form to its content. The purpose of this assessment (which required the drafting of specific detailed assessment criteria and was weighted at 30%, with the split between transcription and report being 90:10) was both to consolidate the students' knowledge of a book's physical features and to encourage them to think about the *relationship* between form and content as preparation for their final assessment, the 2500-word essay or project. This, weighted at 70%, addressed a topic chosen by the student with my approval and was designed so that students could apply their newly-acquired understanding of printing processes and the book trade in the period to texts of interest to them.

Experiences

In the first session, apart from the 'book and blindfold' exercise, students received a detailed A5-sized module handbook (complete with a 190gsm mould-made cotton-paper cover printed in red and black) and cotton gloves for handling books in class or in the assessments. I explained the objectives, structure and assessments of the module, stressing those aspects that differed from the 'typical' English module. Each seminar opened with a 'book of the week', an early printed book or facsimile which would be described and handed round; in the first session, the title page from this book was used to highlight the visual differences between early modern and modern books. This first seminar concluded with a leap from an old technology to a very new one: Blackboard, a commercially available web-based 'learning system' or 'Virtual Learning Environment'.

I used Blackboard as a repository of information, whether already supplied in class (lecture slides, handouts and so on) or supplemental to that week's topics or books. I also created several discussion boards to structure and support students' learning *outside* the classroom. One, for example, allowed students to post (anonymously if necessary) any query they had about the subject.

Over the first half of the course, students had to post a comment on a task assigned weekly. These tasks were intended to lead students into experiencing the range and diversity of the field of the 'history of the book' without feeling overwhelmed. In week one, they browsed the HoBo website in order to get a sense, from the events listed there, of the 'history of the book' as a field and commented online about any aspect which surprised or interested them.[11] This exercise enabled them to locate the field through a snapshot of academic 'practise'; it also encouraged them, in an embryonic way, to consider what aspects of the subject might be worth focusing on for their final assessment. Another online task introduced them to EEBO by asking them to search for their hometown or favourite hobby, as a way of cutting through the immensity of EEBO's holdings at the same time as discovering the scale of the published output from the period (students were often genuinely taken aback that their town or village was mentioned in an early modern work); it also gave them confidence in using EEBO's searching and navigational interfaces.

I established a discussion board specifically for the final assessment. In the week prior to the essay tutorials (in week 7), students posted preliminary thoughts about possible topics; this advance notice allowed me to identify useful secondary sources in time for the tutorial, and in many cases I posted a reply either before or after the tutorial giving, where relevant, some guidance about primary and secondary texts. Students were encouraged to post updates about their research over the rest of the semester and to post comments about other students' projects; in practice, students rarely did either partly, I believe, because of my own over-enthusiasm to reply to students' postings myself, which created an unfortunate expectation among students that *I* would respond to any query and hence there was little reason to intervene themselves. (This improved when the course ran a second time as I deliberately limited – or at least delayed – my interventions.)

Different strategies were needed for inside the classroom. As much of the weekly reading for this course was descriptive, historical or analytical, the students, used to poems, plays and novels, were often at a loss about how to discuss the texts. Initially, I assigned the task of leading seminar discussion for each week's reading to a group within the seminar (they were also to post their notes on Blackboard afterwards) but after several weeks it was clear that this was prompting protracted synopses of texts that everyone else had already read. Accordingly, I introduced worksheets that asked the students to identify what they felt to be the main three points of each article; these worksheets also included general questions about issues raised by the reading. This seemed to focus discussion much more effectively. However, during the course's second run, discussion tended to broaden out again – usually in response to the students' interest in how a particular point related to a wider issue. Timings were increasingly difficult: in the first half of the semester, a single two-hour seminar included: feedback about the previous week's task; 'book(s) of the week'; detailed explanation about forthcoming assessments; extended discussion about the reading; and, if possible, some further group work on a particular aspect of 'history of the book'.

Student feedback was very positive: 'brilliant, refreshingly different and worth any amount of effort'; 'a whole new perspective'; 'fab and original'; 'will continue to study the history of books outside of university'; 'adjusted my ideas about literature and books'; 'learnt a whole new range of disciplines'. A number of students deemed it one of the best courses they had taken, and quite a few wished that other English courses included 'history of the book' approaches. The only substantial reservation concerned the readings: its amount, level and how best to handle it. Ironically, then, the main inhibiting factor for teaching history of the book to undergraduates is the secondary material, not the books or concepts.

The real testament to the success of this course lies with what the students achieved in their research essays. The sixty-four essays I have marked for this course have covered a wide range of topics: translations of *Utopia*, Thomas Shadwell's plays, cookery books, music printing, Thomas Swetnam's *Arraignment of Women*, shorthand books, translations of the *Aenid*, the impact of the plague on the London book trade and so on. Frequently, student research and effort has been impressive: students made their own research trips to the Bodleian and to the cathedral libraries of Wells and Salisbury. One student even used her savings towards a new car to purchase her own early modern book. In preparing their essays, a number of students expressed anxiety that their essays were 'too historical' but the majority managed to strike a deft balance between literary interpretation and historical context. Students could submit an editorial project instead of a conventional essay: an extract from a literary text for which there was more than one early modern edition presented as if it were a scholarly edition in its own right, complete with a detailed textual introduction, explanatory footnotes and full collations. Students chose *Titus Andronicus, Romeo and Juliet, Hamlet, Othello* and even *Catiline*. No student had any prior experience with this skill yet, unexpectedly, several became thoroughly engrossed in the project producing work that was often of very high quality. In fact, more than one of these students pronounced editing to be, of all things, 'addictive': such, then, is the potential power of the history of the book.

Notes

1. D. F. McKenzie, *'What's Past Is Prologue': The Bibliographical Society and History of the Book* (Hearthstone Publications, 1993), pp. 3-7.
2. Ibid, p. 7.
3. Elaine Showalter, *Teaching Literature* (Oxford, Blackwell Publishing, 2003).
4. John Biggs, *Teaching for Quality Learning at University*, 2nd edn. (Maidenhead, Open University Press, 2003)
5. I am grateful to all sixty-four students in the course during 2003-04 and 2004-05 for their patience and enthusiasm.
6. B. S. Bloom, *Taxonomy of educational objectives: Cognitive domain* (New York, David McKay and Company, 1956)
7. D. C. Greetham, *Textual Scholarship: An Introduction* (New York and London, Garland Publishing, 1994). See the companion website for the list of readings.
8. John Barnard, D.F. McKenzie, and Maureen Bell (eds), *The Cambridge History of the Book in Britain: Volume IV 1557–1695* (Cambridge, Cambridge University Press, 2002); Nigel Wheale, *Writing and Society: Literacy, Print and Politics in Britain, 1590–1660* (London, Routledge, 1999); Philip Gaskell, *A New Introduction to Bibliography* (Oxford, Clarendon Press, 1972); David Finkelstein and Alistair McCleery (eds), *The Book History Reader* (London, Routledge, 2002); Jennifer Andersen and Elizabeth Sauer (eds), *Books and Readers in Early Modern England* (Philadelphia, University of Pennsylvania, 2002); D. F. McKenzie, 'Making Meaning' in Peter McDonald and Michael Suarez (eds), *'Printers of the Mind' and Other Essays* (Amherst, University of Massachusetts Press, 2002)
9. I am grateful to the generous assistance of Nick Drew (English Subject Librarian), Julie Parry (Head of Library Services), Nicola Morrison and Helen Rayner (Sion Hill librarians) at Bath Spa; Stephanie Round (Local Collections Librarian) at Bath Central Library; and Howard Nicholson (Head Librarian) at Bath University.
10. I am grateful to Michael Turner for hosting these visits, and to Bill Clennell who gave a 'behind-the-scenes' tour of the library.
11. Available at http://www.english.ox.ac.uk/hobo/ (accessed 7 May 2006).

Preparing Library School Graduate Students for Rare Book and Special Collections Jobs: Assignments and Exercises That Work

Deirdre C. Stam

I had been teaching book history surreptitiously for years before I was lucky enough to teach it openly in the new Rare Book and Special Collections Concentration at the Palmer School of Library and Information Science of Long Island University. So secret was my pursuit that even I was barely aware of it. The discipline of 'book history' or 'print culture' was distinctly marginal when I began my academic career in the 1960s, identified then, and through the 1980s, as variously old-fashioned, elitist, antiquarian, and impractical. But having taught at four graduate schools of library and information science, I have developed a good sense of what works well in graduate settings and what doesn't.

First, I offer some ideas toward a pedagogy of book history. In teaching, book historians seem to agree on the importance of focusing upon detail in contrast to abstraction. That detail can be of several kinds: bibliographic description, collation and comparison, condition reports, provenance, pricing, hands-on experience with the elements of book-making and book-illustration. Yes, context – the times, the economy, and geography, and so forth – is important, but students learn such abstract concepts in most other areas of their academic preparation. Students in book history courses then must reorient from working deductively (from a priori assumptions) to working inductively (from physical evidence to such abstract concepts as authorship, meaning, and significance). This ability – to encounter an original item and make a case for it, either in financial or intellectual terms – is fundamental and essential for library science students. Yet for the most part, students lack experience with the tangible realities of evidence and the skills to work from the object to the interpretive level. In other words, they lack *hands-on experience* with books.[1]

Therefore, in the classroom it's essential to make 'rare books' live, but even in New York City – with its extensive collections of rare books, prints, and related splendors – it's hard to do when rare books aren't available for handling,[2] and when classes are held in the evening when special collections are closed. These classroom exercises inexpensively transcend that difficulty. Further, they are designed so that everyone in the class can benefit from the work of each student. While these exercises are particularly suitable for professional training in library science, most would be appropriate for students in other programs: the distinction is one of emphasis rather than essence.

These activities are designed to engage students and to minimize preparation and anxiety for the teacher. They are also virtually plagiarism-proof: they are very hard to do by simply pulling information off the internet. Lasting from thirty minutes to two hours, most are relatively brief so that they can be added or subtracted as time allows; and they are structured so that students do them quickly, thus keeping up the momentum of the session. Generally I can assume a degree of sophistication and general information, except in the area of illustration processes where we start at the very, very beginning. (Don't kindergartens teach art any more?). Further, judging from student evaluations, they are a worthwhile use of class time.

The pedagogical pattern is to introduce new information (via reading, a film/video/DVD, or a brief lecture with images) and then require students to apply that new information within a fairly brief period of time. If the class is eight or fewer, we work together; if larger, we break into groups, varying group membership with each assignment. After completing the activity, each group reports back to the whole class on its findings/product/outcome. Class participation factors in the final grade, in part to provide me with a basis for grading and in part because most professional work requires collaboration and students have to get used to that fact during their training.

Homework and other out-of-class assignments

One year in the history of printing.

Objective: to develop quickly a deep, if narrow, expertise in one category of publishing

Students track the producing of publications for a given year in a given area; they also must describe all world happenings during that year including economy, wars, natural disasters, politics, etc. Students can present their results as a paper, time-line, web-page, outline, etc.[3]

Biography of a book before 1800.

Objectives: to apply research skills, to become familiar with a rare book 'room', and to observe closely and analyze one specific copy

Each student locates a nearby *copy* of any book published before 1800 to visit in a rare book room and handle repeatedly during the semester. Drawing from Robert Darnton's frequently reprinted essay 'What is the history of books',[4] the student considers all aspects of that copy including authorship, bibliographic description and collation, provenance/ownership, condition, structure and binding, 'ancestors' and 'progeny', production, distribution, design, intellectual content of the work, intellectual milieu, and their encounter with the copy. Reports of 1500 words, excluding notes and bibliography, use at least fifteen sources (most of them printed).

Note: this assignment does not work as well for 1800 onward. Variations of this approach are the Adopt-a-Book assignment, and the device of choosing a title at random from the short-title catalog and concentrating on its many aspects over the semester.

Reading and writing by candlelight

Objectives: to experience the difficulties of reading/copying under 'medieval' or pre-modern conditions; to understand images of monks copying.

Students sit by themselves in a completely dark room with a lighted candle; they then read one page of text aloud and copy one long paragraph. Students write a one-page description of the experience and prepare to discuss in class. Some will mention how reading aloud helped in copying.[5]

Making lists and checking them twice.

Objective: to learn the publication history of specific works and the bibliographic resources used by curators, and examine the publishing history of geographical areas or categories of works.

Students choose a narrow subject or a single author. They provide recommendations for building stock (for a bookseller) or expanding a collection (for a library), using standard bibliographies, footnotes from critical works, holdings records from libraries and booksellers, and other bibliographical tools.[6]

Creative Forgery: Designing a title page for the year x in the region of y

Objective: to analyze historical typefaces and layout traditions.

Provided with three examples of title pages from a particular place and period, students emulate (via computer) the general look of a title page, making up bibliographical data that is reasonably convincing. Have students include some modern content so they cannot simply submit a facsimile of a real title page. Students display these 'forgeries' in class, beside the photocopies of the sample title pages. Students explain – very briefly – the principles that they were attempting to embody and the difficulties they encountered. For a larger class, divide students into groups, giving each group a different set of examples from a different place/period.

Collection management: Crafting policies for a small special collection

Objective: to consider all aspects of overseeing a special collection.

Students choose one real collection of relatively small size, then produce a series of short papers that combine at the end to constitute a set of policies. Topics include collection development, preservation, security, public relations, budgeting, staff development, cataloging/description, educational programming, and more.

Professional Conversation: subscribing to ExLibris and Sharp-L[7] listservs

Objective: to learn the mores of communication and the hot topics in the fields of special collections and book history.

Students join both electronic listservs. In class from time to time, discuss hypothetical contributions and responses to current issues. Encourage students not to clutter the lists with submissions as part of their course work. They may, of course, submit postings if they have a good reason for doing so.

Shop Talk: visiting a book shop or attending a professional event

Objective: to socialize into the profession

Early in the term instruct students to talk to a book-person either in a book shop or at a scholarly/professional conference. Students submit a two-page summary of their experience and tell about the experience in class. This report performs the additional function of providing the instructor with a diagnostic writing sample early in the term. Students enjoy hearing about each others' adventures and the writing samples are examples of creativity and humor.

In-class activities and exercises

Memory: experimenting with words and pictures.

Objective: to understand the abstraction of writing and the power of the image, especially as pertaining to the medieval book

Divide the class into two groups (left and right sides of the room). Group I members cover their eyes. Show Group II a *written list* of seven objects (water glass, feather etc.) that is projected on a screen. In silence, the instructor points to each item for a few seconds.

Group II members then *cover* their eyes, and Group I *uncover* their eyes. Show Group I the list. Again in silence, the instructor *holds up an object dem-*

onstrating each term while pointing to each term on the list. Remove the list, and Group II then uncover their eyes.

Working from memory, the students then write down the terms in the list. The instructor shows once more (to all students) the written list and asks how many got all seven terms right, how many six terms, etc.

Typically, students who had visual clues as well as written texts perform better on the memory test. Encourage students to draw the lesson from experiment, moving to a discussion of medieval book illustration and cathedral sculpture.

Book structures: binding a codex that opens well.

Objective: to become conscious of book structures and their functioning.

The instructor provides a big box of materials and asks students, working in groups of three, to produce a little book in about a half hour. Materials include scissors, thread or unwaxed dental floss, scissors, duct tape, wire, brads, staplers, hole punches, scotch tape, paper clips, spring clasps, wrapping paper, cardboard/manila folders, plastic sheets, and more, including a few 'daffy' items that will probably not be used. The instructor should *not* provide explanations or suggestions during the exercise.

When done, students show and explain their structures to their peers.

Note: I usually follow this exercise, in the following session, with an illustrated lecture on the history of binding.

Collation formula: folding paper and sewing signatures.

Objective: to understand how to read a collation formula (relating to descriptive bibliography)

Explain some simple collation formulae and demonstrate paper folding, then assign to each small group a unique (but short and simple) collation formula for its 'book'. Provide lined notebook paper (to simulate chain lines), large-eyed needles, and unwaxed dental floss so that students can sew the signatures together in the order specified in the formula. Students can also add signature marks. When the activity ceases, each group must explain and demonstrate its assigned collation formula, using its 'book' as the exemplar. Keep books under sixteen leaves; even twelve can be challenging.

The Carter quiz: learning definitions from *ABC for Book Collectors*[8]

Objective: to use technical terms when discussing and describing books and to understand shared concepts and references.

Instruct students to learn Carter's terminology in specified chunks during the opening weeks of the course, then quiz them on the terms.

Note: This assignment has become standard for the History of the Book in library circles, due largely to Terry Belanger's example at Columbia in the 1980s.

Reluctantly, I have been won over to it as a pedagogical tool because it works. A multiple choice approach produces less anxiety than Belanger's practice of asking students to read and reread Carter and write out accurate definitions, and I believe it as likely to produce beneficial long-term results. One can break this assignment into alphabetical chunks and give several quizzes during a term.

Buy and Sell: Assigning a condition level to a used book

Objectives: to learn standard condition concepts and terms, and practice using technical terms for the description of books.

Assumption: students have already begun to use technical terms for the parts of a book (See 'The Carter quiz')

Introduce the terms for condition; in the rare book trade, such terms are very close to standard. One version can be found at in the glossary of terms provided by Abebooks.co.uk: direct students to the Abebooks 'Help' menu, then have them click on 'Features', then 'Glossary'.

Then divide the class into an *even* number of small groups. The instructor provides each group with three books. Telling the groups that they are going to *sell* the books, the instructor asks them to assign a condition status to each, using technical vocabulary for the parts of the book.

When the groups have finished this first step, students exchange their pile of books with another group. This time, the students are going to *buy* the books that have been given to them, and they again assign a condition status. (Do *not* warn students ahead of time that they will both sell and buy).

Finally, in a class discussion, groups explain their condition assignment, using technical terms for the book. For each stack of books, give the 'selling' description first, followed by the 'buying' description. The groups should be encouraged to argue – gently – about differences in assigned condition levels.

Note: If the instructor has eBay and PayPal accounts, they may want to use the following variation on the describing exercise. The instructor has the class describe, evaluate the condition, and price a few books in preparation for the instructor's posting of the books on an eBay auction. This works best if the posting on eBay, and steps in the subsequent auction, can be shown live during class time, using an computer projector.

Introducing a (dead or alive) 'guest speaker' from the printing/book-making/publishing sphere.

Objective: to experience biographical sleuthing in the field, and to gain experience in a public speaking experience that is common for professionals.

For this quick-paced exercise, students prepare a five-minute introduction to some luminary in the field whom they have, hypothetically, asked to come as guest speaker. When undertaken in a light-hearted spirit, sometimes at the end of class when a few extra minutes are remaining, this exercise introduces 'biographical moments'. Assign 'speakers' early in the term, but have students make the presentations whenever there is a bit of free time. Students usually approach this assignment with a touch of drama and humor – both of which are appropriate for the rhetorical form.[9]

The images quiz: recognizing bits of famous pages.

Objective: to become sensitive to type and page design and to recognize major designers

Using illustrations, discuss twenty-five pages from famous works; give students the twenty-five images, with identifying data, to learn before the next class. During the following class give students a quiz on twenty of those examples.

Notes: In some instances the quiz image includes only part of the original page given to the student for study purposes – eliminating, for example, the title and author, or the illustration. A multiple choice approach is easier on the students, but the fact that five of the possibilities do not have corresponding images adds a note of tension that is probably stimulating. The grades are very good on this exercise, but students do not particularly like it. The exercise requires a degree of memorization, and many graduate students seem to consider that beneath their dignity.

Paper: look and feel

Objective: to learn about major paper types and manufacturing processes

Out of class, the instructor creates a little collection of papers such as papyrus, rag-based laid paper, nineteenth-century wood-pulp paper, coated paper, Japanese rice paper, a sheet of modern photocopy paper, and so forth. (Children's museums, art supply stores, and the instructor's own collection of broken/used books and prints can be good sources for examples).

In class, pass these examples around for handling. Make this exercise a game: all students touch the papers once, then a few volunteers close their eyes and feel the papers again. The students should try to identify the papers by touch alone, explaining their guesses aloud as they feel the papers.

Note: I sometimes give rewards of a light-hearted sort (a bookmark or postcard from a research library) to people who succeed at these games, or indeed to anyone who will volunteer. Admittedly, this is not a serious academic exercise, and though it is somewhat passive for most of the class, it succeeds well in raising awareness. Students become almost fixated on paper from this point onward in the course.

Legibility of type and page design: reading aloud from selected English Bibles.

Objective: to become sensitive to type faces and issues of legibility, to the effect of intended use on artistic decisions, and to public reading of religious texts.

Before class, the instructor obtains photocopies of the same passage from a few Bibles famous for their design, such as the *Geneva Bible, King James, Bruce Rogers, Bradbury Thompson*, etc. Facsimiles of the first page of the Old Testament are fairly easy to obtain, but images from other passages would probably be more effective. The instructor should make overheads of the facsimile pages.[10]

Students – one for each Bible – read aloud the comparable passages from the various Bibles. (It might be best to chose some 'hams' among the class members for this rhetorical exercise). While the students are reading, project images of the texts behind them.

After all have finished reading, ask the readers to talk about difficulties they encountered (e.g., did any words trip them up?, how did they figure out the phrasing?, could they see the page adequately?, did the layout suggest any particular emphases?). Ask the class to suggest how the layout or type might have been altered to make the reading easier.

Note: This exercise might be most effective if students, on subsequent visits to rare book rooms, could see originals and consider the factors of size and paper tone and quality as contributive factors to legibility.

Don'ts

My list of what not to do is blessedly short. I eliminate many assignments typical to book history courses because, in my experience, they don't work for adult students who attend graduate classes after a long day on the job. Accordingly, I also offer these admonitions: don't put students on the spot in class, or embarrass them, or patronize them, or simply entertain them, or waste their time and hard-earned tuition.

- *Don't* assign long term papers. The results are too vague, sometimes essentially undergraduate papers; take too much of students' time; and only the writer benefits, not the rest of the class.
- *Don't* assign case studies of great books. The resulting papers are too derivative and predicable.
- *Don't* deliver facts via lectures that have no illustrations, though I do occasionally tell 'stories' including facts. Given my students' broad range of interests and backgrounds, I cannot figure out what facts would be useful or interesting to everyone. In my opinion, after 30 minutes most factual lectures are a great bore.
- *Don't* require attendance at group field trips outside of class. Students are too heavily booked already, and they are too old to herd around. That said, I occasionally make available an extra field-trip opportunity, such as a visit to a rare book auction. They do visit rare book collections on their own and share their experiences with the class.
- *Don't* lead in-class discussions of readings. I never can figure out how to do this without some overly obvious assignment like asking for three observa-

tions per student about the reading. This strategy works with undergraduates, but I have yet to find a natural, collegial way to stimulate discussions about reading that some have completed, and others have not.

Last words

These pedagogical devices have worked in a variety of contexts, though the degree to which these devices work vary with the personnel of the class, the mood of the group, the number of students, the energy-level of the instructor, and the time of day.[11] Adjust to your circumstances and enhance with your own repertoire of examples, stories, and jokes.

Notes

1. Used in conjunction with hands-on experiences, films/videos/DVDs – especially those distributed by Rare Book School at the University of Virginia – can be very helpful. (See Resources pp. 187–8).
2. In some rare book rooms, students cannot handle materials – or they are required to wear gloves. This latter practice is highly debated: some professionals contend that the damage done by the oils from ungloved hands is far less than that done by clumsily gloved fingers. Tactile experience, however, is essential; therefore, I have built a collection of battered books of various kinds – all very cheap, usually obtained from library book sales – and I encourage students to handle them to their hearts' content. I have also accumulated pieces of binding leather, buckram, planks of wood, cross-cut pieces of wood, prints, feathers, and other realia that I regularly pass around to give tangible reality to abstract explanations and terminology.
3. Derived from an exercise reportedly used by William B. Todd. When I remember who suggested a pedagogical device, I acknowledge the source, begging indulgence for sometimes getting it slightly wrong. In other cases, I have so fully internalized the devices that I can't remember where I got the idea. In those cases, too, I apologize for oversights and other slights.
4. Robert Darnton, 'What is the History of books?' *Daedalus* (Summer, 1982), pp. 65-83.
5. Developed by Terry Belanger of Rare Book School at the University of Virginia for his undergraduates.
6. Suggested by Daniel De Simone, Curator of the Lessing J. Rosenwald Collection at the Library of Congress.
7. Exlibris: palimpsest.stanford.edu/byform/mailing-lists/exlibris. Sharp-L : www.sharpweb.org/sharp-l.html (accessed 7 May 2006).
8. John Carter, *ABC for Book Collectors*, 8th edn. With corrections, additions, and an introduction by Nicolas Barker (New Castle DE, Oak Knoll Press; London, British Library, 2004).
9. Developed by Joseph Ripp of Southern Illinois University
10. This exercise elaborates on one suggested by Mary Kay Johnson of Carnegie Mellon University.
11. I am indebted to those who generously responded to my requests for help with this essay: Bill Cole of Barcelona, William Klimon of Cornell University, Eric v. d. Luft of SUNY Upstate Medical University, Rich Ring of John Carter Brown Library, and Paul Wright of the University of Massachusetts Press.

Book History and Librarian Education in the Twenty-first Century

Erik Delfino

What relevance does book history have for those just beginning their library careers at the start of the twenty-first century? Despite the explosion in electronic resources, reports of the death of the book are still greatly exaggerated, and the book remains an important medium in the community at large, as well as within the library. Today's Masters in Library Science (MLS) students will inherit the existing book and other 'analog' collections which their predecessors have been building for hundreds of years, and they will be responsible for the fate of all the millions of physical print objects in their care. As they have in many other transition periods in book history – from the scroll to the codex, for instance, or from manuscript to print – librarians will have to decide which materials to preserve in their original format, which to transfer to new media, and which to leave behind. In short, they will make key decisions about the future of significant quantities of humanity's recorded legacy.

Likewise, they will face the even thornier issue of deciding what new print collections their libraries will build in this increasingly digital era. What will be the value of print compared to electronic resources? Does the printed codex book (and the printed journal, for that matter) still have a role for researchers? For what purposes? If the new role of libraries is to provide access to information that resides elsewhere and which is no longer under local custodial control, who will ensure that information is available to future generations?

A grounding in book history can help librarians face these and other issues by presenting past periods of transition in the history of the book, and analyzing how similar problems in those periods were faced and, perhaps, resolved. The book is now so common and ubiquitous that we often don't see it or think about the profound effects it has had on our history and culture, and an introduction to 'the book as object' can help librarians consider the implications of its changing nature and roles.

Further, book history should continue to have an important role in any MLS program, and librarians likewise need to stay engaged in the book history field. First, book history embraces so many other issues of consequence to the library profession - literacy, education, and society; the relation of books to other information (and entertainment) sources;   the changing nature of reading and writing; the business nature of the publishing industry. Second, librarianship has had a long partnership with other disciplines studying book history. Our profession has recently developed theoretical models for the relationships among bibliographic 'entities' that we feel offer new opportunities for both librarians and our book historian colleagues.

Techniques

In order to provide a historical perspective in a relevant context in my book history class, I include two types of examples wherever possible: lessons from book history that resonate in present situations, and current events that illustrate recurrent historical themes. In a one-semester course, there simply isn't enough time to explore all periods and examples in depth. We try to identify a few key instances that illustrate a variety of points. Here are two examples that deal with major transition periods in past book history.

Gutenberg and Beyond

Johann Gutenberg and the invention of printing with movable type have become unquestionably central to any discussion of book history. It was the reexamination of the effect of printing on early modern Europe, beginning with studies by Elizabeth Eisenstein and others in the 1970s and 1980s, that helped lead to the current widespread interest in book history.[1] With Gutenberg as a starting point, scholars have since moved out both chronologically and geographically, examining earlier and later forms of the book in the West, the Near East, and many other cultures. Outside the academic world, general interest in Gutenberg remains high, as seen in the media's high-profile coverage of the ongoing debate about the nature of the technology he used.

Gutenberg and the invention of printing have also been frequently employed as a metaphor for the advent of the World Wide Web, and for our transition from a society based on print to one based on networked information.[2] In the classroom, this analogy is often used to compare printing and the Web as technologies that increased the volume of available information and facilitated its widespread dissemination. Students readily see these parallels; too often, though, this is where the comparison stops.

The conversations become more interesting – and the analogy more complex – if taken a bit farther. For library school students, the 'Gutenberg gambit' can introduce many other relevant topics:

- contrasting the roles of the medieval scribe, the Renaissance printer/publisher, and the modern webmaster;
- factors involved in the acceptance of, and resistance to, new technology;
- changing roles and relationships of writers and publishers; the fate of the editorial function; the impact of 'self-publishing' via the Web;
- technology's effects on the volume/speed of production and dissemination of information;
- new information tools and their effects on society and the economy;
- new technologies and their impact on the needs/strategies of researchers, and the nature of research itself;
- control of information content, and the implications for authority and authentication of information, censorship, etc.
- conversion of existing information to new formats, and preservation of old formats.

Comparing the introduction of printing with that of the Web has been a good way to explore with students the relation of the means of information production and its use, as well as the impact of new 'user interfaces'. For instance, printing technology did not fundamentally change (at least at first) the book medium itself, or the way the user related to the medium. It was the technology of *production* that changed, not the product. Late medieval manuscripts and early Renaissance printed books often shared physical similarities and a common 'interface': they looked alike, they were held the same way in the hand, and they were read in much the same manner. *Liber Chronicarum* (the 'Nuremberg Chronicle', 1493) is a good illustration of this point – an early printed book that has a certain medieval 'look and feel'. These examples can help students explore how the Web, in contrast, is having fundamentally different effects on reading and writing precisely because it is both a new means of production *and* a new textual medium.

I also use the introduction of printing to raise the issue of just what is 'new' about a new information technology. This is a constant issue for librarians, who must evaluate each new medium, technology, and information product and decide if it will supplement, complement, or replace existing resources.

The Scroll and the Codex

Gutenberg's innovation certainly isn't the only transition in book history worth examining by MLS students. Another intriguing one is the eventual success of the codex over the scroll as the dominant form of book in the West between the first and sixth centuries. Unlike printing (or for that matter, the Web), the codex neither improved production (with its folded quires, sewing, and binding, a codex was inherently more difficult and expensive to create than a scroll), nor facilitated dissemination of information, and yet it supplanted the form of book that had dominated for thousands of years.

The codex, like the web, did have significant 'user interface' improvements over its predecessor: relative compactness, more efficient use of the writing surface, direct access to particular pages, 'bookmarkability', etc. These are similar to the modern contentions that electronic resources have features that make them more efficient and 'user friendly' than print.

However, what makes this topic so appealing for discussion with students are the scholarly arguments that it wasn't technological factors which most contributed to the codex's eventual success, but rather social ones – particularly its early adoption by the new Christian church.[3] In an attempt both to break with the past and establish their separateness from other religions, early Christians (it is thought) chose the codex rather than the scroll as their medium almost from the beginning of the movement ('it's not pagan, and it's not Jewish, and neither are we'). As Christianity came to dominate the Roman Empire, so its adopted book form came to dominate the book world.

This introduces interesting societal and political notes into the discussion of book history. In the classroom, this argument can serve as an opening for all sorts of discussions on the sociology of reading and writing, the role of the printed book (codex) in the modern world, the generational aspects of children growing up with new technology (be it a manuscript codex, print, or the Web), the effect of technology on reading habits, and non-technical reasons for embracing a particular technology.

Modern Events, Historical Lessons

A major goal of the book history class in our MLS program is to help prepare students for the 'book world' as it exists in the twenty-first century. Librarians will have to deal with a host of challenges, including the following:

- issues of copyright and censorship;
- costs/benefits of print and electronic resources;
- emerging book- and information-related technologies;
- changing priorities of governing bodies;
- consolidation among book publishers and jobbers;
- the changing demographics and needs of their users.

In class, we look for current events that can both reflect these issues and serve as starting points for class discussions on historical precedents and related topics. For example, consider the ongoing debate about unauthorized sharing of digital music, movie, and other files, a familiar topic on college campuses around the country. Students are usually willing to voice strong opinions on both sides of the issue, and their interest has led to successful conversations on the changing nature of intellectual property, rights of authors, publishers and users, etc. I have used this subject as an introduction to copyright law, its changing nature from the British 'Statute of Anne' (1709) and the present, gradual shift from individual to corporate control of rights, etc.

In addition, recent history has provided a wealth of events with wonderful potential for classroom conversations and topical examples. Below are some examples of news events (from 2003 and 2004) and related teaching points used successfully to expand on concepts in our class discussions.

Books and other media

- the release of the latest Harry Potter book(s)
- the return of Oprah's Book Club with the 'revival' of *East of Eden*
- the release of Bill Clinton's *My Life*
- the publication of the 9/11 Commission's report

Teaching points: books as media events; the Author as Celebrity – and as Commodity; the effect one person can have on reading and book buying habits; publisher marketing techniques; the role, appeal, and success of print books in an increasingly digital age.

Preservation and content vulnerability

- the flood at the Peabody Library at Johns Hopkins University
- the Hurricane Isabel blackout, and the East Coast power failure

Teaching points: juxtaposition of the relative strengths and weaknesses of print and electronic resources; vulnerability of print materials to environmental damage; vulnerability of electronic resources to power and network failures; the concept of LOCKSS ('lots of copies keep stuff safe').

Books and emerging technology

- Barnes & Noble's decision to stop selling e-books
- Amazon's release of its 'search within the book' feature
- Google's book scanning project
- National Endowment for the Arts study on American literary reading habits

Teaching points: unreliability of technological predictions ('print books are out; e-books are in'); expectations running ahead of technology's ability to deliver; unexpected synergy between electronic and print tools (using online content search as tool to sell print books); future of print collections; control and access issues; changes in reading habits and demographics; need for studies of online and non-fiction reading.

A Final Thought

Beyond practical teaching examples, library science also has an important contribution to make to the theory of book history, of potential use to those teaching the subject in all disciplines. Many existing library computer systems do a poor job of clearly identifying, collocating, and presenting the many versions of a given work which may be represented in a bibliographic database. In an attempt to bring the power of computers to bear on this problem, the library profession, through the International Federation of Library Associations, recently developed a theoretical model called *Functional Requirements for Bibliographic Records,* or FRBR ('ferber').[4]

At its core, FRBR presents a four-level hierarchy for the bibliographic representation of intellectual endeavors (such as books), from the most abstract conception down to a specific, physical copy. At the top of the hierarchy is the 'Work' as it exists in the author's mind, without regard to any particular physical representation. That Work can take many forms - known as 'Expressions' at the next level in the model – such as a written text in English, or a film in French. Each Expression can then have one or more 'Manifestations', which equate roughly to an 'edition' (in the case of books), or a 'release' (in the case, say, of a sound recording, film, or video). Finally, each Expression is given physical form in one or more individual 'Items', or copies. The shorthand for this relationship is usually given as:

> 'WORK
> is realized through
> EXPRESSION
> is embodied in
> MANIFESTATION
> is exemplified by
> ITEM'

FRBR was developed specifically to resolve a number of problems in the representation of bibliographic data in library database systems. It is still new and only now beginning to be implemented in library technology systems. However, its basic concepts and terminology, as outlined above, will be readily recognized by those in many branches of book history, such as textual criticism. The study of 'Items' (copies) from numerous 'Expressions' is one of many tools, for instance, used in ascertaining the author's intent.

In some preliminary experiments with my library school students, I have found FRBR extremely helpful in introducing them to such concepts as authorship, intellectual property rights, and descriptive bibliography. The model seems to offer huge potential as a new tool in the teaching of book history, whether for the study of a particular title, or an organizing principle in the classroom, and it bears much further exploration and study.

Notes

1. Elizabeth Eisenstein, *The Printing Press as an Agent of Change* (Cambridge and New York, Cambridge University Press, 1979); and *The Printing Revolution in Early Modern Europe*. (New York , Cambridge University Press, 1983).
2. See for instance James Dewar, *The Information Age and the Printing Press: Looking Backward to See Ahead*, (RAND Corporation, 1998); accessed at: http://www.rand.org/publications/P/ P8014/ (accessed 7 May 2006).
3. Colin H. Roberts, and T. C. Skeat, *The Birth of the Codex*, (Oxford and New York, Oxford University Press, 1983).
4. Barbara Tillett, *What is FRBR? A Conceptual Model for the Bibliographic Universe* (Washington DC, Library of Congress, 2004); accessed at: http://www.loc.gov/cds/FRBR.html (accessed 7 May 2006).

Making the Medicine Go Down: Baggy Monsters and Book History

Sean C. Grass

In February 1999, as I prepared the syllabus for my first course in British literature, an article appeared in the *Chronicle of Higher Education* that terrified me.
According to James Shapiro of Columbia University, recent trends indicated
that university professors were beginning 'to abandon longer works . . . [in
order] to rescue their favorite authors from oblivion':

> novels that are more than 350 pages long – even if they are by celebrated
> writers like Charles Dickens, James Joyce, George Eliot, and Henry James
> – are regularly rejected by professors who have learned from experience that
> it's wiser to play it safe and substitute a shorter work, one that students will
> be more likely to finish.[1]

As a specialist in Victorian fiction, I had sudden visions of teaching *A Christmas
Carol* and *Silas Marner* until my dotage. My course for the next semester was
ambitiously titled 'Traditions of English Literature', and there, I decided, amid
obligatory selections from Chaucer and Shakespeare, I would fight against Shapiro's grim observation. Literature syllabi might someday dispense with baggy
monsters, but not on my watch.

By October, we were 400 pages into *Bleak House*, and all seemed well. We
had navigated the novel's prickly opening chapters, and pop quizzes showed
that most students were reading; in another hundred pages Krook would spontaneously – gloriously – combust. Then, one day, as I walked to our classroom,
I casually asked one of my best students how she was doing. She replied, 'fine',
then blurted, 'why are you making us *do* this?' I don't want to overstate the
importance of her question or make it seem more epiphanic than it was. But
that day, setting aside my plans, we took up her question and my response. As
I explained my sense of Dickens's – and, by extension, *Bleak House*'s – place
in English literature, I realized I was talking less about Dickens's artistic right
to be in the canon than about his place in the development of the novel as a

popular and profitable genre. That class session was our most important of the semester, because it helped students and teacher alike to understand why we should bother with *Bleak House*'s sprawl. Since then, *Bleak House* – and discussions of nineteenth-century book history – have remained staples of my undergraduate survey. Early in the semester we spend a week discussing literacy rates, book prices, triple-deckers, circulating libraries, novels in parts, and related issues. Even this can't make the baggy monsters of Victorian fiction as sleek as Mary Shelley's *Frankenstein* or Bram Stoker's *Dracula*. But for students, baggy monsters are more comprehensible, at least, when they are taught within the broader context of the nineteenth-century literary market.

When we talk about book history in my Victorian survey, I tell students up front that I want to help them understand why novels like *Bleak House* are so extraordinarily long. But discussing book history has other salutary effects. Talking about the complex relationships between authors, publishers, booksellers, and readers shows students that our semester's literature was shaped by contextual considerations that we can try to reconstruct. As we discuss, Victorian fiction is often meticulously context-specific, whether about geography or money or events like the Great Exhibition or the Sepoy Rebellion. Talking about book history, then, actually reinforces the aim of other assignments: readings from Daniel Pool's *What Jane Austen Ate and Charles Dickens Knew*, student presentations on historical matters, and extra-credit problems involving Victorian money. Book history also gives undergraduates a point of contact between the Victorians and themselves. My students arrive knowing little about Victorian England, but they can wax eloquent on the problem of expensive books and the dynamic between textbook publishers, bookstores, and 'the literate poor'. Such discussions help us clear a formidable hurdle: my students, to read a novel double or treble the size of any they have tried; I, to conquer their aversion to long books and disabuse them of their notion that Dickens was 'paid by the word'.

I don't know where this idea comes from – whether it is urban legend or a line from *The Simpsons*, or whether high-school teachers are exacting revenge for having to force discontented teenagers through *Great Expectations*. Whoever instills this belief does me the inestimable service of providing a perfect pretext for introducing book history. By our third week, having discussed things like Parliament, the Anglican Church, and the Industrial Revolution, I prompt our transition into more literary subjects by brandishing *Bleak House* and asking, 'Why are Dickens's novels so long?' On the rare occasion that no one takes the bait, I volunteer that perhaps Dickens was paid by the word; some students will always admit having heard that scurrilous lie. Then I ask, if Dickens was paid by the word, why are his novels so *short*? Even in *Bleak House*, after all, someone with Dickens's talents might surely have sprinkled in a few more adverbs or prepositions. A clever student will sometimes suggest that Dickens was limited by technology and could not write longer novels because old bindings could hold only so many leaves. But as I tell them, Dickens's novels were published mostly in monthly installments, and even whole novels during the nineteenth century were commonly published in multiple volumes. So far as material limitations were concerned, I point out, a Victorian novel could have run as long as an encyclopedia. Students recognize through all of this that Dickens was paid just as modern novelists are: according to the shrewd calculus of publishers who gauge the market value of an author's work. If Dickens wrote long novels, he did so because the Victorian literary market required that he should – because readers and publishers wanted them. Though students are initially aghast at the sheer perversity of Victorians (they *really* wanted hideously long novels?), they soon realize that a complicated market dynamic shaped Victorian literature, a dynamic we must understand to make sense of the texts.

To impose order upon the complex subject of book history, I divide the topic into two differently-themed days of lecture and discussion: (1) the cultural and material factors that for a long time limited the audience for the British novel; and (2) the technological and publishing innovations that eventually eroded those factors and made the novel the literary form of popular choice in England by the mid-nineteenth century.

At first glance, this scheme may look a little *too* neat. But I am using book history to prepare my students to read Victorian novels, and anyway our actual discussion is more nuanced. We begin by talking about the low literacy rates in England during the eighteenth century and the fact that the novel was the 'disreputable' genre, compared with poetry, well into the century that followed. Few students are surprised that the adult literacy rate was just 10% in England during the second half of the eighteenth century, [2] and some usually know that these literate Britons were typically aristocrats or members of the clergy. But they rarely realize that Anglican clergymen were all trained at Oxford or Cambridge, or that the clerical profession was largely a refuge for the second and third sons of the British upper-class. The fact that readers in eighteenth-century England were predominantly genteel, we discuss, had profound effects on the literature of the day. Contrasting passages from Alexander Pope's *The Rape of the Lock* and Daniel Defoe's *Moll Flanders*, we examine the way that some early novelists – because they came from the educated working-class – were more willing than poets to address the gritty concerns of the lower, working, and middle classes, which contributed to the sense that the novel was not respectable 'art'. On the one hand, this was bad for the novel since it meant that genteel readers (those with money to buy books) were unlikely to become a wide popular audience for British fiction. On the other hand, *because* the novel was less reputable than poetry, it afforded women and educated working-class men an unprecedented chance to enter the literary market.

Students recognize that this was a slender audience, especially considering the high price of books. In an age of computers and desktop publishing, students know little about the way that printers and publishers produced books two centuries ago. But they often are genuinely interested in the oddities of the process. They are invariably amused to learn that England made its paper from rags in 1800, and that the cost of paper peaked in 1810 when the Napoleonic Wars halted the importation of rags from France. During that decade the cost of a ream of paper rose from twenty to thirty-two shillings, or the modern equivalent of as much as $150.[3] Students draw the logical inference: with paper so expensive (25% of the production cost of a new title), the market favored short books, which meant that publishers of new works were more likely to deal in poetry than fiction and that books of poetry were cheaper than novels.[4] We also discuss the appallingly low standard of living in England around 1800, when few could buy candles, let alone books. With a small, static number of upper-class consumers for literature, it made sense that publishers brought out most new books in expensive editions of no more than 1,000 copies though England was home to some nine million people.[5] Adult literacy probably doubled between 1790 and 1820, but without expanding considerably the market for British novels. The low standard of living, high price of books, and disreputable nature of the genre ensured that new fiction could not have a wide popular audience in England.

On day two, we talk about the way that technological and publishing innovations broke down these barriers and helped to propel the novel's rise as a popular genre. We examine first how the invention and growing use of paper-making machines helped to restore the cost of a ream of paper to just twenty shillings again by 1835, and how greater efficiencies in printing procedures allowed printers to manage longer books.[6] With paper and printing costs contributing less to the overall cost of a book, poetry's old marketplace advantage over fiction began to shrink. We also talk about the way that falling paper prices helped to foster the growth of a periodicals market in England, so that many readers of poetry turned to cheaper magazines and journals where they could find poems by their favorite poets nestled among timely essays on current events. The roughly simultaneous rise of steel engravings, I point out, also had important consequences, since it made beautifully illustrated texts 'the next big thing' in the literary market. Buyers wanted pretty pictures, and they created a market for literary annuals that functioned as poetry anthologies and emphasized illustrations rather than written words. As we talk about these things, my students realize these innovations tended especially to erode the status of poetry in the literary market.

The other major part of our discussion on day two includes three sub-topics that I place under the heading of 'publishing innovations': (1) the growth of circulating libraries; (2) the rise of the triple-decker; and (3) the advent of the novel in parts. While I often wish students would show *more* familiarity with modern libraries, they understand the concept of a library well enough to make the conversation easy. The big difference, I tell them, is that circulating libraries were not free; rather, readers paid for a subscription that entitled them to check out a certain number of books at once. The more one paid for a subscription, the more volumes one could have. Though a price tag of £2 per year (or $200 in modern equivalent) sounds high, students understand it was far cheaper than buying books. For £2, a reader might read several dozen novels in a year instead of purchasing just a few. Students see readily that circulating libraries probably encouraged reading, though they simultaneously discouraged economically marginal readers from buying. They also see, with prodding, that this phenomenon had two related effects: first, it gave circulating libraries enormous clout in the literary market; and second, it encouraged libraries to stock works published in multiple volumes, since a reader who wanted the entire work at once would have to pay more for his or her subscription. Using Charles Mudie as the example, I point out that circulating libraries might account for as much as 75% of a novel's sales, so if Mudie wanted multiple-volume works, that's what he got. Publishers knew that they could sell such works to their certain buyers – the libraries – so they insisted that authors write books that would occupy multiple volumes. Sir Walter Scott and his publisher stumbled across the winning 'triple-decker' format with *Kenilworth* in 1821, and the market never looked back. As we close our second day on book history, I remind students that a triple-decker cost 31s. 6d. and point out that as long as books were this pricey, they made circulating libraries necessary. The circulating libraries wanted baggy monsters.

For the purposes of my Victorian survey, this discussion of book history leads us back to Dickens and the serialization of *The Pickwick Papers* in 1836-1837. By the 1830s adult literacy rates were nearing 35%, which meant that increasing numbers of lower-, working-, and middle-class Britons were becoming potential readers. But such readers could not afford to purchase triple-deckers, nor were they likely to live in areas that had circulating libraries. Under these circumstances, I tell students, the publication of *The Pickwick Papers* was the literary equivalent of a perfect storm: the right author in the right place at just the right time. We spend half of our first day on Dickens talking about the almost accidental way in which he came to write it: the novel's origins with illustrator Robert Seymour, the decision to publish the novel in parts, Chapman and Hall's search for an unknown (and, as they thought, irrelevant) writer, and Dickens's immediate success in dominating the project. The story shocks students who cannot imagine Dickens as an insignificant young journalist with no obvious literary 'gift'. It also drives home the point that the success of *The Pickwick Papers* was as much about opportunity as about literary genius.

The rest of the session is dedicated to discussing the innovations that Dickens introduced to adapt the novel to publication in parts. We talk about the lower cost of novels in parts, the new classes of readers they attracted, and the shrewd and pioneering way in which Dickens used lower- and middle-class characters to appeal to this new audience. We also discuss the problem of holding a reader's interest through nineteen months when, at any moment, the reader can decide they had had enough of the story. I compare such novels to television serials and have students examine Dickens's works for soap opera gimmicks: melodrama, mystery, and cliffhanger endings to installments. They also begin watching for certain techniques of characterization – oral litanies, synecdoche, multiple characters who reiterate and amplify themes – that helped readers keep things straight in a story delivered to them at one-month intervals. We talk about these things as devices that Dickens used to make sure there would be *no forgetting* in his novels, and I read students a passage they will find again in *Bleak House*:

> What connexion can there be, between the place in Lincolnshire, the house in town, the Mercury in powder, and the whereabouts of Jo the outlaw with the broom ... ? What connexion can there have been between many people in the innumerable histories of this world, who, from opposite sides of great gulfs, have, nevertheless, been very curiously brought together![7]

In other words, I tell students, their bewilderment at this long novel is already written into the plot, and it is okay if at first they don't see all of the connections. The passage reflects Dickens's recognition that the content and form of his novel are interdependent, and perhaps, too, that the novel in parts posed particular challenges for the writer and his readers. This is what Victorian novels do *generally*, I tell them: they show that what literature *represents* depends intimately upon the pressures that *produce* it. I could not teach that lesson about Dickens and the Victorian novel without teaching them first about nineteenth-century book history.

I cannot say with absolute certainty that students like *Bleak House* more because we have had 'the talk' about book history, but about one-quarter of them write essays on the novel when they could opt for perennial favorites like *Jane Eyre*, 'Goblin Market', or 'Porphyria's Lover'. Also, even students who enter the class apparently hating Dickens write in their course evaluations that *Bleak House* was not as bad as they thought it would be – high praise from juniors who have just read a thousand-page novel. I can also report that undergraduates responded favorably to a special course I offered recently on Dickens, making it the first senior-level course to fill when registration opened, though students knew from the description that they would read long novels like *Nicholas Nickleby*, *David Copperfield*, and *Great Expectations*. None of this means that Shapiro was wrong to report the slow demise of baggy monsters.

But it may mean that for those of us who wish to resurrect them, book history will be the literary galvanism of the post-modern age.

Notes

1. James Shapiro, 'When Brevity Rules the Syllabus, *Ulysses* is Lost', *Chronicle of Higher Education*, 45 (February 12, 1999), p. A60.
2. William St. Clair, *The Reading Nation in the Romantic Period* (Cambridge, Cambridge University Press, 2004), p. 478.
3. Lee Erickson, *The Economy of Literary Form: English Literature and the Industrialization of Publishing, 1800-1850* (Baltimore, Johns Hopkins University Press, 1996), p. 20.
4. St. Clair, p. 506.
5. See St. Clair, pp. 578-664 for details regarding the print runs of new novels by authors like Jane Austen, Ann Radcliffe, and Sir Walter Scott.
6. Erickson, p. 27.
7. Charles Dickens, Nicola Bradbury (ed.), *Bleak House* (London, Penguin, 1996), p. 256.

'They are Not Just Big, Dusty Novels': Teaching *Hard Times* within the Context of *Household Words*

Jennifer Phegley

Teaching Charles Dickens's *Hard Times* within its original publication context in *Household Words* (serialized from 1 April to 12 August 1854) helps students think about the novel in more complex ways.[1] It allows them to understand the Victorian literary marketplace and to engage in higher-level reading practices by analyzing the periodical form's 'seemingly radical incoherence' that 'coexists with order'.[2] This periodicals-centered approach also provides students with a richer sense of literature's ability to intervene in social and political debates. In particular, considering the periodical context of *Hard Times* helps students arrive at more satisfying answers to critical questions such as those posed by the call to reform at the novel's end.

At the conclusion of *Hard Times*, Charles Dickens entreats his readers to recognize and act on their power to change society: 'Dear Reader!' Dickens exclaims, 'It rests with you and me, whether ... similar things shall be or not'.[3] This appeal to action has troubled readers at least since George Gissing claimed that the novel was too exaggerated to be an effective protest against industrialism.[4] In fact, on the basis of this entreaty, Nicholas Coles argues that

> [d]espite [Dickens's] appearing to assume by his appeal that his novel has shown us what form our activism should take, *Hard Times* is the Dickens novel which readers have least known what to do with, and about which there has been least agreement... Dickens presents a vision of society on the basis of which socially redeeming action, including his own reforming practice, is effectually impossible.[5]

The problem seems to be that during the serial run of *Hard Times*, Dickens, a notoriously controlling editor, aimed to produce a unified magazine that appeared to speak with one voice – his own – using non-fiction and fiction in complementary ways. Thus, while the non-fiction journalism in *Household Words* offers an overt advocacy for abused industrial workers, *Hard Times* offers a fictionalized, anti-union, and some would say overly sentimentalized account of workers' lives. This complementarity partly explains R. D. Butterworth's decision to explore Dickens's attitude toward industrial workers in *Hard Times* and *Household Words* in two separate articles: 'Dickens the Novelist' and 'Dickens the Journalist'.[6] Butterworth's decision highlights the division that Dickens's fictional and non-fictional responses to industrialism invite. As a result, after discussing Dickens's sympathetic journalistic account of the Preston Strike (printed in *Household Words* two months before the serialization of *Hard Times*), Butterworth reconciles the differences between the calm strikers depicted in *Household Words* and the dangerous rabble-rousers portrayed in *Hard Times* by claiming that 'In his journalism, derived from real life, Dickens makes some acknowledgment that unions may serve in the immediate term a valid purpose... Fiction, on the other hand, is no place in which to make compromises, but to argue for what the writer thinks is right'.[7]

However, within *Household Words*, fiction and non-fiction are less distinct than Butterworth claims. The lines between the two are blurred, and it is often difficult to distinguish between them, fiction and non-fiction frequently serving the same purposes. While this claim may explain Dickens's anti-union stance in *Hard Times*, examining the interactions between the novel and the articles in *Household Words* to determine how they work as parts of a unified whole enables us to see how the novel humanizes and personalizes the cause of industrial reform, while the non-fiction articles provide a more political context that frames our understanding of *Hard Times's* characters. Thus despite critical disagreement over the novel's message, when read within the context of *Household Words*, Dickens's plea for reform does indeed offer a vision of 'socially redeeming action'. Though the novel may not concretely describe what readers should do to change society, the magazine's non-fiction articles suggest that they should do *something* and that the novel's tragic events are, at least in part, a result of their own passivity.

This critical disagreement over the efficacy of *Hard Times's* call to reform is mirrored by my students' responses to the novel. I began teaching *Hard Times* in its serial context in part because of my research interest in Victorian periodicals, but also because of the drastic contrast between my own response to the novel and that of my students. Like my students, I first read the novel as an undergraduate (in a history course on the Industrial Revolution), but unlike them, I was deeply moved by Dickens's depiction of the living and working conditions of the characters. My students however were more dismissive of the power of the characters and cynical about Dickens's desire to effect change. Largely non-traditional, commuter students paying their own way through college, working full time, and taking care of families, my students consistently (and convincingly) argued either that the novel neglects the working classes or idealizes them. They claimed *Hard Times* does not support political action or engage directly in the lives of workers. And they typically concluded that Dickens's sentimentalization of Stephen and Rachael thwarts the impact of any potential protest against their living and working conditions – complaints that I found compelling despite my very different initial reading experience. Students typically supported their conclusion that Dickens's agenda was more conservative than activist by focusing on the following three aspects of the novel: 1) that the manipulative labor unionizer Slackbridge causes Stephen's ostracization rather than saving him; 2) that Stephen dies by accidentally falling into a pit (though the pit is an abandoned industrial site) rather than as a direct result of his working conditions; and 3) that Stephen's greatest obstacle to happiness is a drunken wife rather than a corrupt and abusive industrial system.

Searching for a way to complicate these adamant student responses, to bring the historical context to light without merely lecturing on it, and, I suppose, to defend Dickens as an advocate for reform, I decided to return the novel to its original serial context by introducing students to articles from *Household Words* that appeared alongside the novel. This essay demonstrates how teaching the novel alongside the articles in *Household Words* radically changed student responses to Dickens, as both a novelist and a reformer.

I began in my upper-level Victorian Literature and Novel courses with advanced undergraduate and graduate students and then tried this approach out in an introductory British literature survey course filled with a combination of English majors and non-majors. In each case, the result was the same: students became more sympathetic to Dickens's approach upon reading the novel in its magazine context. At first, I used a handout that included excerpts from *Household Words* articles that expose the horrors of working class life such as Henry Morley's 'The Quiet Poor', 'Ground in the Mill', and 'Death's Doors', and unattributed articles on topics like pollution and women's rights.[8] These excerpts introduced the students to the kinds of articles featured in the magazine and sparked discussion about how the non-fiction articles might have influenced the original audience.[9] The next time I taught *Hard Times*, I started with the handout but also asked students to look at the magazine themselves, to read background information about the magazine, and to come to class prepared to talk about the ways in which the themes and approaches in the articles reflected or conflicted with the novel. Finally, in my survey course, I added a required essay analyzing the relationship between the magazine and the novel.[10] Whether engaging with the handout or the magazine itself, whether discussing the novel and the surrounding articles or writing about them, most students began to see how original readers' understanding of Dickens's protests may have been heightened by the complimentary articles – published anonymously and thereby seemingly emanating from Dickens himself – that more overtly clamor for political change on behalf of the working classes. Particularly in their essays students were able to identify more interesting connections than those I had discovered myself. For example, one analyzed the class implications of limbs (legs, arms, and hands) in the novel and in an article called 'Legs'.[11] This student enriched her understanding of Dickens's social purpose by connecting a seemingly irrelevant article directly to Dickens's use of symbolism in the novel.

My handout modeled this contextualized reading by including, for example, the following excerpt from 'The Quiet Poor' where Morley's straightforward description of the living conditions of the poor contrasts with Dickens's novelistic ones:

> The summer heat lifts out of the filthy courts a heavy vapour of death, the overcrowded rooms are scarcely tenantable, and the inhabitants, as much as time and weather permit, turn out into the road before their doors. The air everywhere is stifling, but within doors many of the cottages are intolerable. [...] There is not a house, a room, ... in which there was not sickness.[12]

In comparing this passage to the novel, students would often focus in on Dickens's more fanciful descriptions of the living conditions of his characters. For example, students found that Dickens's depiction of the Jupe house as 'haggard' and 'shabby, as if, for want of custom, it had itself taken to drinking, and had gone the way all drunkards go, and was very near the end of it' seemed fantastical and unreal compared to Morley's more visceral description.[13] One student noted in her paper that Morley's scene starkly contrasts with Mr. Bounderby's refrain that his factory workers expect to be set up in a coach and six and fed on turtle soup and venison. Indeed, she claims that 'in seeking a broad audience [... Dickens] effectively limited the nature of his social comments [in the novel]. However, combining his satirical brilliance with other articles [... he remedied the public's] ignorance of the reprehensible factory conditions, desperate lack of sanitary living quarters and overall dismal level of enormous poverty'.

Likewise, Morley's 'Ground in the Mill' includes a series of horrific deaths caused by industrialization that contrast with Stephen's more subtle death in *Hard Times*:

> A man was lime-washing the ceiling of an engine-room: he was seized by a horizontal shaft and killed immediately... A youth while talking thoughtlessly took hold of a strap that hung over the shaft: his hand was wrenched off at the wrist. A man climbed to the top of his machine to put the strap on the drum: he wore a smock which the shaft caught; both of his arms were then torn out of the shoulder-joints, both legs were broken, and his head was severely bruised: in the end, of course, he died. [... These workers were a] sacrifice to the commercial prosperity of Great Britain.[14]

Upon reading Morley's graphic account of the destruction of industrial workers, many students agreed that Stephen's death is rendered more significant by its proximity to Morley's powerful statement about the results of unfettered industrialism. They were especially convinced by Morley's call for the enforcement of the Factory Act of 1844, which required the fencing of open shafts like the one Stephen falls into. Understanding that 'The Old Hell Shaft' violated the Factory Act shifted students' attention from the pathos of Stephen's death and its distance from the factory to the failure of industrialists to follow safety regulations. As Joseph Butwin points out, Dickens had written a footnote to Stephen's death scene that referred readers back to 'Ground in the Mill', but eliminated the note and a more powerful speech by Stephen on behalf of workers before publishing it in his magazine.[15] Possibly Dickens felt the overt reference was unnecessary and even redundant since his novel already implicitly pointed outward to the non-fiction works surrounding it. While students had previously focused on the pathos of Stephen's death, upon reading the novel in its periodical context they understood how Dickens used Stephen to put a sympathetic face on the nameless and faceless victims Morley described. One student even wrote about the parallel between Morley's physical descriptions of mutilation and Dickens's portrayal of emotional disfigurement wrought by the novel's educational system: 'Dickens is directly relating the dangers of life and limb in the factories with the dangers to emotions in the education factories. The children come out of school missing vital pieces of their minds, just as child workers sometimes came out of the factories missing limbs'.

Students also came to see *Hard Times* as an activist statement that called on readers to work for change as they read the novel in tandem with Morley's 'Death's Doors'. This article appears in the same issue of *Household Words* as the chapters of *Hard Times* that deal with unionization in a very unsympathetic manner. Morley appeals to readers directly to act on behalf of the working classes:

> You must act, we must act, every soul must act... Now is the hour, if ever the hour will strike, when every man with a firm arm must stretch it out, and when every man who can get a hearing must speak for those weak and silent sufferers among us whom it would now be more cruel than ever to forget. We must unite to be helpful – helpful each in his own sphere.[16]

Students generally contended that this plea, echoed in the last lines of the novel, counterbalances the negative depiction of Slackbridge by placing responsibility on every citizen to act on behalf of the working class. Morley's call for action thus lends strength to the novel's conclusion. As one student wrote: 'A close reading of *Hard Times* in its original context, accompanied by the supplemental information contained in the magazine, gives contemporary readers a much deeper understanding of the societal issues Dickens sought to address... *Hard*

Times is not concrete – to be fully understood and appreciated it must be read with all the subtleties allowed by its original inclusion in *Household Words*'. My experience teaching *Hard Times* as a part of a unified text called *Household Words* refutes Coles's claim that Dickens's concluding call to action is rendered powerless as a result of the internal logic of the novel. Rather, as this student notes, it is the external logic, contained in the magazine, that completes the novel and renders Dickens's call to action powerful.

When students in both upper-division courses assessed in written surveys what they had learned by reading *Hard Times* in its periodical context, they consistently claimed that the experience transformed their understanding of Dickens. Most students came to see Dickens's magazine and novel as a single text speaking with one complex voice. One student claimed that finding coherence amidst the chaos required being patient with 'inconsistencies' and understanding that differences in the non-fiction and fiction in *Household Words* could actually work intertextually to form a unified whole. She explained: 'I think I see Dickens as a lot more of a cunning businessman and entrepreneur than I previously did... I better see his determination to reach a variety of audiences (and sell more copies) and to market ... his work'. This student concluded that since most readers bought the magazine for its fiction, Dickens was smart to infuse his novel with more overtly political statements that came from the periphery rather than the center. In this way, Dickens could maintain a broad audience while also pushing readers toward socio-political reform. Another student stated that Dickens 'used material based on real life to lend credibility to the world he created in *Hard Times*. The novel allows entrance into the consciousness of the people the writers of the articles use as subjects for their pieces'. Thus, these students began to see Dickens as more complex and interesting after considering *Hard Times* within the context of *Household Words*. One student summed up the experience of reading serialized novels in magazines this way: 'what's *around* the novel ... truly impacts how you read the novel... The whole idea of publication history enlivens the period. They are not just big, dusty novels, but works, when seen through the history of publication, are more indicative of a fascinating social culture'. Reading novels in magazines thus teaches students to attend to intertextuality, to the production history of literary texts, and to the connections between literature and media that are relevant to the understanding of our own cultural context. Not only did my students read Dickens in a more sophisticated way, they also readily recognized the roots of modern media practices in the nineteenth-century literary realm. As a result, the Victorians came to life for them in surprising ways.

Notes

1. I thank Margot Stafford for generously offering to help track down relevant essays from *House-hold Words*; the University of Missouri – Kansas City English Department's Grand Street Group for valuable feedback; and my students for being continually engaged, honest, and challenging.
2. Linda K. Hughes, 'Turbulence in the 'Golden Stream': Chaos Theory and the Study of Periodicals', *Victorian Periodicals Review*, 22 (Fall 1989), p. 119.
3. Charles Dickens, *Hard Times* (London and New York, Penguin Press, 1995), p. 298.
4. George Gissing, *Charles Dickens: A Critical Study* (London: Blackie and Son, 1898), pp. 201-2.
5. Nicholas Coles, '*The Politics of Hard Times*: Dickens the Novelist versus Dickens the Reformer', *Dickens Studies Annual*, 15 (1986), p. 173.
6. R. D. Butterworth, 'Dickens the Journalist: The Preston Strike and "On Strike"', *The Dickensian* (Summer 1993), pp. 129-138; and 'Dickens the Novelist: The Preston Strike and *Hard Times*', *The Dickensian* (Summer 1992), pp. 91-102.
7. Butterworth, 'Dickens the Novelist', p. 101.
8. Henry Morley, 'Death's Doors', *Household Words* (10 June 1854), pp. 398-402; 'Ground in the Mill', *Household Words* (22 April 1854), pp. 224-7; and 'The Quiet Poor', *Household Words* (15 April 1854), pp. 201-6.
9. See companion website for the handout.
10. See companion website for the assignment.
11. Morley, 'Legs', *Household Words* (15 April 1854), pp. 209-12.
12. Morley, 'The Quiet Poor', pp. 202-3.
13. Dickens, *Hard Times*, p. 33.
14. Morley, 'Ground in the Mill', *Household Words*, p. 224.
15. Joseph Butwin, '*Hard Times*: The News and the Novel' *Nineteenth-Century Fiction* 32:2 (September 1977), p. 180.
16. Morley, 'Death's Doors' pp. 398, 400.

'In a Bibleistic Way': Teaching Nineteenth-Century American Poetry Through Book and Periodical Studies

Susanna Ashton

Bringing students into the conversation about the value of material book history opens up exciting critical possibilities for literary questioning. From the mechanical (using the history of the book as manufactured object to capture the attention of engineering and technical majors) to the more abstract (invoking the ways book history forces a nuanced analysis of the politics of canonization, or the ways it highlights the differences between reader–response criticism and formalist analysis), a book history context spurs questions I define as distinctly literary, questions addressing ideas about representations, language, and sign systems of meaning.

In particular, book history has a special relationship to poetry: it is a history that calls into question the very concept of representations and images – best exemplified by the compressed nature of poetry. As we analyze the history, transmission, crafting, and social role of the material text, we necessarily foreground the question of representations. How does the physical ink transform itself into a shape that takes on such immense meaning or how does the physical heft of a literature anthology signify the role of cultural capital for the average undergraduate? How does a page allow (or force) us to make meaning? What do those black squiggly marks we call letters represent to us that inform our understanding of the textual world? Because the issue of representations is always present when analyzing books, using book history – with care – to push students to analyze the role of representation in poetry works beautifully.

In teaching Emily Dickinson, for example, I instigate conversations about the relevance of analyzing the medium of transmission in poetic analysis. If we saw Emily Dickinson's poem on a greetings card, would that change how we understand it? Is there a pure text? What might she herself think about that notion and can we garner any clues from her own work? Is poetic form a medium of transmission no different theoretically from the physical forms of private letters, say, or printed anthologies?

To show how shocking Dickinson might have seemed to nineteenth-century readers, I distribute some popular poetry of the era which would have appealed to a profoundly different aesthetic. At the same time, I ask questions about why people receive certain types of literature differently at different times. However, pulling out maudlin Victorian verse to show how terrific Dickinson was in comparison hardly seems like a productive way to teach literary analysis.

I've taken, therefore, to having two 'lab sessions' to examine nineteenth-century gift books and to think about sentimentality, notions of cultural value, and the excitement of hands-on scholarship. Popular in the 1830s–1870s, gift books were lavishly illustrated anthologies of poetry and prose, with elaborate bindings often covered with gilt embossing. Intended primarily as gifts, they graced most middle-class parlors of the era. I've found them superb tools to move students out of their comfort zones of literary and historical analysis. The library staff of our university's rare book room – excited to have students involved with the collections – provide an elegant library meeting room for us, and many students remarked in class evaluations how much simply holding the class in a rare book room meant to them. The library staff and I had selected enough nineteenth-century gift books for every student or pair of students to have one. Some were standard gift books with titles like *A Friendship's Offering,* but others had political, holiday, temperance and abolitionist themes. Usually illustrated, these books easily impress the students into thinking they are handling exceedingly rare books; while I caution them to be careful, I reassure them that they can indeed touch the books and handle them gently.

After learning how to handle the books physically (with care not to bend the spines all the way open), students simply inspect 'their' book and take notes with their partner, describing it as best they can. Students examine the physical book with special attentiveness, noting individual markings such as fingerprints, stains, or inscriptions. In ten minutes or so, when the students read from their notes, most simply talk about the size, shape, and color of their book. (Since our focus is observation, I don't provide specialized terminology in advance. After they have completed taking notes, I do give some specific terms – 'flyleaf', 'embossed gilt', 'paste downs', 'cloth', 'frontispiece' – and students often take up these terms in their ensuing descriptions.)

The purpose of their examination was to imagine the readership and the role of the gift book itself. 'Why would it be small', I asked, 'Why might it have featured so many pictures of dead children?' 'What might the frequent inscriptions suggest about how gift books were received and shared?' Taking the questions seriously, students raised many good ideas about how these poetry anthologies might have functioned in a society that, despite all of its advances, still suffered terrible infant death rates, an elaborate mourning culture and complex notions of the afterlife.

Though several gift books featured canonical writers, such as Nathaniel Hawthorne and Ralph Waldo Emerson, the majority of gift-book poems were written by women writers largely unknown today. To prompt textual analysis, we read through selections the students had noted as especially intriguing and discussed them in serious terms as art forms that resonated with a particular audience at a particular time. Ultimately, handling the gift books altered the tone of student discussion about sentimental rhetoric from condescending to reflective. Once students read the marginalia inscribed on the flyleaves, they better understood the power of generic poetic forms they had earlier discounted.

The next class period, we examined how Dickinson's poetry both echoed and revolted against many of the gift-book conventions. I was delighted to hear their discussion of Dickinson move away from the facile biographical analyses I'd heard churned out too many times such as Dickinson was 'a crazy lady who never left the house'. Knowing that she was both part of and resistant to a gift-book tradition gave students a new dimension to imagine her work as both private and in circulation, as a common form for cultural communication and as a radical departure from communicative norms.

Book and periodical history also helps move students from literal to figurative understandings, as I found when teaching Edgar Allen Poe's 'The Raven'.[1] For example, a brief discussion over the role of periodicals, plagiarism and copyright led my students to profoundly literary questions about how the poem's repeated 'Nevermore' might actually function to articulate the inherent contradictions of meaning systems. I had unwittingly launched my class into a proto-Derridian mode and the intellectual disquiet it raised was one of the best classroom experiences I've ever had.

I first overviewed Poe's experiences with magazine publishing and the mutual plagiarizing practiced by many nineteenth-century journalists. I hoped this information would broaden their notions of Poe from being the gothic, alcoholic, child molester of undergraduate myth to being instead, or perhaps additionally, a canny and calculating genius. As we moved onto a detailed discussion of the poem's language and images, one student posited that Poe's experience in plagiarizing and being plagiarized might have led to an understanding of all truths as merely a matter of projection. She didn't, of course, exactly phrase it this way. She pointed out that what she called the 'mindless and annoying' repetition of 'Nevermore' was really a plagiarism itself. 'The bird,' she explained, 'stole someone else's words!' The raven, she argued, was copying what someone else had said, just as all the other people who had been stealing Poe's work in magazines over the years. With the help of another student, she expanded her point to argue that the bird was speaking words it hadn't written and couldn't know the meaning of. It was a thief guilty of copyright infringement! Clearly, my brief overview of how Poe complained about (and participated in) spats over plagiarized articles in the fast-moving world of nineteenth-century periodicals had enabled students to shift from historical context to rather sophisticated semiotic deconstruction.

When the class later analyzed Poe's essay 'The Philosophy of Composition' and how he claimed to have begun 'The Raven' simply with a fascination with the sound of 'o' and 'r', students argued excitedly about whether or not sound itself had meaning.[2] (In one particularly fun moment a lively student demonstrated the different ways he could say 'Oh!' and we all confessed that that we were *definitely* inclined to read meaning into his various interpretations.) Another student proudly pointed out that the letter 'r' had a particular meaning – since it was also simultaneously the word 'are'. True, I agreed, but I returned them to the problem of how Poe claimed to have begun the poem with a letter rather than a word. If meaning is simply a matter of projection, then one might see the frustrated speaker of the poet confronting an empty signifier. The 'Nevermore' of the raven might indicate how desperate we are to project meaning onto everything, even when there is nothing there. Using my student's observation about 'r' and 'are' having simultaneous meanings bolstered this notion further. Perhaps, I suggested, the confusion of having too many meanings forces us, as readers, poetic protagonists, genius poets or just humans, to project meanings onto nothing just to calm ourselves down. The students were puzzled by my point, until we then returned to the poem and walked through the increasing frustration of the speaker as he tests out different meanings on an elusive, empty signifier – the ever-irritating bird.

I pointed out that we shouldn't take 'The Philosophy of Composition' at face value – like many of Poe's works, there is much reason to believe that he was manufacturing a notion of labor and composition to give people something they wanted to hear. I asked my students how Poe might have wanted to be viewed; they concluded quickly that since he was considered a lazy drinker and possible plagiarizer (they were really stuck on that idea) he would want people to think that he worked very hard – just the way 'normal' (as one student put it) workers work. When pressed, a student elaborated that Poe would want writing to seem like cooking or brick laying. Delighted, I ran with this for a bit – 'So, perhaps he uses tools then…like letters? Just the way we use ingredients and then follow a recipe? But does that really sound like the way you think a poet thinks that he or she works?' Facing a confused silence, I tossed out notions of romantic inspiration and reminded students that Poe's world identified the role of inspiration itself as the creator of all meaning. For a true romantic writer, the idea of poetry as manual labor with easily quantifiable tools in the forms of letters would be an anathema. By the end of the session, the students seemed to conclude that 'The Philosophy of Composition' was a load of nonsense, created by Poe as a prank to illustrate how limited notions of the creative impulse might work. I'm not sure I agree with that conclusion myself (he always struck me as a gritty-minded journalist who mocked romantics as much as he was one). Nonetheless, I was pleased that my students had come to that point without me lecturing on ironic interpretation. Instead, they had arrived at that position through a thicket of history and imaginative theory. Although many unanswerable questions were raised, I was delighted by how incorporating periodical and book history moved us away from the predictable analysis of 'The Raven' and opened up a consideration of textual meaning that incorporated sound analysis, proto-deconstruction, and problems of reader-response (both their own and that of the poem's speaker).

Book history also works in unexpected moments, such as when I taught three poems published in Paul Lawrence Dunbar's 1896 poetic collection, *Lyrics of Lowly Life*: the dialect poems, 'When Malindy Sings' and 'An Ante-Bellum Sermon' and the non-dialect poem 'We Wear the Mask' (originally published in 1895).[3] I intended to point out that William Dean Howells, one of the era's most prominent and influential literary critics, wrote *Lyrics's* introduction and that this imprimatur meant Dunbar's work was published with an eye to an educated white audience – a rare literary event for an African American author. I thought this juicy bit of publishing history would offer good fodder for discussions about the politics of the literary canon and provide a nifty segue into a brief analysis of 'We Wear the Mask' and how publishing dialect poems might have been a self-conscious production of an ironic and culturally self-conscious mask. Approaching the dialect poems with a nuanced sense of how a literary form might be self-consciously manipulative and doubly conscious (I add a little W.E.B. Du Bois here) was my primary goal.

So I only expected to provide a little publishing anecdote, yet weeks of consciously using book history to spark student analysis had made me attentive to the creative opening a student spontaneously offered. Indeed, it led to one of the most provocatively interdisciplinary discussions I've ever had in a classroom. The context is this: in 'When Malindy Sings' the narrator offers a disdainful directive to a presumably white Miss Lucy who relies upon sheet music to sing:

> G'way an' quit dat noise, Miss Lucy—
> Put dat music book away;
> What's de use to keep on tryin'?
> Ef you practise twell you're gray... (I. 1-4)

I juxtaposed that passage with one from 'An Ante-Bellum Sermon' in which a black preacher stands in the wilderness ('We is gathahed hyeah my brothahs, / In dis howlin' wildaness' [I. 1-2]) and in heavy dialect recounts the story of Moses's liberation of the Jews, all the while assuring his slave audience that he means no heresy: 'Now don't run an' tell yo' mastahs / Dat I's preachin' discontent.' (VI. 47-8).

To open discussion, I asked the students to create some thematic or creative connections between the two dialect poems. One student pointed out that the first poem was about singing and the other was about talking. 'Isn't that a little funny,' I asked, 'considering that both are in a written form that is permanent and opposite of the transient character of speech or song?' I continued, 'Is Dunbar hypocritical?' My students offered observations that 'probably a lot of the slaves listening to the preacher in the woods wouldn't have had a Bible' and 'maybe', one student noted, 'even the preacher didn't have one.' (This student said the Dunbar poem reminded her of a scene in the movie version of Toni Morrison's *Beloved* when an illiterate grandmother was nonetheless considered a holy woman when she preached in the woods.) 'I wonder,' queried one young woman, 'if Dunbar wants to remind people that speaking and singing and listening are more important than reading'. A young man responded, 'Well, if this was supposed to be read mostly by white people, maybe it was using sound to remind white people, in particular, that book knowledge wasn't as important as they thought it was'. Since this was an observation worth interrogating, I returned them to the moment when the narrator in 'When Malindy Sings' specially addresses not only book knowledge but the very mechanics of materiality in books:

> Easy 'nough fu' folks to hollah,
> Lookin' at de lines an' dots,
> When dey ain't no one kin sence it,
> An' de chune comes in, in spots;
> But fu' real melojous music,
> Dat jes' strikes yo' hea't and clings,
> Jes' you stan' an' listen wif me
> When Malindy sings. (III. 17-27)

And in 'An Ante-Bellum Sermon', students read the following stanza with a new dimension for how they wanted to understand what might have been at stake in 'Bibleistic' knowledge.

> So you see de Lawd's intention,
> Evah sence de worl' began,
> Was dat His almighty freedom
> Should belong to evah man,
> But I think it would be bettah,
> Ef I'd pause agin to say,
> Dat I'm talkin' bout ouah freedom
> In a Bibleistic way. (IX. 65-72)

The stanza's irony and wry intentions were apparent to the students (who seemed very fond of this poem) but mere cleverness in the preacher's rhetoric was now fleshed out by notions that, in this context, the spoken word necessarily took precedent over the printed one just as the truth of the message about freedom and justice took precedence over a narrow understanding of a 'Bibleistic' interpretation. In a final exchange, a student raised her hand and quietly wondered, 'Maybe if the Malindy narrator was a slave he might have not liked books because he wasn't able to have any himself. And so, instead, he thought *not* having books was just plain better. Because look at how some white people wanted to understand the Bible'. Another student expanded upon this with the observation that: 'Well, slaves were considered things, right? And so were books. So maybe the narrator didn't like to be a thing and he didn't like things. Instead he liked singing and God better than regular things'. Delighted, I let the class return to 'We Wear the Mask' – this time testing out the interpretative notion that while dialect might be a mask, maybe poetry was a mask. Or maybe even the material book and the material world were just masks for 'true' selves. We never resolved these issues, of course, but the tools book history had provided us with and which we had used throughout the semester, lent the class a metacritical awareness of medium to interpret poems not in the context *of* history but as texts intrinsically constructing and creating their own textual moment.

Notes

1. Edgar Allen Poe, 'The Raven' in T.O. Mabbot (ed.), *Selected Poetry and Prose of Edgar Allen Poe* (New York, The Modern Library, 1951), pp. 33-7.
2. Edgar Allen Poe, 'The Philosophy of Composition' in Mabbot, ibid, pp. 363-74.
3. Paul Laurence Dunbar, 'When Malindy Sings', 'The Antebellum Sermon' and 'We Wear the Mask', *Lyrics of Lowly Life* (Dodd, Mead, 1908), pp. 195-9, 26-30, 167.

The Bibliography and Research Course

John T. Shawcross

Many students have found a course in bibliography and research meaningful for their future work, teaching, publication and oral presentations; conversely, others whose later teaching and writing would have benefited from such study have come to regret the lack of such a course. Three matters are important in setting up the course:

A. 'Bibliography' covers more topics than simply documentation forms. Though knowledge of the *Chicago Manual of Style* or the *MLA Handbook for Writers of Research Papers* is important, these handbooks do not investigate 'bibliographic' matters that research will encounter.

B. The course should present content and activities that relate to many fields, approaches, and interests as well as many periods of literature and all genres. Content and activities should encompass the fields and interests of the students, the methodologies of writing and criticism, and the kinds of work that the future may require of a dedicated professional. Therefore, the course should not be devoted, for example, to a study of T. S. Eliot's *The Waste Land* (the instructor's particular interest), but its study may very easily be included.

C. The course should include such topics as editing, resources for information, the significance of past 'knowledge', the revision of past knowledge by updated study, and sources of correct and up-to-date information. Memory can often be faulty; knowing where to find information is ultimately more important than actually knowing it.

What follows are representative suggestions for a syllabus, built on a few important principles: 1) provision for the students' experience in accomplishing various tasks that may prove helpful in the students' current and future work; 2) in-class review of the results of student assignments and employment of such activities in their current projects; 3) opportunities for students to produce shorter papers and talks, drawn from their own interests and presented to the class in full or in summary; 4) assignments that purposefully require the student to engage different subjects and approaches, while other written requirements may build upon and expand a topic that the student is examining independently or for another current class. The latter not only reduces a student's scattering of work, but emphasizes the varying tasks that usually must be accomplished before a meaningful paper or talk is ready for presentation. For example, one task is the acquisition of background information; another, the awareness and evaluation of scholarship on a specific topic, thus producing what will become equivalent to a 'Works Cited' page; another, for some, would be the establishment of a specific text or justification for the use of a specific text (for example, an Elizabethan play, or development and alterations of Walt Whitman's 'Song of Myself'); another, the significance of 'Reception Theory' in interpreting and evaluating a literary work, or in demonstrating the revisionism an author may undergo over time (for example, the reputation of Edna St. Vincent Millay or John Donne).

My point should be clear: the course should aid the student both in current educational activities and in potential future activities, as based on the experience and observations of the teacher. For example, one student produced the required final paper on a subject of interest to him; with additional research, that paper became a master's thesis, later a published article in a learned journal. Eventually, his dissertation explored for other topics the methodology employed in the original paper; and later, the dissertation was published by a university press. Or, in another example, a former student was working on a book about a novelist and Hollywood screenwriter. She wished to establish a full list of screenplays to evaluate the literary corpus of this overlooked but popular author, but she was unable to unearth much information until she recalled such suggestions and procedures from class which led her to research various archival materials and potential repositories for materials and pertinent correspondence.

The following course description is based on a fourteen-week semester with three class periods per week, with around ten students. Meeting once a week is less effective and more limiting than two or three meetings, and class size should be no larger than fifteen and closer to ten. There are five units.

Unit 1: Finding Information, Considering Past Information, Updating Information (three weeks)

A series of exercises familiarize students with such resources as the *National Union Catalogue*, *National Union Periodicals*, *British Library Catalogue*, concordances, variorum editions, *Dictionary of National Biography* (*DNB*) and *Dictionary of American Biography*, *Columbia Encyclopedia*, geographic indices and atlases, Short-Title Catalogues (such as Pollard / Redgrave / Pantzer, or Donald Wing, or the Eighteenth Century volumes), *Oxford English Dictionary*, and Charles Evans's *American Bibliography*. Class discussions will undoubtedly raise the problem of current validity of some information (as in the *Columbia Encyclopedia*) and the bias – social, political, intellectual – of *DNB* entries. Discussion should also note the inclusion and omission of authors in these reference works and in series like *Contemporary Authors*, or *Dictionary of Literary Biography*, or *Encyclopedia of American Literature* or compendia of women writers or authors of color. Classroom examination of student work is necessary for a full and instructive covering of these materials: one student may have found only older information or not found an entry to make identification, but another will have discovered more compilations with more recent authors and works.

Exercise sheets might ask for identification of the following:

- Persons – John Wycliff, Margaret Roper, Mary Astell, Richard Lewis, Horne Tooke, Lucy Aikin
- Pseudonyms – Saki, Ouida, Boz, Amanda Cross, Henry Handel Richardson
- Titles – *Julian and Maddalo*, *The Apple Cart*, *The Free-Lance Pallbearers*, *Spoon River Anthology*, *Exiles*
- Literary terms – metonym, roman à clef, ecphrastic, hermeneutic, sestina
- Events, influences, and dates – Shays's Rebellion, Ashcan School, 2-14 September 1752, Lady Day, Ramism

Such items pull into awareness not only the specific identification, but the milieu and continued importance that each may hold. Raised may be the frequent appearance of collections of shorter pieces that actually constitute one long work (as *Spoon River Anthology*, Edward Dorn's *Gunslinger*, Sherwood Anderson's *Winesburg, Ohio* or James Joyce's *Dubliners*). The masculine persona of Richardson continues the masquerade that women felt obliged to assume from the Renaissance onward, George Eliot being, perhaps, the best known. Language matters are significant: etymology (silly), meaning (caliber), pronunciation (either / neither), origin (donnybrook), origin and first altered usage (snowbird or pork).

Assignments should take advantage of the Web but make clear the pitfalls that exclusive reliance on it may bring. Reliance on the Web has created a body of researchers who derive information and texts solely from the Internet, but very often that information and those texts are inaccurate, incomplete, nonspecific of source, and biased. Moreover, many students simply accept whatever answers appear without further verification or without full information that the project being pursued should engage.

Unit 2: Bibliographic Research and Documentation (two weeks)

The varieties of enumerative bibliography are important to define: a *primary* bibliography of works by an author requires decision as to type (title page reproduced or modernized and abbreviated; collation included or not; mechanics of form; and separation of genres or composite); a *secondary* bibliography may list all items the compiler thinks useful or only those directly pertinent to the author/subject, all presented in one listing or in separations of books, articles, talks, or as only a 'Works Cited'. Each type has its advantages according to the specific study, but without experience few compilers are aware of the nature of these variations. Set forth (and examine through exercises) sources for unearthing pertinent published and manuscript materials, including the *MLA Bibliography, Year's Work in English Studies, Books In Print*, and various annual bibliographies produced by professional societies like the American Society for Eighteenth-Century Studies or the Spenser Society (in *Spenser Studies*).

Unit 3: Textual Matters: Setting Up a Text and Approaches to Discussion (four weeks)

Since standard literary classes seldom address the nature of a text, the ill-informed student assumes that printed texts are accurate and stable, and that the notes supplied with an edition need no further study. Neither the text nor its treatment is necessarily always to be accepted without question or without qualification. The text of Whitman's poetry, for example, may reprint the so-called 'death-bed' edition, which some scholars reject in favor of earlier versions. A poem with a long line, perhaps an alexandrine like the last line of Milton's 'On Time', may be printed in two lines because of page dimensions, thus obfuscating the effect of the continuance of time that the long line provides in that poem, particularly in contrast to its shorter lines (five being trimeters), representing the brevity of a human being's life.

While modern literature, particularly prose, is little annotated, introductions for texts intended for student use may benefit from allusive reference. For example, in the beginning of James Baldwin's *Go Tell It On The Mountain*, the main character, John, goes to an unnamed motion picture which is commented upon. The film – the cinematic version of W. Somerset Maugham's *Of Human Bondage*, starring Bette Davis and Leslie Howard – is an important allusion for a meaningful reading. Not only is the human bondage that pervades the novel a result of racial bondage, it is the bondage one has with family and friends and especially the bondage that one must bear because of who and what one is.

Experience in creating a text and in editing a text are important activities that a professional critic may have to engage, and cogent examination of a class text will lead to a deeper understanding of that text, and one hopes a more competent 'teaching' of it. A class's assignment of working up a variorum text (of a poem like William Butler Yeats's 'At Galway Races') will depict what the author goes through in writing to arrive at a satisfactory version; what the author's concerns for the poem are and especially for its 'meaning'; and perhaps what influences or intentions have fashioned the final product. Possibilities include Allen Tate's poem 'Ode to the Confederate Dead' which went through numerous printed versions before Tate settled on the anthologized text, and William Faulkner's three- or four-part version of his short story, 'The Bear'. In editing the text, students will have to face an unanswerable question – which should be the anthologized version?

Another exercise is to edit part of John Donne's 'Expostulation' in the much-quoted seventeenth devotion of *Devotions on Emergent Occasions*. Collation of the first three editions (1624, 1624, 1626, widely available on microfilm) reveals spelling, punctuation, and capitalization variants. Attention to the text points to two errors: marginal reference 2 Pet. 2:13 should be 2 Pet. 1:13-14, and 'the old Testament', should be 'thy old Testament'. But the original does not note that the text also quotes John 14:2; in its commentary, a modern edition of the work annotates the quoted lines incorrectly as John 14:3. None of the original or recent editions makes the important connection in the 'Expostulation' between Donne's 'My God, my God' and 'O my God, my God' (twice) and Jesus's last words on the Cross: 'My God, my God, why hast thou forsaken me?' (Matthew 27:46), which has much to say about the author's despair in the midst of his expected death from typhus. The 'Prayer' that concludes this devotion (each 'devotion' has three parts: 'The Meditation', 'The Expostulation', and 'The Prayer') quotes the biblical text more fully twice, although the reference is not given in the early (only in the recent) editions. An introductory statement or annotations should also point out the numerological significance of the twenty-three devotions (rather than twenty-four, positing the metaphor of the passage of a day), of the trinal sectioning of each, and of this being the seventeenth (an indivisible number, here metaphorically pointing to period of the darkening of the day with the possibility of dawn or of no dawning for the author). The answer to the often quoted concept of this devotion asking 'for whom the bell tolls' – 'thee' – places the author (and reader) in the position of recognizing this as a turning point in life-death, whether this is a continuation of the dark which is death or ultimately 'of drawing light out of darknesse'.

Whatever text or texts are employed to demonstrate the work that a text may require (the language, the introduction, the annotations) provides a basis for the numerous critical approaches that may be valuable in interpreting the text, evaluating the author's achievement, or placing all of this within a spectrum of intellectual currents and influences. Introduce critical methodologies, allowing students to apply different ones and discussing these methodologies in the classroom to establish meaningfulness for a text (perhaps not for all texts), the interrogation of a text, or the referentiality of the specific text. A number of up-to-date volumes define and illustrate critical methodologies; *A Handbook of Critical Approaches to Literature*, for example, models multiple approaches to a single work, and includes an extensive bibliography for further study and a useful index.[1]

Another effective exercise for demonstrating annotation or commentary is to edit an unedited personal letter – the kind of work a student of the eighteenth century might investigate in pursuing intellectual currents of those times. A letter can serve to require a general background introduction, identification of people or events alluded to in the letter, possible significance of date, and discussion of basic ideas. It can be fairly short and therefore appropriately handled in a class assignment. For instance, a letter from John Ward (a literary personage) to Andrew Millar (an important publisher) in British Library Additional MS 4320 (dated 14 April 1738), or one from George Vertue (the artist) to Edward Harley, Earl of Oxford, among the manuscripts of the Duke of Portland in Welbeck Abbey, Nottingham, dated 24 February 1738. (Texts of both are available.)

A useful ancillary text – Alexander Petit's *Textual Studies and the Common Reader* – supplies a number of examinations and results of such matters as those above, including important discussions of hypertext and electronic editing which the future scholars in the class will be dealing with.[2]

Unit 4: Writing and Presentation Skills (one week)

A week should be given to a review of effective writing: organization, logical development, coherence, style (levels of language and expression), length, the 'thesis' (or intentionality of the written material) and its establishment. Graduate students need such retrospection on composition, as any reader for a journal or publisher knows. This leads to an examination and review of documentation, of different kinds of footnotage and positioning of such notes, of 'Works Cited' and/or 'Bibliography' and the differences between the two, and indexing the book. Of importance will also be specific suggestions on beginning, developing, and completing the master's thesis and the doctoral dissertation. In turn, necessary revision of either for publication as an article or a book should aid the prudent student in the future. Students will also appreciate hints on how to submit papers for oral delivery or for publication. Sources for writers to determine what journals or presses might be interested in their work – its subject, its treatment, its length, its audience – where and how to submit, and what is expected with submission, are available in numerous reference books (as well as on the Web) and through observations of examples. Work should include a couple of contrasting texts that may or may not represent a publishable piece of writing, texts that students will be able to footnote, texts that can serve as springboards into the question of where to publish, what should accompany such inquiry and the final version.

Unit 5: Presentations (four weeks)

At the end of the term, students present for the class's criticism and evaluation a longer paper (or talk) to be submitted to their course and/or to another current class. At the time of the presentation, some students will still be developing the paper or talk; a few will have completed the writing. For the class members, content and authorial ideas will add to their knowledge and (one hopes) interests, as well as providing exemplary procedures of what to do in pursuing a specific topic and how to accomplish the intent of a piece of writing. Often suggestions for the author to consider in completing (or revising) the paper, and the procedures and thinking on which it is based, will aid the author and, of course, lead to the class's awareness of additional kinds of research and of the nature of audience reactions. An author has to recognize his or her audience – its knowledge of the material presented, the communication of content and ideas that the author hopes to achieve, the followability of the paper or talk for the audience – in many cases, improvement of authorial writing affects immediate understanding; the class, in other words, provides a surrogate professional audience.

An author, much involved in and knowledgeable about the subject, may make invalid assumptions about certain audiences. Readers and listeners may, for example, know of the Harlem Renaissance and perhaps generally of its importance in American culture, but only a few will have meaningful understanding of times and places, of authors such as Sterling Brown or Angelina Weld Grimké, of the important Schomberg Center for Research in Black Culture of the New York Public Library, all of which may need identification or even commentary. Or a paper on John Milton's *Samson Agonistes* which discusses lines 465-6 will need to define the word 'connive' whose meaning ('shut the eye', 'ignore') is quite different from that it holds today. Allusions like Henry Thoreau's to Evelyn (that is, John Evelyn) and to Sir Kenelm Digby in *Walden* when he describes the bean-field he farmed require some identification, particularly since Thoreau does not identify the works from which he quotes and "vital spirits" from the air' (whatever they are) seem to account for his being able to harvest 'twelve bushels of beans'. These are matters that many writers, knowledgeable and involved in their specific subject, overlook as not being part of a reader's or listener's understanding. All these pieces of information that should be made clear in the paper or talk represent the kind of 'information gathering' included in the first unit of the course.

Further, the oral presentation will point up the presenter's skill in communicating to the audience so that they are addressed instead of the words being directed downward and possibly mumbled ('not hearing' is less a matter of loudness than a lack of speaking to the audience), and so that they can follow and not experience hiatus in listening because of something not being immediately understood. The problems of time-limits, especially when reading a poetic text is included, become evident, and a need of correction may arise. Here will also emerge the substance of class periods devoted to writing, to publication, and to oral presentation of a paper.

Notes

1. Wilfred Guerin, Earle Labor, Lee Morgan, Jeanne C. Reesman, and John Willingham (eds), *A Handbook of Critical Approaches to Literature* (Oxford and New York, Oxford University Press, 1998).
2. Alexander Petit (ed.), *Textual Studies and the Common Reader: Essays on Editing Novels and Novelists* (Athens, University of Georgia Press, 2000).

Integrating 'Bibliography' with 'Literary Research': A Comprehensive Approach

Maura Ives

ENGL 603, Bibliography and Literary Research, introduces Texas A & M English graduate students to a wide range of topics and issues:

- MLA documentation format
- Print and electronic reference sources in English and the humanities
- The special characteristics of humanities research
- The history of books and printing
- Enumerative, analytical, and descriptive bibliography
- Editorial theory and practice

The course's title, as well as this laundry list of contents, raises a question that we pursue throughout the semester: what is the relationship between 'bibliography' and 'literary research'? To the extent that the course covers enumerative or reference bibliography, the answer seems obvious; students understand that they need to know how to use major serial bibliographies and other secondary sources. But the relevance of other forms of bibliography is less easily understood by students who have never thought about the process by which the texts they study became books. The lack of exposure to bibliography, textual scholarship, and the history of the book among English graduate students should come as no surprise; as Jerome McGann has observed (in an essay that is required reading for my students), these fields have been marginalized within English studies for some time.[1] In McGann's view, we are facing an 'educational emergency' because the digitalization of literary and other texts requires scholars trained in 'the histories of textual transmission and . . . scholarly method and editing' – fields that have all but disappeared within most graduate programs in English.[2] Thus our attempt to reintegrate 'bibliography' and 'literary research' is doubly difficult: for my students, much of the course material, challenging in itself, also appears irrelevant and disconnected to the English graduate curriculum as currently defined. But if McGann is right, a class such as this one is desperately needed to equip our students for the 'digital future'.[3]

ENGL 603 integrates bibliography, book history, and literary studies through its emphasis upon a pair of related assignments: a research guide and an edition proposal. Teaching literary research by demonstrating databases, assigning sections of Jim Harner's *Literary Research Guide,* and sending students on a few library 'treasure hunts' is equivalent to teaching writing through grammar drills: students gain information but cannot apply it to their own work. Only actual research develops research skills. Students must practice using a variety of reference sources and materials, and they must work through the recursive process of forming a question, finding an answer that changes the question, researching the new question, and so on. Thus 603's research assignments introduce students to the joys and frustrations of a process that begins with serial bibliographies, library catalogs, and other enumerative tools, then branches off into a more focused, individualized project that requires them to identify, locate, analyze and interpret books and manuscripts.

But before students launch upon these assignments, they do some introductory reading that explains and situates the course content. To demonstrate the coherence of the semester's work and to convince skeptical students that they do need to take a 'bibliography class', I begin the semester by distributing the Association of College and Research Libraries' Literatures in English Section (LES) draft 'Research Competency Guidelines for Literatures in English'. Although the LES guidelines are geared towards undergraduates, most outcomes are also part of our semester's work. Even better, while the Guidelines include headings relevant to enumerative bibliography (things like 'Identify and use key literary research tools to locate relevant information' and 'Plan effective search strategies and modify search strategies as needed'), the very first heading, 'Understand the structure of information within the field of literary research', includes the following book-related goals:

> I.6 Understand that literary texts exist in a variety of editions, some of which are more authoritative or useful than others
> I.7 Understand the process of literary production, from authors' manuscripts through publication in a variety of printed editions and formats and including availability in bookstores, libraries, and the Internet[4]

Before we talk about the Guidelines, I ask the students to complete a brief survey based upon them. Invariably, students fare well on questions about reference bibliography, but few can answer questions such as 'what constitutes an edition of a literary work': most will list components such as an introduction or section of critical responses, with no mention of the possibility of changes or corrections in the literary text itself.

Next, we read Rebecca Watson-Boone's 'The Information Needs and Habits of Humanities Scholars' and Stephen Nissenbaum's essay 'The Month Before "The Night Before Christmas,"' in which he discusses the beginnings of a project that eventually became a monograph (*The Battle for Christmas*). Noting that books and journals are the main research materials for humanities scholars (who rely particularly upon primary sources), Boone identifies a number of common humanities research strategies and practices, such as browsing, footnote chasing and working independently. Nissenbaum's essay engagingly demonstrates the points made by Watson-Boone, by focusing upon a particular text, Clement Moore's 'An Account of a Visit from St. Nicholas'. Nissenbaum's discussion of illustrated versions of the poem, his comparison of Moore's poem with earlier, similar works, his use of a variety of textual and graphic primary sources (biographical information, city maps and ordinances, Moore's pamphlets), and his step-by-step discussion of the sometimes straightforward but more often serendipitous and recursive process of forming and developing his topic, set the stage for our course's focus. The relative lack of literary research on Moore's poem (compounded by inconsistency in how reference sources list its title), the poem's rich and complicated bibliographical and textual history, and the recent debate over its authorship, all provide for interesting discussion and provide a touchstone for later topics.[5]

We then discuss the research methods and strategies that Nissenbaum, writing in 1989, uses (asking colleagues what they know about a topic, browsing journals and books, scouring works cited lists for sources, not going immediately to the library). Students then consider what Nissenbaum might do differently now after the explosion of print and electronic resources. Like Nissenbaum, most tenured faculty learned to do research before desktop access to MLAIB, WorldCat, and full-text electronic archives of primary and secondary sources. I recount how a senior faculty member told me, when asked how she found ideas for research, 'I read around' – a classic, old-school humanities researcher's response. As Stephen Wiberley argues, humanists retain these methods because they give good results.[6] But every research project demands its own strategies, and students must learn what works for a particular research goal and what doesn't. Our discussions increase students' awareness of their own research skills while introducing them to new ones, serving also as a safety valve for the anxiety many feel in the face of the vast and potentially treacherous ocean of scholarly resources now available to them.

Thus introduced to a variety of research tools and strategies, students begin the semester's two major assignments, which are interrelated and cumulative. The first – a research guide for a British or American author – asks students to survey and analyze primary and secondary materials for an author of their choice. To help the students avoid foreseeable pitfalls, I limit their choices in several ways: they must choose a writer who published their work in English; to ensure access (or at least the possibility of access) to archival materials, that author should probably be one who lived in the United States or Britain (though other possibilities, such as Canada and South Africa, are not entirely off limits); and to ensure that the student will have a full range of secondary sources to consult, contemporary authors are ruled out, as are newly rediscovered writers for whom little published scholarship is available.

To complete the assignment, students must first master the basics of literary research conducted through secondary sources: print and electronic bibliographies and indexes to scholarship (such as MLAIB and ABELL), biographical reference works (*DNB*, national biographies, etc.), relevant library, union and consortia catalogs (WorldCat, RLIN, RLG), and any available materials specific to their author.

Over several weeks, students complete drafts (which I review) of various segments of the guide: sections for reference guides and bibliographies, biographies, primary sources, archival holdings, and critical works, all build upon each other and follow in sequence. Students must also meet at least once with our humanities subject specialist librarian. This required meeting helps hone the students' reference skills, but (I hope) it prevents them from internalizing one of the best-documented traits of humanities researchers: avoiding reference librarians.[7] As the project grows, students struggle with problems familiar to accomplished researchers, but new to them, such as the lack – or overabundance – of resources for particular authors, and common annoyances ranging from bibliographical ghosts, missing library books, and interlibrary loan materials that arrive too late, to the shortcomings of standard reference sources (and the degree to which those shortcomings are ameliorated, or not, through electronic access).

Students quickly seize upon the essential scholarship for the author they have chosen, and just as quickly learn not to take the quality, comprehensiveness, or reliability of author bibliographies, biographies, and other secondary materials for granted. A few students find bugs in electronic sources, which provides much food for thought; others find out, either on their own or through my comments, that one really must look in more than one place to find everything.

But the goal of the assignment is not simply to engage students with the reference materials and strategies that they learn about in class; rather, after having used those tools to discover what their author wrote, and how scholars have responded to that writing, their task is to make sense of it all. How much of the author's canon is currently in print – and why? Which texts are most frequently read and studied, which are neglected? What historical and current trends appear in scholarly reception? What are the prevailing critical or theoretical approaches? What might account for a rise or fall in scholarly attention? The patterns that emerge in the mass of data invite larger discussions. As new theoretical approaches and fields of study emerge or decline, so do new articles and books about particular authors or works. Students working with women writers might pinpoint the moment when feminist criticism brought renewed attention to a writer who had disappeared from the scholarly landscape. Suddenly the seemingly mindless task of combing databases and flipping pages for every scrap of information about an author's life and works becomes a valuable window through which students see how the field of literary studies has grown and changed over time.

After completing the research guide, the students go one step further by preparing a proposal for a scholarly edition of one of the author's works. The resources and insights gained from the first assignment are essential for the second, but the editorial proposal also builds upon a new set of readings in printing history, analytical and descriptive bibliography, and editorial theory. Readings from William Proctor Williams and Craig Abbott's *An Introduction to Bibliographical and Textual Studies*, D. C. Greetham's *Textual Scholarship* and Philip Gaskell's *A New Introduction to Bibliography* are supplemented by a visit to a working replica of a hand press housed in our special collections library. Films such as *The Making of a Renaissance Book* and *The Anatomy of a Book* also help students visualize book production in the hand press era. Students study machine printing by examining nineteenth-century books to find evidence of the date and method of printing, and they explore descriptive bibliography by transcribing title pages and through an in-class workshop in which they compare a set of published bibliographical descriptions to copies of the books they describe.

To this point, students have gained a working knowledge of the processes of the hand and machine press periods and seen how bibliographers investigate and record the particular processes that resulted in published books. As our attention turns to how books represent and change texts, we read in editorial theory and practice. Peter Shillingsburg's invaluable *Scholarly Editing in the Computer Age* introduces key issues in contemporary scholarly editing, while essays by G. T. Tanselle and Jerome McGann provide essential concepts and vocabulary.

Along with reading Williams and Abbott's chapters on textual transmission, students participate in a collation workshop that vividly demonstrates how, and why, printed texts vary from manuscripts and from each other. Students examine a portion of text as it occurs in manuscript and printed versions, then collate various pairs, seeing firsthand the changes that occur between manuscript and print. This often leads to spirited debate about the manuscript itself (how does one decide if a particular blob is a comma or a period?). The class then works through case studies of actual print and electronic editions, such as the Nebraska Cather edition, and the Rossetti and Blake electronic archives, all major, noteworthy and well-documented projects.

In the edition proposal assignment, students identify a text to be edited, provide a rationale for selecting that text, discuss the history of the text's composition and publication, and propose an editorial project that takes our readings in editorial theory as well as the particular characteristics of the text into account. Students provide a sample of the proposed edition, including a portion of the text and proposed apparatus. Students may use any methodological or theoretical perspective, provided that they ground their project both in contemporary editorial scholarship and in careful study of the text's transmission history. While a few students propose an eclectic text, most choose some form of documentary edition. I encourage students to choose a frequently published poem or short story, especially work published in periodicals, often treasure-troves of textual variants and of rich and interesting juxtapositions of text and image. Students must examine physical documents closely. When manuscript sources exist but travel to an archive is impossible, students must try to obtain copies; students must examine firsthand as many books and periodicals as possible. The project emphasizes books published during the author's lifetime, so students wrestle with questions of agency (did the author make revisions? who approved the illustrations?).

Some students make dramatic discoveries, significant variations that invigorate editorial work. Others find few textual changes, but notice compelling aspects of the material text that become the focus of their project. Because students approach this project after reading in printing history and descriptive bibliography, they are especially receptive to the concepts of bibliographical and conceptual codes (as discussed in McGann and Bornstein). Their knowledge of book construction makes them keen observers of the interactions between the text and its material context. Perhaps because of their sensitivity to the visual and material as well as the verbal communicative features of texts, many students imagine electronic projects that would incorporate illustrations, page images, and other representations of the physical book. Since we have no time for training in digital media, students are not required to create electronic projects, but they do explain why, and how, a particular project would be most appropriately pursued in that format. Here too, students wrestle with practical problems: limited access to archival material and copyright restrictions offer healthy reminders that editing texts is conditioned not only by textual theories but also by material, legal, and economic aspects.

By the end of the semester, the class's limited understanding of literary 'bibliography' as 'a list of books' has deepened into a more sophisticated understanding of bibliographical scholarship, the technology of printing, the theory and practice of scholarly editing, and the significance of the text as artifact. They gain respect for books as material objects, and for the range and value of the scholarly contributions of librarians, bibliographers, editors, and book historians. They are informed users of a wide variety of scholarly tools, from ancient codexes to digital archives. In short, they now understand why literary scholars might need to know something about books.

Notes

1. Jerome McGann, 'A Note on the Current State of Humanities Scholarship', *Critical Inquiry*, 30 (Winter 2004), pp. 409-10.
2. Ibid, p. 410.
3. Jerome McGann, 'Literary Scholarship in the Digital Future', *Chronicle of Higher Education*, 49:16 (13 December 2002): B7.
4. ACRL Literatures in English Section Ad hoc Committee on Literary Research Competencies, (Anne Jordan Baker, Jeanne Pavy, and Judy Reynolds), 'Research Competency Guidelines for Literatures in English Draft', http://www.ala.org/ala/acrl/acrlstandards/researchcompentenciesLES.htm (accessed 7 May 2006).
5. For example, collation of various nineteenth-century versions of the poem introduces nineteenth-century house style and compositional practices, and the publishing history of the poem, in which many versions, often illustrated, were printed without the author's involvement becomes newly relevant when students read editorial theory at the end of the semester.
6. Stephen Wiberley's work is helpful in explaining and at times defending humanists' choice of some strategies over others (culling citations from footnotes as opposed to using bibliographies); see also Rebecca Green's 'Locating Sources in Humanities Scholarship: The Efficacy of Following Bibliographic References', *Library Quarterly* 70:2 (2000): 201-33.
7. See Wiberley, 'Habits of Humanists: Scholarly Behavior and New Information Technologies', *Library Hi Tech*, 9:1 (1991): p. 18.

The Hidden Lives of Books

D. W. Krummel

Readers search for the writings they may want to see, librarians for titles they may want to acquire and catalogue, dealers for the books they handle. Usually this is routine work. For difficult cases, special strategies are often needed, and rewards often ensue. Those who look for obscure titles in out-of-the way sources pick up a range of odd stories about books and their historical contexts, along with impressions of the nature of our bibliographical record. The strategies of searching (finding citations for what you want) and verification (making sure what you find is what you really need) are usually learned by experience But can they be taught?

I have attempted to teach them in two settings: in library school (University of Illinois, Urbana) over a semester, to students mostly with humanities backgrounds; and at Rare Book School (Columbia University, now University of Virginia), over a very busy full-time week, mostly to librarians. My model was a course with R. C. Stewart (then head of acquisitions at the University of Michigan library); my interest was sustained by discoveries in Richard Altick's *The Art of Literary Research*, in the Library of Congress's long-abandoned 'Weekly List of Unlocated Research Books', and in my library work.

Teaching Strategies

A whole course devoted to searching and verification would be impossible without a strong library collection like that at Illinois. While the wonderful reading room in the Butler Library at Columbia was a particular joy to watch the class use, the smaller setting in Charlottesville proved almost as effective. Joel Silver's enviable setting in the Lilly Library at Indiana encourages a close study of the major bibliographies themselves. Book history courses are bound to benefit from searching experience, whether informally, as will happen naturally, or formally, as I attempted.

Preparing the mind to be fortunate entails immersion in scholarship and its bibliographies. Assignments must be instructive but not patronizing. Planting needles in haystacks is the wrong strategy; treasure hunts are more like it – although some students will skip from step one to step seven, bypassing the five interim steps carefully devised for some 'mini-eurekas'. Knowledgeable reference librarians are always helpful. Assume a willingness to try foreign-language titles, even for searchers not fluent in them. Organizing and teaching a course built around such learning experiences is not easy, but it is fun to teach and challenging to good students.

We began with general sources (universal lists, histories and bibliographies of bibliography, library catalogues, indexes to anonyma and pseudonyma, subject lists, foreign language guides, etc.). It continued with incunabula and then proceeded linguistically: British, Romance language (French, Italian, Spanish and Portuguese), Germanic language (Germany, Scandinavia, Holland), other languages (here limited by alphabet: and would that more Third World citations could be included!), ending up with the United States. Alternatively, one could switch the incunabula and United States units, so as to start with the easiest and end with the hardest.

Each unit began with a lecture on the sources (about 500 for the course, and one task is to make sure that these are available). Students were assigned titles to search (see examples at the end of this essay), and two hours in the next class were devoted to discussing results. During the searching, it helped to be with the students as they figured out the sources, guiding and cajoling them into their mini-eurekas, also encouraging them talk to each other: they are often better teachers than you. Nor should one hope to assign grades any way but subjectively. (One should not hope to assign grades any way but subjectively.)

Principles of Effective Searches

Most searching manuals serve library in-house training; Bill Katz is among the few to suggest what skills are involved. His principles are summarized thus:

1. Instinct for sources: when you know the answer is in a source, it is.
2. Distrust: don't depend on prior research for accuracy or completeness (qualified, of course: sometimes I trust, and sometimes I don't).
3. Total context: remember the indexes.
4. Record the search: keep a list of where you have looked.
5. Deliberate speed: take your time.
6. Diversity of access: try various entry points.[1]

These principles are especially important today, with so many rich options. My course came into focus around 1980, when books were still the main sources. Online sources, with multiple access points, have forever changed the bibliographical search process mostly but not entirely for the better. Our vast databases of union catalogues, like Worldcat and RLIN, are wonderfully handy and provide most of the citations in smaller sources, along with the latest facts. (Life will be even happier when online catalogues can give us a screen that says, '*Did you mean ...*') Random order, furthermore, denies its citations any structure of collocation, while fixed citation practices often exclude details found in specialized sources. The final example below illustrates the problem.

The enemy of focus is always breadth, the enemy of breadth is focus, and searching calls on both. Rarely can one single source tell the whole story, and small, delimited lists often juxtapose the entries so as to allow one to see what comes before and after: one gets a sense of the neighborhood. They also allow searchers to separate 'failures' from 'negative successes'. (The former require one to say, 'I can't find it, but it may be there somewhere'; the latter enable one to say, 'I can't find it, and I now know it's not there.')

To Katz's principles let me thus add two more:

7. At the outset one never knows whether a search will be simple or complicated; or how much one will be tempted to make a simple search complicated or a complicated one simple. Therefore, among the important sensitivities of a good searcher is the instinct for knowing how likely a search is to being definitively complete – or definitive but unsatisfying, i.e., finding everything but a final answer.

8. Searching yields unexpected (often) and interesting (almost always) results. It is important to remember what one started out looking for in the first place; but what else one learns may prove to be no less relevant – especially to book historians.

Out of the bibliographical woodwork – from citations both formal and casual, in vast and famous lists as well as in countless brief and forgotten ones – the hidden lives of books emerge. How does one encourage the probing of the bibliographical infrastructure of our civilization? *Habent sua fata libelli:* books have their own fates. Terence's aphorism applies to books both specifically and collectively. Large theories, meant to work from the top down, are exciting to play with, but small facts – and one needs to know how and where to find them – also work from the bottom up to suggest how books both reflect and influence their history.

Sample Searching Assignments

The following anthology suggests some tricks and techniques. [2]

1. William Rudolph Smith, *The History of Wisconsin: in Three Parts,* 3 vols., Madison, Beriah Brown, 1854

Many citations do not explain that volume 2 was never published at all: the State Legislature chose not to fund it. A few citations mention Sabin[3], who summarizes the story, along with the location of the manuscript (the Wisconsin Historical Society).

2. Anonymous, *Eremita, Of the Visible Sacrifice of the Church of God,* Brussels, 1637

This recusant tract was attributed to Sir Edward Dering (vol. 6 of Halkett & Laing[4]), later to St. Simon Stock (vol. 9), and now to Thomas Doughty (pseud. John Hunt). This book's reception history is inevitably reflected in the scholarship behind the changing attributions.

3. Margaret Blount, *The Wronged Wife, or The Soul of Hate,* New York, 1870

One learns to recognize genres by their titles: this is a dime novel by an unknown hack. Publishers, however, know the value of name recognition. The respected source here is Johannsen[5], who attributes it not to Blount (who is elusive) but to Septimus R. Urban (about whom a bit is known, but not much). Other sources put it under Mrs Mary O'Francis (or Mary O. Francis), Malcolm J. Merry (or Rymer, or Errym), or Mrs Mary Fleming. (Might not his reading of dime novels have inspired Michel Foucault to ask, 'What is an author?') The author is less important here than the intended readers, although library cataloguers and scholars often feel very guilty when they fail to make an author attribution.

4. *Pauline, the Prima Donna, or Memoirs of an Opera Singer,* Boston, 1868

Task: Which is the best edition of this work?

We learn (in libraries often from mischievous adolescents) what to do when seemingly innocent inquiries turn out otherwise. Here we enter the world of porno-bibliography, of Pisanus Fraxi, Guillaume Apollinaire, and Rose's *Register.*[6] This book is the purported memoirs of the famous Wilhelmine Schroeder-Devrient (1804-1860). Her life was not without juicy scandals, but the repertoire described here may be a bit much. This English translation was probably actually printed in Altona outside Hamburg. (Like seditious writing, pornography often bears fictitious imprints; and determining the 'best' of the many editions probably depends mostly on the illustrations, and on one's predilections for leather or chains.) It can be argued that this elusive literature is one more appropriately cited by word of mouth rather than in written citations. Many distinguished libraries today have an *enfer,* but its contents are not in the public catalogue, and many administrators (of course) do not even know that they even exist.

5. *The Whole Prophesie of Scotland, England, & Somepart of France, and Denmark,* 1603

Sir Anthony Panizzi's ancient 'ninety-one rules' for cataloguing at the British Museum are a landmark in library history[7], but their demise is not widely lamented, since they often asked modern readers to a play guessing game with the original cataloguer. The game is called 'I'm thinking of a word, what is it?' In this case, the entry for many years (a real groaner) was awarded to the unnamed author, who was (isn't it obvious?) – Merlin.

6. *The Queenes Maiesties Entertainment at Woodstocke*, 1575

No, the Rolling Stones were not there, but the events did take place that year, although the unique surviving fragment is from 1585. But where do you find it? Often it appears under the title; *The Hermit's Tale* first appears here, so George Gascoigne sometimes gets the honors. The British Museum cataloguers were inspired by the Panizzi rules to park it under 'Elizabeth, Queen.' Greg has a wonderfully detailed citation, and A. W. Pollard introduces a modern reprint.[8]

7. An indulgence issued by Alexander VI, dated 26 February 1498, printed by Pynson

Task: Begin with *GW* and Goff[9].

The world of incunabula is not for small children. The languages are late medieval Latin or vernaculars not yet standardized; in the absence of title pages, cataloguing works from the colophon; and the scholarship on the books is often as vast and exciting as it is opaque. IISTC-2[10] helps immensely, but those who work with the books will always need as full an array of bibliographies as possible. Neither *GW* nor Goff pays much heed to cataloguing rules, and perhaps wisely, since the rules call for entries like (as for AACR-2[11]) 'Catholic Church, Pope, 1493-1503 (Alexander VI).' A few sources cite the work under Robert Castellan. Goff uses A; *GW* which has it in a small pre-war supplement under (so help me God) *Einblattdrucke*, i.e., broadsheets; but neither tells the complete story. It helps to know that Pynson worked in London, and to know how 'Proctor order' works. Duff[12] (for practical purposes, the English volume in Proctor) cites three variant printings, under 'Indulgences'. The implications on printing history and religious history are probably worthy of further study.

8. Maj. Gen. Thomas Davies, *Con. in Zoology and Ornithology*, 1798

Task: Start with Allibone.[13]

Allibone may be based on Watt[14], but it is vast and useful (for instance, for pamphlets and articles) and literature students can benefit from its quotations of early critical reviews. This citation itself is a lazy cop-out, but devious strategies can lead to the *Transactions* of the Linnaean Society, and to the bemusing prospects of ending up either with a jumping mouse from Canada, or a flycatcher from New South Wales.

9. G. Boccaccio. *Historia molto dilettevole, novamente ritrovata,* Venice, I. A. & fratelli di Sabbio, for N. Garanta, 1526

Task: Find at least five copies in U. S. libraries.

This is pseudo-Boccaccio, listed after the authentic sources. Mansell[15] reports copies at Harvard, Yale, Princeton, and Stanford; the North-American Italian short-title catalog has Folger and Kansas. WorldCat fares not as well. Instances like this lead one to ask: how much in American libraries lies buried in local OPACs, or entirely uncatalogued, for instance in un-analyzed 'bound-with' volumes?

10. Fr. de Cepeda, *Artes de las lenguas Chiapa, Zogue, Celdales, y Cinacanteca*, Mexico, 1560

Many linguists would love to see this treatise of early dialects, but it (also titles under some variant forms) has never been located. Medina (and Garcia Icazbalceta) can trace the title no further back than Pinelli.[16] The tale of Peter of Ghent ('the Franciscan grasshopper') probably deserves a novel.

11. *Ein Sendbrieff so eyner von Venedig herauss geschickt hat, darynn begriffen wie es zu Rom ergangen ist*, Erfurt, Melchior Sachse, 1527

Panizzi again shows his evil side: the copy I know of this published 'circular letter' (a report on the sack of Rome), was long available only to those who thought to look under 'Rome (the City).'

12. Johann Heinrich von Thünen, *Der isolierte Staat*

Task: Construct the publishing history of this major work in economic theory.

This landmark text in economics (it proposed that the evils of society come from separating the worker from the product) began as a pamphlet in 1826. It was expanded, a second part was added, then a second 'volume', all later revised and supplemented. It is hard to construct the genealogy: no single general source, not even the GW^{17}, has everything.

13. Isaiah ben Abraham Horowitz, *Libro yntitulado enseña a pecadores*, Amsterdam, 5426

One must convert the calendar, and think 1666. The Sephardic diaspora produced this Ladino text, which is in the British Library catalogues.

14. *Die Ghetyden van onser liever vrouwen*, Delft, 1484

This books of hours should officially be cited under 'Catholic Church. Liturgy and Ritual. Hours. Dutch.' Scholars often find this painful pedantry. Goff, for instance, settles for 'Horae'.

15. Collection d'Anciens Evangiles, ou Monumens du premier siécle du Christianisme, extraits de Fabricius, Grabius et autres Savans, Par l'Abbé B*** [Bigex], A Londres, 1769

Numerous sources tell us that the abbot in question was in fact Voltaire. London is almost certainly a fictitious imprint.

16. Theodorus Gaza, *De aniumalibus*, 1493

Modern thought may be based on Plato and Aristotle, but when do commentators (or commentators on commentators, etc.) add enough to deserve a main entry? Even now among geographers early atlases are often called 'Ptolomies'. Historical precedent rules, rightly or wrongly. I do not know who deprived poor Theodore of a main entry, or why, but this book is almost always entered under Aristotle. How does one find this out? With luck, one stumbles across a cross-reference.

17. Iacobo Fabro Stapulense, *Ioan. Damasceni quae orthodoxae fidei, lib. IIII*, Basel, 1548, 95 pp.

This situation is complicated in this work of John of Damascus, since the Renaissance commentator is also known as Jacques Lefebre d'Etaples. (Happily he is never Jack Smith, but Lefevre may be under F, and the v may be b, or bv.) Cross references are wonderful, but they should not be so plentiful as to serve the needs of dummies. So when are we learned enough to be out of danger?

18. José Maria da Silva Albuquerque, *O operatro e a associão*, 1879

Knowledge of onomastics is invaluable. For this citation, it helps to forget New Mexico and remember that in Spanish, the partronym comes before the metronym, but in Portuguese it is the other way around. (The implications led many Portuguese bibliographers – Silva [18] is a case in point – to list his many thousands of entries by the author's first name: watch out for João!)

19. M. Everaert, *Tleven ende vrome daden vande Doorluchtigen Griecsche end Romeynsche mannen ... door Aemilius Probus*, Leyden, 1601

For the foreign-language-disadvantaged, sounding out words can lead to mini-eurekas. In this case, 'illustrious Greek and Roman men' says Plutarch. The British Library ('the second best collection of everything') naturally has a copy.

20. Te episetole i te mau hebera ra, e ta iacobo: te mau episetole a ioane, e te apocalpo hoi, iritihia ei parau tahiti, Tahaa, 1826

Sounding out the words here leads to another mini-eureka: this is mostly a New Testament, printed by South Seas missionaries. Du Rietz [19] cites it and locates copies. Not surprisingly, Darlow and Moule lists a copy. [20]

21. Michel-Ange. *Poesies*, Paris, 1826

It's easy to miss the point of this search – the author is not the Archangel St. Michael but the sculptor Michelangelo, filed under B for Buonarotti – when the answer is so deceptively easy. One of my best students called it a day after finding it under M in an online Bibliothèque Nationale catalogue, with no cross-reference. No eureka here: how does one encourage critical evaluation with sources as authoritative and easy as this?

Notes

1. *Introduction to Reference Work,* 4th edn. 2 vols. (New York, McGraw-Hill, 1982), vol. 2, p. 85.
2. In the text, I refer to sources minimally, as librarians or book dealers often do, and the notes that follow offer abbreviated citations. For full citations see Robert Balay, *Guide to Reference Books* 11th edn. (Chicago: American Library Association, 1996), or vol. 3 of *Walford's Guide to Reference Material* (London: Library Association, 1993).
3. Joseph Sabin, *Bibliotheca Americana: A Dictionary of Books Relating to America, from its Discovery to the Present Time* (1868-1936).
4. Samuel Halkett and John Laing, *Dictionary of Anonymous and Pseudonymous English Literature* (1926-[62]).
5. Albert Johannsen, *House of Beadle and Adams and its Dime and Nickel Novels* (c.1950).
6. Pisanus Fraxi, *Encyclopedia of Erotic Literature* (1969); Guillaume Apollinaire, author of the erotic *Les Onze Mille Verges*, worked to publish banned books during World War I; Alfred Rose's *Register of Erotic Books* (1965).
7. Anthony Panizzi, 'Rules for the compilation of the catalogue' Catalogue of printed books in the British Museum, Vol. 1. London, 1841. pp. [v]-ix.
8. W. W. Greg, *Bibliography of the English Printed Drama* (1939–59); A. W. Pollard, 'Introduction', *Queen's Majesty's Entertainment at Woodstock* (Oxford, H. Daniel and H. Hart, 1910).
9. *Gesamtkatalog der Wiegendrucke* (1972–); Frederick R. Goff. (ed.), *Incunabula in American Libraries* (1972).
10. *Illustrated Incunabula Short Title Catalogue,* 2nd edn.
11. *Anglo-American Cataloging Rules,* 2nd edn. (1980).
12. See E. Gordon Duff, *Early Printed Books* (1893) and Robert Proctor, *An Index to the Early Printed Books in the British Museum: from the Invention of Printing to the year 1500* (1960).
13. S. Austin Allibone, *A Critical Dictionary of English Literature, and British and American Authors, Living and Deceased, from the Earliest Accounts to the Middle of the Nineteenth Century* (1859-1871) .
14. Robert Watt, *Biblioteca Britannica* (1824).
15. *National Union Catalog,* pre-1956 imprints.
16. José Toribio Medina, *Biblioteca-Hispanoamerica*, reprinted 1968 Garcia Icazbalceta; *Biographia Mexicana del Siglo XVI* (1954) .
17. See note 7.
18. Innocencio Francisco da Silva, *Diccionario Bibliographico Portuquez* (1858-1923).
19. Rolf Du Rietz, *Bibliotheca Polynesia* (1969).
20. T. H. Darlow and H. F. Moule, *Historical Catalogue of Printed Editions of Holy Scripture in the library of the British and Foreign Bible Society* (1968).

Learning from Binders: Investigating the Bookbinding Trade in Colonial Philadelphia

Thomas E. Kinsella and Willman Spawn

I assign the following question in my undergraduate *Literary Research* course:

> In the cluttered and dusty rare book stacks at the university library, you find a large folio printed in Paris, 1557, bound in sheepskin with a gilt central ornament. On closer inspection you find a name 'Gilbert Erle of Cassillis' embossed in a circle around the ornament. The word 'Cassillis' has been written on the title page; this is evidently provenance, and the hand looks contemporary with the imprint. Your local book historian believes that the binding is about the same age as the volume (certainly no earlier, and no more than twenty years older); it is typical of sixteenth-century French binding styles. For whom was this book bound? Why do you suggest this ownership?

This question is difficult for most students. They don't know what 'folio' or 'provenance' means; they have never regarded 'gilt central ornaments' as belonging on books. When they consider the details, however, students identify three lines of research: Parisian printing, French bookbinding, and the name, 'Gilbert Erle'. They find, to their surprise, a large body of research on Parisian printing. The answer, alas, is not found through that avenue. They also discover extensive scholarship on Renaissance bookbinding. Unfortunately, the volume in question is not ornate enough or famous enough to have been described in print. Students work through biographical dictionaries, hoping to find a Frenchman (or anyone!) named Gilbert Erle. They discover that Erle is an obsolete spelling for earl, and that Cassillis is the name of an earldom. Cassillis in the *Dictionary of National Biography* directs readers to Kennedy, and the Third and Fourth Earls of Cassillis, both named Gilbert Kennedy, are the ultimate candidates.[1]

Students have not been frustrated by the equivocal nature of the final answer – without additional information, no choice can be made between father and son. Instead they are excited by the investigative nature of the research ('It's like CSI!') and astounded by the amount of scholarship on issues they never knew existed. What they are experiencing, often for the first time, is the seductive power of book history.

I offer below three case studies – projects distilled from research within the Philadelphia library community and in libraries across America. Many towns and cities have similar resources to support the study of local book history, and many research universities have archival materials that enable similar studies outside of their geographic area. Trade records and historical resources also frequently survive. Most importantly, the primary sources for studying the book trade also survive: the books themselves.

Completing these cases is probably beyond the reach of semester-long study; developing fundamental research skills is not. Students can identify reference sources, target institutions and resources, develop questions, and carry forward research. Remember: research does not have to be exhaustive to be useful to students. At the undergraduate level, such activity teaches the centerpiece skills of liberal arts education – research, analysis, and synthesis. At the graduate level it contributes to a deeper understanding of the relationship between media, culture, and the dissemination of knowledge. At either level, worthwhile goals to pursue.

Research Tools

1. Standard works of American bibliography.

Charles Evans' *American Bibliography* and Roger Bristol's *Supplement to Evans* remain solid if imperfect bibliographies for the colonial period. Clifford Shipton and James Mooney's *Short-Title Evans* corrects Evans while incorporating additional titles. Bristol's *Index to Evans* usefully identifies imprints by printer, publisher, or bookseller and by geographical location.[2]

2. Works on printing and publishing

Isaiah Thomas's *History of Printing in America* (1810) is still useful. William McCulloch's *Additions to Thomas's History of Printing* amplifies Thomas's work for Philadelphia.[3] Douglas C. McMurtrie's *A History of Printing in the United States* (1936) and Lawrence C. Wroth's *The Colonial Printer* (1938) are helpful, but significant scholarship has been completed since their publication, and students should be familiar with contemporary work, well represented by Hugh Amory and David D. Hall's *A History of the Book in America: The Colonial Book in the Atlantic World* (2000).[4]

3. Colonial bookbinding trade

Hannah D. French's *Bookbinding in Early America: Seven Essays on Masters and Methods* (1986) is a good place to start. Two catalogues also offer overviews: *Early American Bookbindings from the Collection of Michael Papantonio* (1972) and *Bookbinding in America, 1680–1910, from the Collection of Frederick E.*

Maser (1983). For colonial Philadelphia, Willman and Carol Spawn explain tool-based identification of bindings,[5] and C. William Miller's bibliography, *Benjamin Franklin's Philadelphia Printing* (1974), identifies Franklin's binders, describes examples of their work, and provides an illustrated tool catalogue. Glenn and Maude Brown's *A Directory of the Book-Arts and Book Trade in Philadelphia to 1820* provides names and addresses of binders, booksellers, printers and other tradesmen.

4. Newspaper indexes and databases.

To research advertisements, consult Benjamin Franklin's *Pennsylvania Gazette* (available online) and long runs of other Philadelphia newspapers (on microfilm) as well as Clarence S. Brigham's *History and Bibliography of American Newspapers, 1690-1820*. To track down immigrant workmen, consult genealogical references such as the *Passenger and Immigration Lists Index*, with multiple supplements, published by Gale, and Ralph Strassburger and William Hinke's *Pennsylvania German Pioneers*. Journals in the field also offer helpful information, especially *Papers of the Bibliographical Society of America*, *Studies in Bibliography*, and the *Pennsylvania Magazine of History and Biography*.

5. Archival Materials.

To examine colonial bookbindings (especially from Philadelphia), visit archives such as the following: the Library Company of Philadelphia, the Pennsylvania Historical Society, the American Philosophical Society, the University of Pennsylvania, Bryn Mawr, Swarthmore and Haverford Colleges, and The Free Library of Philadelphia.

Surviving archival material when used skillfully helps identify bookbinders and understand their trade. The minutes of the Library Company record binding orders that can be traced to extant volumes. The cashbook of Isaac Norris describes bindings and identifies binders. The account books of Benjamin Franklin, William Bradford the second, Hall and Sellers, and Mathew Carey name binders and give details about the trade. Despite loss over time, much evidence remains: the difficulty is in drawing connections between this evidence.

Case Study 1: Franklin's binder

Benjamin Franklin's *Autobiography* mentions Stephen Potts, 'a young country man of full age, bred to the same, of uncommon natural parts, and great wit and humor, but a little idle.'[6] According to Franklin, Potts was articled to Samuel Keimer, a printer working in Philadelphia during the 1720s. When Franklin agreed to manage Keimer's printing shop, he apparently trained

Potts in bookbinding. Who was Stephen Potts and what can you learn of his career in the Philadelphia book trade?

Since Franklin left voluminous papers, the first path of inquiry starts there. But the Yale edition of Franklin's papers provides surprisingly little information. In 1733 Franklin gave power of attorney to his wife, Deborah, and Potts witnessed the document. In 1738 Franklin asked the tailor Mr. Corin 'Please to let the Bearer Stephen Potts have a pair of Leather Breeches', charged to Franklin's account. A biographical note reveals more:

> Stephen Potts (d. 1758) was a member of the Junto, a bookbinder, bookseller, and in his last years a tavern keeper. BF first knew him as a fellow employee at Keimer's and described him in his autobiography . . . BF's ledgers show that the two men had extensive business relations from 1733 to 1757.[7]

This suggests another line of inquiry: Franklin's account books. George Simpson Eddy has published portions of Franklin's accounts, with notes.[8] Consulting them, students find that Potts and Franklin shared accounts for nearly thirty years. Throughout the 1730s Potts was indebted to Franklin for small sums of cash, pasteboard, and leather. The accounts also show that Potts paid Franklin for room and board during this early period; the business relationship appears to have been close. Unfortunately, ledgers providing specific details of Potts' binding are missing. During the 1740s and 1750s, transactions between the two men decrease significantly, but do not cease entirely until 1757.

Eddy points students in another direction. In 1732 Franklin began to advertise bookbinding in the colophon of his newspaper the *Pennsylvania Gazette*. Binding was to be 'done reasonably in the best Manner', presumably by Potts. Review of the *Gazette* (in a searchable database) turns up four advertisements for Potts, three dating from 1743 and one from 1749 (not including repeats). The advertisements reveal a bookbinder/bookseller with a reasonably large inventory of book titles that changes from one advertisement to the next. Franklin's *Pennsylvania Gazette* was not the only newspaper in Philadelphia at this time. An additional advertisement from October 1742 appears in the *American Weekly Mercury* (*AWM*). Four more advertisements, December 1742 to September 1743, appear in the *Pennsylvania Journal* (*PJ*). They reveal an active tradesman working independently from Franklin.

In 1742 Potts lists his address as 'Over against the Pewter-Platter Alley, in Front street'. By 1743 at the same address his establishment has acquired a name: 'at the Sign of the Bible and Crown'. The imposing shop name and small number of advertisements may suggest that Potts was well known and needed little advertising.[9] Also, it is intriguing that Potts advertises in the *AWM* and *PJ*, two competitors to Franklin's *Gazette*.

Accounts reveal a close business relationship between Franklin and Potts during the 1730s, and advertising suggests a new phase in Potts' career during the 1740s. A final advertisement in the *Pennsylvania Journal*, dated 4 January 1759, reads

> Whereas at the death of Stephen Potts, late of this City Bookbinder, many books which had been left to bind, remained on hand, and as the owners never call'd for them, this is to give notice, they may yet be had at the Widows house in Church Ally [sic], and those not call'd for before this day 3 months will be exposed at public auction to pay the binding. Philadelphia, January 4, 1759.

We have yet to uncover what sort of bindings Potts executed. Students might be prodded: If any Potts bindings have survived, where are they likely to be found? Franklin again provides a starting point. If Potts was not working exclusively for Franklin during the 1740s and 1750s, perhaps he has branched out to Franklin's associates. The Library Company of Philadelphia, the first subscription library in the colonies and the brainchild of Franklin, retains records from its earliest days. An examination of its Minute Book provides the missing specific details; the record for 11 April 1743 reads

> [T]he said Secretary [Joseph Breintnall] had taken to the Library last Saturday Parkinson's Herbal new bound by Stephen Potts, also vols. 4 & 5 of Bayle by Stephen newly bound, and Bayle Vol. 1st (sent by Stephen with the others) that was formerly bound. (*Minute Book*, I:129)

These volumes, John Parkinson's *Theatrum Botanicum* and Pierre Bayle's *Historical and Critical Dictionary*, survive in their original bindings at the Library Company. Further diligent search reveals that the Library Company also owns J. Lyon's *Infallibility of Human Judgment* with the title-page inscription: 'Joseph Breintnall May 1730 who had it bound by Stephen Potts, Philadelphia. Given to the Library 19 February 1732'. These bindings, with several decorative tools in common, at last provide examples of Stephen Potts's work.

After extensive research, a picture emerges. For more than a decade, starting about 1730, Stephen Potts was associated with Benjamin Franklin's printing establishment, apparently serving as in-house binder. This arrangement dissolved by 1743, and Potts opened his own shop where 'The Said S. Potts Binds Books in the best manner' (*Journal*, December 28). In this location Potts concentrated on bookselling, but accounts of printers and bookmen testify to his continued binding activity: William Bradford paid him for work between 1742 and 1746, likewise James Logan in 1749, John Watson in 1750, and Stephen Paschall in 1752.[10] He executed both edition binding and individual orders, remaining in business until his death in 1758. His work is typically solid and undistinguished – sheepskin over binder's board and decorated conservatively with blind fillets, rolls, and stamps.

Case Study 2: The Widow Ottin

> You receive a tip from a correspondent: 'Seek George Otto in the *Journals of Henry Melchior Muhlenberg*'. Where does this information lead you?

The published *Journals* describe Otto as a bookbinder whom Muhlenberg visited several times during his last illness and buried in February 1762. After receiving 'the papers of the deceased', Muhlenberg wrote a brief sketch of Otto's life, beginning with his birth in 1716 in Würzburg.[11] On 6 July 1746, in Reutlingen, Otto married Anna Maria, daughter of Jacob Neusser. He moved to Freudenstadt with his wife and lived there several years, arriving in Pennsylvania in 1752.[12] Muhlenberg concluded with the following assessment of Otto: 'His chief fault was an inclination towards drunkenness, but God, in His compassionate love, cast him on a sickbed for seven weeks and delivered him as a brand from the fire.' Muhlenberg provides us with no evidence about Otto's binding activities nor his place of residence, although it was probably in or near Philadelphia.

After the death of Otto, Muhlenberg mentions four transactions with Widow Anna Maria Ottin (the feminine form of Otto). On 19 November 1762, Muhlenberg gave the widow 7s. 6d., 'in part payment for stitching books'. On 29 January 1763, Ottin 'brought copies of Johann Arndt's *Garden of Paradise* which she had bound'.[13] On 11 February of the same year, Ottin brought 'the last of the books which she had bound' with a bill for 18s. 9d., which Muhlenberg paid in full. Finally, on 20 July 1764, 'The poor widow of a bookbinder asked me to give her some binding to do in order that she might earn something, as she had nothing to live on'. Muhlenberg must have honored the request, for the next day he records that the 'Widow Otto brought back the bound notebooks and received her payment, 13s. for paper, 5s. for binding'. This is not much to go on: a sporadic record of binding transactions between a binder's widow and one client during the early 1760s.

Students will find their next clue in the comprehensive index to the *Pennsylvania Magazine of History and Biography*. The *Notes and Queries* section of volume 5 (1881) provides the following note:

> In the 'American Almanac for 1765', printed by 'Henry Miller, on Second Street', is the following: –
>
> *Notice.*
>
> 'The widow of George Otto deceased (late book binder) continues the business on the south side of Race St., aside of Mr. Daniel Etters, and almost opposite Mr. Magnet. She does all manner of binding, and keeps for sale all kinds of small and large books, at fair prices.'

From this, we learn that Ottin was located in Philadelphia and advertising with Henry Miller. Our next clue is Miller who, research reveals, was a printer and publisher who began the *Der Wochentliche Philadelphische Staatsbote, The*

Weekly Philadelphia State Messenger, in 1762. Might Ottin have advertised in this German-language newspaper? Since the *Staatsbote* is not indexed, one's only recourse is to read the text, available on microfilm.[14] Since reading eighteenth-century German fraktur font can be difficult, divide the work among the students.

Patient review of *Staatsbote* advertisements turns up eighteen that mention the Widow Ottin, between 1764 and 1779 (not including repeats). Her earliest place of business was indeed on Race Street, next to Daniel Etters, where she sold religious texts and schoolbooks and did bookbinding. In 1771 she advertised a new shop in Second Street opposite Mr. Schweighauser, at the sign of the Golden Ball, third house from Mr. Kidd. We see the widow independently advertising her shop wares and services. We also find yearly advertisements for the newest and most reliable calendar, available from Ottin or other booksellers and bookbinders. The picture starts to focus. The widow became an active participant in the German language book trade, along with printer Henry Miller (Heinrich Müller), and bookbinders George Reinhold and Andreas Geyer. A search of the *Philadelphia PAGenweb Archives* discovers a record of Anna Maria Ott's will, dated 14 September 1784.[15] After a trip to the Philadelphia city archives to examine the will, students arrive at a suitable ending to this project.

Case Study 3: Robert Aitken's wastebook

> A librarian from the Library Company, knowing your interest in colonial bookbinding, shows you a thick, bound manuscript dating from the last quarter of the eighteenth century; he then hands you a xerographic copy of the same. 'This is Robert Aitken's wastebook.' He informs you. 'It's a bit late in the period, but it may be of use.' Who is Robert Aitken and how can this record best be put to use?[16]

The *Dictionary of American Biography* summarizes Robert Aitken's career. Born in Scotland on 22 January 1734/5 and trained as a bookbinder and bookseller, Aitken first arrived in Philadelphia in 1769 with a stock of books; after selling them he returned to Scotland. In 1771 he and his family immigrated to Philadelphia where he opened first a book and stationer's shop and later a printing shop and bindery. He achieved fame as the printer of the 'Bible of the Revolution', the first English bible openly printed in the colonies. His business generally flourished, and throughout his life, he was a well-regarded tradesman. He died on 14 July 1802.

Examination of the wastebook – the copy allows students to work outside library hours – reveals 700 pages of closely written accounts, generally arranged in chronological order. Tracing Aitken's business transactions from 1771 through 1802, the waste-book was Aitken's log of daily business, providing a record of sales such as silver knee buckles, snuff boxes, and needle cases. More important to our study, it lists completed print jobs and binding work for hundreds of customers, some well known such as John Adams, Benjamin Franklin, Thomas Jefferson, Benjamin Rush, and John Witherspoon.

The wastebook contains an overwhelming amount of cryptic, detailed information. To make sense of it, one needs to make two indices: one, an index of customers, listing purchases, especially the titles of books described as printed or bound by Aitken, and second, an alternate index of book titles, listing customers and details of binding. Titles, however, present problems. Like most booksellers, Aitken used short-titles for many works that he printed, bound, or sold. Thus the wastebook mentions *The Fourfold State*, but Evans lists no such title. Identifying difficult entries requires considerable study of the works of the day: Thomas Boston's *Human Nature in its Fourfold State; Of Primitive Integrity, Entire Depravation, Begun Recovery, and Consummate Happiness or Misery; subsisting in The Parents of Mankind in Paradise, The Irregenerate, the Regenerate, All Mankind in the Future State* is the full title that Aitken reasonably shortened to *The Fourfold State*.

Following indexing, one begins the hit-or-miss process of identifying extant titles. Online catalogues are not yet reliable sources for the holdings of older, well-established libraries, so trips to various promising institutions prove necessary. At the Free Library of Philadelphia, customer and title indices in hand, one finds a copy of Hugh Blair's *Lectures on Rhetoric and Belles Lettres* in an elaborate gilt red binding. An inscription shows that Gerardus Clarkson gave it to his son in 1788. A brief entry in the wastebook makes the connection: 'Blair bound for Clarkson, 1788'. One can identify dozens of other bindings in this way, including two presentation copies of William Thornton's *Cadmus*, printed and bound by Aitken in 1793, and duly noted in the wastebook (copies owned by the Library Company and the American Philosophical Society).

The wastebook is an invaluable tool for identifying bindings executed in Aitken's shop. It also provides details that help explain the organization and output of the shop. From 1773 to 1776, for example, Aitken recorded payment of quarterly wages to three journeymen binders. In 1774, at least 5,000 plain bindings were executed, along with 400 gilt bindings, and unnumbered folded and stitched pamphlets, memorandum books, ledgers, journals, and some rebinding. The wastebook allows the output of Aitken's shop to be studied over a period of more than thirty years.

Notes

1. The Third Earl, captured at the rout of Solway Moss and in the service alternately of the English and Scottish crowns, died in France while part of the Scots delegation at the marriage of Queen Mary to the Dauphin in 1558. The volume was probably bound for him; however, it could have lain in sheets and been bound for his son, the Fourth Earl. The volume is part of

the Annenberg Rare Book & Manuscript Library at the University of Pennsylvania: Flavius Josephus, *Les sept liures de Flauius Iosephus de la guerre et captiuité des Iuifz, traduitz de Grec, et mis en francoys par N. de Herberay* . . . (Paris: Estienne Groulleau, 1557).

2. The full title of Bristol's *Index* reads *Index of Printers, Publishers, and Booksellers Indicated by Charles Evans in his American Bibliography* (Charlottesville, 1961). The digital edition of Early American Imprints, Series I. Evans (1639-1800), available online as a paid service, is invaluable.

3. This entertaining and important work (American Antiquarian Society, 1921) compiles letters and documents sent from McCulloch to Thomas between 1812 and 1815. It is in need of republication with annotation.

4. McMurtrie's study, subtitled *The Middle & South Atlantic States*, appeared in 1936 as volume II of a projected national study. The only volume completed before McMurtrie's death, the text is available in a Burt Franklin reprint (1969).

5. Articles by the Spawns relating to Philadelphia bookbinding include 'The Aitken Shop; Identification of an Eighteenth-century Bindery and its Tools', *Papers of the Bibliographical Society of America*, 57 (1963), pp. 422-37; 'Jane Aitken', *Notable American Women 1607-1950* (Cambridge MA, The Belknap Press, 1971); 'Identifying Eighteenth Century American Bookbinders', *Guild of Book Workers Journal*, 17 (1978), pp. 25-37; 'Notes on American Bookbindings: Extra-Gilt Bindings of Robert Aitken, 1787-88', *Proceedings of the American Antiquarian Society*, 93 (1983), pp. 415-17; and 'Francis Skinner, Bookbinder of Newport: an 18th-Century Craftsman Identified by his Tools', *Winterthur Portfolio* 2 (1965), pp. 47-61. This last addresses the use of similar binding tools in Newport and Philadelphia.

6. Leonard W. Labaree, Ralph L. Ketcham, Helen C. Boatfield and Helene H. Fineman ed., *The Autobiography of Benjamin Franklin* (New Haven, Yale University Press, 1964), p. 108.

7. Leonard W. Labaree *et al* ed., *The Papers of Benjamin Franklin* (New Haven, Yale University Press, 1959-2004): vol. I, p. 332; vol. II, p. 209.

8. George Simpson Eddy ed., *Account Books Kept by Benjamin Franklin: Ledger 1728-1739, Journal 1730-1737* (New York, Columbia University Press, 1928); *Account Books Kept by Benjamin Franklin: Ledger "D": 1739-1747* (New York, Columbia University Press, 1929); and *A Work-Book of the Printing House of Benjamin Franklin & David Hall, 1759-1766* (New York, The New York Public Library, 1930).

9. To understand the significance of Potts's advertising, students should research advertising patterns of bookbinders at mid-century.

10. William Bradford Account Book, 1742, 1746 (PHi); James Logan Account Book, B: 201, Sept. 21, 1749 (Stenton); John Watson, 'Journal', see *PMHB*, v. 39, 7; Stephen Paschall Account Book, 1 (PHi).

11. Henry Melchior Muhlenberg, Theodore G. Tappert and John W. Doberstein trans., *The Journals of Henry Melchior Muhlenberg*, vol. 1 (Philadelphia, Evangelical Lutheran Ministerium of Pennsylvania and Adjacent States, 1942-58), p. 491.

12. Strassburger & Hinke, vol. I, p. 498, list 190-C, confirms Otto's arrival, identifying him as Johann Georg Ott.

13. The works of Johann Arndt (1555-1621) were popular during the eighteenth century. The text is *Des Gottseligen und Hocherleuchteten Lehrers Johann Arndts ... Paradies-gärtlein: voller christlichen tugend-gebäte, deme beygefüget Johann Habermanns erbauliche Morgen- und abendandachten nebst Caspar Neumanns Kern aller gebäte*. The edition is uncertain.

14. A nearly complete run of the *Staatsbote* is available on microfilm from Readex: http://www.readex.com/readex/ (accessed 7 May 2006).

15. *The Philadelphia PAGenweb Archives*, a sub-page of *The PAGenWeb Project* and the *USGenWeb Project*, provides web-based copies of census data, church registers, land records, and will and estate records, along with other documents of genealogical interest: http://www.rootsweb.com/~usgenweb/pa/philadelphia/ (accessed 7 May 2006).

16. A similar event occurred in the early 1950s when Edwin Wolf, 2nd, future Librarian of the Library Company, approached Willman Spawn and suggested that analysis of Aitken's waste-book would be productive in his ongoing study of colonial bookbinding. Much of the information described in this project is found in an article by Willman and Carol Spawn, 'The Aitken Shop: Identification of an Eighteenth-century Bindery and Its Tools'; see note 5 above. We have also made use of the Spawns' 'R. Aitken: Colonial Printer of Philadelphia,' *Graphic Arts Review*, January-February, 1961.

Papermaking, History and Practice

Timothy Barrett

I teach a fifteen-week, semester-long class on the history and technique of Asian and European papermaking, using a mixture of lectures, hands-on papermaking demonstrations, and assignments. I spend relatively little time on labour /management relations, the economics of paper production, the international paper-market, the relationships between papermakers and publishers, etc., because book specialists need a gut-level appreciation for what went into paper production. Such sensitivities allow a scholar to know, before having specific publishing information, that book A was well made of high-quality materials, while book B was hurriedly executed. This physical 'read' on a book can provide valuable insights regarding the producer's motivations, intended audience, etc.

When teaching papermaking in a book history or bibliography course, I focus on advances in the technology of papermaking during the period in question. Depending on course focus and resources, I advise combining readings[1] and discussions on the history and technique of the craft, with a trip to special collections, an actual wet hands-on papermaking session, and ideally, visits to a modern paper mill and a hand papermaking workshop. I'm continually amazed at how important seeing or participating in live papermaking is.

This essay concentrates on a 500-year period in the West: roughly 1300 through to 1800 with brief attention to the earlier invention of the craft in China, its movement east into Korea and Japan, and at about the same time, its movement westward into the Arab Mediterranean area. I also touch on the later invention of the paper machine and events leading up to the manufacture of modern permanent and durable book papers.

Historical Background

Scholars debate exactly when and where the first paper intended for writing purposes was invented, but it's safe to say 'around the time of Christ, in China'. The earliest form of papermaking employed a mould made of a wooden frame covered with stretched fabric. The mould was floated in water, fabric side down, and water soon seeped up through the fabric. A small amount of prepared pulp was poured into the water in the mould and distributed by hand. The mould was then lifted out of the water, leaving a layer of fibre on the wet fabric. After drying in the sun or around a fire, the dry paper was peeled off the mould. This technique is still practiced in Nepal and some surrounding countries.[2]

Because of its simple technology, this process is generally accepted as the first widely used papermaking method. One major problem, however, restricted daily production. Since paper had to dry on the mould, a papermaker either had to wait to make another sheet or needed many moulds to keep busy all day. Two major technical innovations improved this situation. One utilized a ribbed open wooden frame mould fitted with a removable woven bamboo or grass covering; this allowed the freshly formed wet sheet to be removed to a gradually increasing pile of damp paper.[3] Immediately, the number of moulds required for business decreased from many, to one. The other innovation involved the construction of a lined pit in the ground that could serve as a reservoir for clean water into which a large volume of prepared pulp could be mixed. Instead of having to add pulp to the mould each time a sheet was made, now, by carefully mixing the fibre in this pit vat, the papermaker could form sheets continuously for hours before having to stop and add more fibre. To remove excess water, large stones were placed on a board atop the stack of formed sheets. Later, the sheets were peeled apart and laid out on the grass or brushed on a masonry wall to dry. These two innovations were probably in place before the craft left China.

Around 600 A.D., papermaking appears to have traveled east into Japan via the Korean peninsula. Sometime before or after arrival of the craft in Japan, papermakers discovered that the addition of a viscous formation aid to the vat, combined with a distinctive sloshing sheetforming action, permitted the production of very fine quality, lightweight, long-fibred sheets. So important is this innovation that exactly when and where this distinctly 'Asian' technique developed is hotly debated by Korean, Japanese, Chinese and other paper historians. Some form of Asian-style papermaking is still used today in a number of Asian countries to produce sheets commonly, but inaccurately, referred to in the West as 'rice paper'.

Curiously, as papermaking moved east from China, it also moved westward into the Arab world, arriving in Samarkand as early as 650 A.D. By the year 800 A.D., papermaking was firmly established in the Arab Mediterranean theater. In the Mediterranean, paper competed handsomely with papyrus – the precursor writing material well established since 1000 B.C. – until about 1000 A.D., when the papyrus industry all but ceased. The Arabs dominated the papermaking craft in the Mediterranean theater until roughly 1100.

Around 1200, the craft entered Italy, and by 1350 or 1400 the Italians had introduced a series of innovations resulting in what we now consider 'European or Western-style handmade paper'. While the Arabs had been using old hempen ropes and rags as raw materials, the Italians refined the rag collection trade, increasing the quality and quantity of raw material available to papermakers. The Arabs originally beat their fibre using a large hammer-headed stamper, foot-operated by one person and fed at the business end by a second person, but the Arabs later developed the use of the water wheel to power multiple stamper heads. The Italians, however, may have been responsible for developing gangs of heads operating in groups. Large amounts of rags were dispersed in enough water in the stone mortar pits to circulate automatically without the need for constant human attention. The Italians also introduced – soon after the development of wire drawing – the wire faced, fixed surface mould which allowed the quick transfer (or 'couching') of the freshly made sheet onto a damp felt. The felts in between the sheets allowed rapid and high pressure removal of excess water, using large mechanical screw presses. The Italians developed a three-person team that worked in unison at the vat: where the Arab vat person could make perhaps 400 sheets in a day, the Italian teammates could make 1500-2000 or more. Italian papermakers began drying paper by hanging the pressed-but-still-moist sheets over ropes stretched across upper floor lofts in their mills. By opening and closing specially designed shutters, they could dry paper in a wide range of weather – a distinct improvement over the Arab method of brushing sheets against a smooth masonry wall to dry.

Arab sheets were sometimes considered too soft; probably a result of insufficient beating and the use of an overly-weak starch surface sizing applied to the finished sheets. The Italians introduced the use of gelatin surface sizes which, combined with careful rag selection and increased beating in the 'automated' stampers, resulted in paper that was much tougher and stronger. In essence, the early Italian papermakers were attempting to produce a material that performed much like parchment or vellum, the competing material of the time used in making books and preparing written documents. They succeeded; by 1400 in Europe, papermaking was a serious heavy industry, generating enough paper to help fuel the rise of the universities, the rapid spread of printing, and arguably, the Renaissance itself.[4]

Papermaking continued roughly in this fashion for four centuries. One major innovation was the invention of the Hollander beater, almost certainly in the Low Countries around 1650. By 1750, except in rare instances, it had entirely replaced the stamping mills because of its much more efficient beating capacity. Around 1800 several major innovations appeared including the paper machine, the introduction of rosin and alum internal size, and chlorine bleach. All three contributed to major increases in annual paper production and decreases in price but, unfortunately, to decreases in overall paper quality and permanence as well. Some early machine-mades (produced before 1830 in England) show surprisingly light color and good strength characteristics today owing primarily to the fact the raw material was still old rags, a source of very high-quality cellulose. But the demand for paper skyrocketed with the increasing performance of power printing presses; by the mid-nineteenth century commercially viable wood pulps appeared.

The earlier papers made from wood pulp contained large amounts of non-celluosic materials that occur naturally in the wood. In paper they contributed to the rapid loss of brightness. In addition, the common use of rosin and alum internal size resulted an acidic paper pH that contributed to the rapid loss of paper strength. The result was decades of poor paper with relatively few exceptions. Finally, in the mid-twentieth century, analyses of exceptionally long-lasting fifteen-century papers resulted in modern formulas for (again) making long-lasting paper. The key components are a purified form of cellulose, an alkaline pH, a non-acidic internal size, and addition of an alkaline reserve such as calcium carbonate.

Evaluating Paper Quality

In general, any high-quality book or writing paper (machine-made or hand-made) when held to the light shows a very even, consistent formation quality and a freedom from knots, clumps, foreign matter or other debris. Often, in sheets known to be handmade (pre-1800), one can also see that the moulds and watermarks were well maintained and that the sheets were skillfully 'couched' when transferred to the wet felts. Poor quality paper often shows irregular or rough formation quality, i.e. cloudy areas of uneven thickness, and/or unwanted debris. Holding the paper to the light, may reveal sometimes bent, broken or badly repaired mould wires, or evidence of poor workmanship in couching.

But paper quality also depends on its intended use. A wrapping paper may be rough in formation quality, but be a superior paper when toughness is the main requirement. A poorly made book paper may be ideal in a cheaply-made reader intended for less well-off children. Similar gross generalizations can be made about colour and apparent mechanical properties: high-quality historical book and writing papers remain light in colour and invite gentle, appropriate handling, while papers made quickly or of inferior materials are browned and brittle. Remember that one of the quickest ways to make paper cheaper is to make it thinner. Therefore, thicker paper, for a given application, is a more expensive item.

Estimating Paper Date and Location of Manufacture

Between 1300 and 1800 the European papermaking process remained more-or-less the same. However, mould surfaces changed at important junctures, a fact helpful in dating. For most of this period, paper was made on 'laid' moulds, where long laid wires were set in place parallel, one next to the other, and held in position with twisted 'chain' wires running across the tops of the ribs. Dard Hunter uses the term 'medieval laid' when referring to some of the earliest sheets made in Europe on moulds with especially irregular laid lines. These were in use more in the 1300s; by the 1400s, much more even and consistent laid lines appear, almost certainly as a result of concurrent developments in the craft of wire drawing. This latter surface Hunter calls 'antique laid'. Both it and medieval laid papers show a distinctive and more or less apparent shadow along and parallel to the chainline/ribs.

In 1757 the first 'wove' papers appeared, made on a mould fitted with a woven wire mesh covering. To avoid the problematic shadows from the ribs, mould makers attached a course laid covering first to the ribs, followed by the wove top covering. Because paper made on a wove mould exhibits an entirely uniform surface with none of the earlier laid and chain pattern, it is possible to confuse it with machine-made paper. Around 1800, paper and mould makers realized they could also eliminate the uneven thickness from chainline/rib shadows in antique laid papers by including a course laid surface under the top, finelaid surface. Hunter terms this result 'modern laid'. Paper made on a modern laid mould can be confused with machine-made paper showing a laid pattern. The latter watermark is applied on the machine during sheetforming with the use of a 'dandy roll'.[5]

Watermarks – twisted wire forms sewn to the surface of the mould – help identify one or more of the following: mill/papermaker, paper size, and/or quality. Watermarks offer the best way of more closely estimating paper date and possibly location.[6] A good student project might be to assign individuals or teams a watermarked leaf and ask them to approximate date and country of origin from the mould surfaces and watermarks.

Hands-on Papermaking

Actual wet papermaking may be beyond the scope of your class, but the following (simple) exercise in Nepalese papermaking can be done easily and with care, even in a normally dry workspace. European and Japanese-style papermaking sessions require more investment in tools, supplies and preparation time.[7] An alternative is to find a local hand papermaker to host your class for a hands-on wet session.

The following process, which I term 'Nepalese papermaking', is still used in some areas of China, Tibet, and Nepal. Many consider it the oldest and original form of papermaking. The more authentic (and time consuming) approach uses actual bast fibre from the mitsumata tree; a second approach uses recycled pulp made in a blender from paper torn from a brown shopping bag.

Equipment required

1 10"x10" stretched fabric mould[8]
Paper pulp (either mitsumata bast or paper bag pulp; see recipe below)
1 black mortar tub (approximately 22"x17"x 6")
3' by 8' worktable
To make a stretched fabric mould
Cut a 1 inch by 2 inch (or equivalent) pine furring strip into four, ten-inch lengths. Nail lengths together to approximate a square, 1 1/2 inches deep on the inside. Cover one open side with thin muslin fabric (stretched tight), using a staple gun or thumbtacks.
Choose a pulp to work with, and prepare according to recipe.

Mitsumata bast fibre pulp

Supplies required:
100 grams mitsumata bark
50 grams soda ash (sodium carbonate)
1 meat tenderizer or 1"x18" dowel
Prepare the fibre as follows: Soak the bark overnight in water. The next morning, heat up 5 quarts or litres of water in a stainless steel or enamelware pot. Add 50 grams soda ash to the warming water and bring to boil. Sprinkle in the damp bark and push down with a mixing stick. Cook at a gently rolling boil for two hours, turning every 30 minutes. Let cool overnight if possible. Use rubber gloves to remove the cooked bark, transfer it to a pot of clear cool water, gently rinse, transfer to the cook pot (rinsed out and refilled with clear water) and continue rinsing until water runs clear or almost clear. Squeeze out the excess water and store the cooked fibre in a plastic bag in the refrigerator. To beat the fibre, first squeeze handfuls of the wet bark to remove excess water. Then spread it out on a firm table top and beat with a meat tenderizer (smooth side) or a 1"x18" dowel for 30 minutes, adding a quarter cup of water every 5 minutes. Return fibre to the refrigerator until you are ready to make paper. The 100 grams of starting mulberry bark will yield about 50 grams of finished paper (about 12 sheets from a 10x10 mould).

Shopping bag pulp

Obtain roughly 100 square inches (4.5 grams) of a lightweight brown kraft paper. Tear the paper into 1 inch squares, presoak briefly in water, and gradually add them to a running blender filled three quarters of the way with water. Give the blender a chance to break up the pieces of paper before adding more. In 4-5 minutes, you should have the entire batch prepared with no chunks of paper remaining in the mixture.

To make paper (from either pulp)

Fill the mortar tub with water about half way, drop the mould into the water, muslin side down. Make sure the fabric is well wet with no air bubbles underneath. If the fabric doesn't wet well, use hot water and/or a bit of soap to wash the surface. Rinse the mould well before returning it to the vat. Let the mould float and flood with water.

For the mitsumata pulp, take a walnut-sized ball of beaten fibre and tear it apart, adding it to a medium sized bowl containing about 4 cups of water. With your hand, agitate the fibre until evenly dispersed. Pour this mixture into the mould and gently agitate the fibre to cover the full area of the fabric.

For the blender-prepared pulp, mix a final time, then pour the blender contents into the mould.

For either pulp, carefully lift the mould out of the water, leaving the fibre deposited on the fabric's surface. Stand the mould up to drain and dry overnight. The next day, rub the fabric behind the dry paper to loosen the sheet, then pull a corner up from the mesh (try using a paper clip with one wire end bent down at 90 degrees). Carefully pull the dry sheet away from the fabric.[9]

Notes

1. My notes refer to the standard text, Dard Hunter's *Papermaking: The History and Technique of an Ancient Craft*, 2nd edn., revised and enlarged (New York, Alfred A. Knopf, 1947); reprinted (New York, Dover, 1978)
2. Ibid., pp. 111-13 and photographs on pp. 78, 79, 82, and 84. My papermaking instructions use this 'Nepalese' process.
3. Ibid., pp. 84-110.
4. Ibid., pp. 435-44, describes forming, pressing, and drying sheets.
5. Ibid., pp. 114-38 discusses mould types.
6. One can survey watermarks, using the Literary Manuscript Analysis (LIMA) database at: http://www2.warwick.ac.uk/fac/arts/ren/publications/lima/paper/describing/databases/ (accessed 7 May 2006). See Resources for additional sources.
7. See Resources for information on suppliers, books, videotapes, etc.
8. With one mould, you can demonstrate making a sheet (and show students a pre-dried one). With multiple moulds, students can form sheets themselves.
9. Formation quality in handmade Nepalese style sheets will be only fair compared to modern handmade or machine-made paper, but it will be very similar to the Nepalese paper in the University of Iowa Centre for the Book Paper Sample set (see Resources).

The Bibliographical Analysis of Antique Laid Paper: A Method

R. Carter Hailey

Once students have been introduced to the history and practice of papermaking, they may become interested in ways scholars have used paper to solve bibliographic problems. A fine introduction to the subject is John Bidwell's 'The Study of Paper as Evidence, Artefact, and Commodity' where he observes that 'By examining paper, scholars have detected literary forgeries, discovered misleading dates in early imprints, and reassembled manuscripts in their proper order after the original sequence had been disturbed'.[1] My purpose here is to introduce a technique for the description and analysis of hand-made antique laid paper that is simple and effective enough to be widely accessible even to nascent filigranologists.

One of the earliest studies to show the importance of paper as bibliographical evidence is W. W. Greg's two-part essay 'On Certain False Dates in Shakespearian Quartos' (*The Library*, 1908). The Pavier quartos, so called for their publisher, are a group of ten plays attributed to Shakespeare which are occasionally found bound together and are variously dated 1600, 1608, and 1619. Having distinguished twenty-six different watermarks as well as some unmarked stock used to print these quartos, Greg found that in a number of instances paper bearing the same watermarks appeared in quartos with different title page dates. Understanding that hand-made printing paper was an industrial commodity produced on moulds whose lifespan was probably something on the order of a year to eighteen months, that paper was typically bought ad hoc by publishers and/or printers, and that stocks of paper were quickly consumed, Greg recognized that the earlier dates must be false.

The true giant in the bibliographical study of paper was Allan Stevenson who crowned his scholarly career with a book-length study on the dating of the Constance Missal (1967) which some scholars had argued was one of the earliest books printed, perhaps even antedating the Gutenberg Bible.[2] Though watermark evidence Stevenson demonstrated that the Missal could not have

been printed earlier than 1473, and while his discovery had in fact been anticipated in the work of Theo Gerardy and Gerhard Piccard, his methodology
represented a significant advance in filigranology – the study of watermarks.
Through his meticulous observations, Stevenson had realized that watermarks
are not static images, but may in fact change dramatically in appearance over a
half-million dips in the vat. But Stevenson also noticed that the pattern of sewing dots – the discrete points at which the watermark was affixed to the mould
by relatively heavy sewing thread or wire – remained fixed as the watermark
itself deteriorated around it.[3] Armed with this data, Stevenson was able to trace
the products of particular moulds through many different states of its watermark. Stevenson's writings on paper are notable not only for their scholarly
rigor and insight, but for the evident delight he takes in literary detective work
and the clarity and liveliness of prose: as Needham puts it, '[Stevenson] was a
lord of language, projecting an authorial persona seemingly ever in high spirits
at the sheer innocent joy of finding things out'.[4]

In terms of methodology, the two twentieth-century landmarks for the
study of hand-made paper are Allan Stevenson's 'Watermarks are Twins' (1951)
and David Vander Meulen's 'The Identification of Paper Without Watermarks'
(1984). As Paul Needham argues, the identification and discrimination of
watermark twins 'is the key to all adequate studies of handmade, watermarked
paper.'[5] To show why this is so, I briefly rehearse below the construction of the
paper mould and the process of papermaking.

The mould for making antique laid paper is a rectangular wooden frame
reinforced by a series of wooden ribs running parallel to the short side and
spaced at intervals, often slightly irregular, averaging anywhere from about
18mm to as much as 35mm. Over this framework a series of 'laid' wires are
placed parallel to the long side, tied to each other with fine chain wires, and
fastened at intervals to the supporting ribs; it is this surface of closely-spaced
wires that forms a sieve which allows the water to drain away, leaving a freshly-
made sheet of paper. Two individuals, the vatman and the coucher (sometimes
assisted by a layer), worked together using a pair of paper moulds and a single
deckle. The vatman dipped one mould fitted with the deckle into the vat of
warmed stuff, let it briefly drain and handed it to the coucher who, having
passed the twin mould and the deckle back to the vatman, turned out the
freshly-made sheet onto a piece of felt. For watermarked papers – by far more
common than unmarked for the earlier hand press period – each mould had a
wireform sewn to its surface, bearing one of many designs which included uni-
corns, fleur-de-lis, foolscaps, pots, hands, and numerous others. The wireforms
of the twin moulds were generally of the same design, though as with all such
handmade artifacts, slight variation was inevitable, quite distinct variation not
at all unusual.

The number of different paper *stocks* is thus half the number of individual watermarks; in Stevenson's succinct formulation: 'The basic equation is: Two watermarks equal one paper.'[6] It follows that, in Needham's words, 'a paper stock is only defined when both its twins can be identified. . . . For in the absence of identified twins, one might easily (for example) record one watermark in one book, and a second similar but nonidentical mark in another, with no way of judging whether one was dealing with the same or two different stocks'.[7] This possibility is further complicated since paper manufacturers frequently used a series of twin paper moulds bearing a similar, even standardized (though not to say identical) design.[8] One must admire the tremendous industry of C.M. Briquet, who understood quite well that watermarks were twins but only rarely reproduced both individuals of a pair. To claim that a watermark is 'like' an example from *Les Filigranes* is to say very little; to say that a mark is the 'same' will frequently be erroneous. Did the watermark in question come from the same paper mould, from its twin mould, or from a mould belonging to different pair which happens to bear a similar watermark design? The effective bibliographical analysis of antique laid paper depends entirely on the researcher's ability to identify and discriminate the product of individual paper moulds, to pair twins, and to distinguish them from the product of other similar moulds and mould pairs.

But watermarks are not the only features that can be used to identify and distinguish antique laid papers. Just as the wireform leaves a visible impression on the paper – the watermark – so do the laid and chain wires, with the impressions of the latter being generally referred to as 'chainlines'. David Vander Meulen's key insight was that these features could be used to identify *unwatermarked* papers. Unlike sewing dots – or watermarks themselves for that matter – chainlines 'are present in every leaf of handmade paper manufactured before the introduction of wove paper in the later eighteenth century'.[9] Since the spacing between chainlines is rarely regular, chain space models – produced by carefully measuring, recording, and ordering of chain spaces to reflect their original arrangement across the length of the sheet – can serve as a fingerprint for the mould. Chain space models are (nearly) as characteristic as fingerprints because there is usually some distinctive pattern in the sequence of narrower and wider spaces that can serve as a sort of genetic marker. Since chainlines result from the impression of fine wires which are secured to the supporting wooden ribs, they are less apt to shift their position or deteriorate than are watermarks. The state of the chainlines will remain relatively stable even as the watermark goes through a number of successive states due to damage or wear. Thus chain space models are particularly useful in establishing the identity of watermarks in variant states and avoiding the misidentification of watermarks in different states as different watermarks.

Allan Stevenson's study of incunabular papers in *The Problem of the Missal Speciale* depended heavily on expensive beta-radiographs of watermarks to reveal the pattern of sewing dots; in this case precise reproductions were crucial to his success. Bidwell has noted that would-be filigranologists have often been daunted by the scientific rigor of Stevenson's methodology and its dependence on expensive, unwieldy equipment.[10] But positive identification need not depend on expensive reproductions: all you really need is a mug shot and a fingerprint. By combining mug shots – in my own case careful freehand sketches of the visible portions of watermarks – with fingerprints – that is the chain space models – I am able in most cases confidently to make identifications, pair twins, distinguish similar sets of marks from each other, and to achieve that 'certainty of recognition' that Stevenson rightly suggests is crucial to using paper evidence convincingly to solve bibliographical problems.[11] The fingerprint is actually *more* important than the mug shot; after all Vander Meulen demonstrated that laid paper *without* watermarks can be identified and distinguished. Scholars should of course employ the best method available to them to reproduce watermarks, but should not be discouraged if drawings or tracings are all they can supply. Any reasonably good reproduction in conjunction with a complete chain space model should enable positive identification. These two pieces of evidence used together form a powerful forensic tool and the necessary equipment is nothing more exotic than a clear, flexible, plastic ruler with a metric scale. And a good deal of patience.

I will now describe the procedure for collecting chainspace data and creating the chainspace model, using examples from my work on Robert Crowley's quarto editions of *Piers Plowman* (1550). The first step is to decide from which side of the sheet the data is to be collected. Paul Needham has succinctly summarized the problem:

> The sheet has, of course, two sides: the *mould* side, which was actually in contact with the wire mesh of the paper mould; and the *felt* side . . . the side which was first laid onto the felt as the sheet was pressed out of the mould. If one examines a sheet with mould side facing, one sees in essence a mirror image of the upper surface of the mould; if one looks at the felt side, one sees in essence the upper surface of the mould itself.[12]

Scholars have differed on which side should be favored; while my own preference is for the felt side, consistency of procedure is paramount. The mould side can usually be distinguished by the slight indentations that are left by the watermark and/or chainlines. When sheets have been washed and pressed, as sometimes is the case with books that have undergone restoration or conservation treatments, distinguishing the mould and felt sides may be more difficult. Looking at the pages with a light raking across the surface may be helpful.

In a quarto book, chainlines run parallel to the top edge of the leaf and perpendicular to the gutter; for consistency chain spaces are best measured along the gutter since this is the latitudinal centre or equator of the sheet. For quarto gatherings, my procedure is to align the book so I am viewing the top half of the watermark from the felt side of the leaf. (With the Crowley *Piers* watermarks it is always possible to identify right-side-upness: the fingers of the hand point up and the pot's top is always up.) I note the leaf and side from which I'm viewing the mark, e.g. 2^r, and then, using a metric ruler, I measure and record the width of the chain spaces to the nearest half millimeter from left to right along the gutter from the top of the leaf in reading position to the bottom. As Vander Meulen notes, the half millimeter is a convenient tolerance, since discrimination can easily be made between chains that fall more nearly *on* or *between* a millimeter marking on the ruler.[13] I then reorient the book, rotating it 180 degrees, so that the complementary leaf – that is the leaf that completes the original length of the sheet – is also viewed from the felt side, and again measure and record the chain spaces from left to right. In a quarto gathering, if, for example, the top half of the watermark viewed from the felt side is found at 2^r, the complementary leaf would be 1^v; if it were 4^r, the complementary leaf would be 3^v. In the former, leaf 2^r will have been measured left-to-right along the gutter from the top edge to the bottom, while leaf 1^v, after the book has been rotated, will also be measured left-to-right, but this time from the bottom to the top edge. When the two halves are combined in the correct sequence, in this case 1^v/2^r, they will form a chain space model representing the length of the whole sheet before folding (less whatever portion is lost to trimming), as viewed from the felt side and reading from left to right.

While at a given latitude chain spaces are remarkably consistent from sheet to sheet of paper from a given mould[14] (and this is their great evidentiary value), adjacent chains lines may often wander from each other as they traverse the sheet. This is why, whatever the format of a book, chain spaces should consistently be measured across what was originally the centre of the sheet, since it represents an identifiable common point of reference. Folios are measured from the gutter across to the centre of the fore edge (or vice versa) in the middle of the leaf, quartos along the gutter, octavos along the top edge, etc. This procedural consistency will allow the same paper to be identified in different formats.

The following is a typical model from a quarto sheet from a first edition copy of *Piers Plowman* (STC 19906), a watermark I've called ^{O}**HAND, PA**^{a}.[15] When taking notes in the field, this is the basic form in which I record the data:

19906 Y: 11^v/2^r Wires: 28/3
4|25|27 | 25|24.5 | 27|23.5|24|10} {11|23|25.5|25.5|24.5|25.5|24|26.5|10|2
              | 16.5 [9.5|8] 16.5 |
              | 13.5 [12.5|11.5] 13 |

In the first line I indicate respectively the STC number of the edition, the copy consulted, the gathering from which the model was taken along with the orientation of the two halves of the model as measured from left-to-right, and the wireline density, that is the number of wires per 3cm. The second line is the chain space model itself, with the vertical strokes representing the chainlines, and the bold stokes indicating the position of the watermark on the sheet. While some paper scholars include the watermark measurements in the sequence, I prefer to abstract them, and record them below the chain space model in the relative position where the watermark occurs, a procedure that makes for a clearer statement of the chain sequence. The gap in the middle of the model, indicated by the curly brackets, represents the trimmed top edge of the quarto sheet. Rather than attempt to approximate the width of the excised chain space and chainline, I am satisfied to accept a bit of indeterminacy in the middle of the model. Since, in this system, positive identification and discrimination of paper stocks is dependant on the combined evidence of watermark reproductions, chain space models, and wire line density, a single indeterminate chain space will rarely if ever prevent Stevenson's 'certainty of recognition'.

Notes

1. Bidwell in Peter Davison (ed.), *The Book Encompassed: Studies in Twentieth-Century Bibliography* (Cambridge, Cambridge University Press, 1992), p. 68.
2. Allan Stevenson, *The Problem of the Missale Speciale* (London, Bibliographical Society, 1967).
3. Distinct sewing dots disappear early in the sixteenth century when watermarks began to be sewn continuously to moulds with fine wires.
4. Paul Needham, 'Allan H. Stevenson and the Bibliographical Uses of Paper', *Studies in Bibliography*, 47 (1994), p. 62.
5. Ibid., p. 29.
6. Allan Stevenson, 'Watermarks are Twins', *Studies in Bibliography*, 4 (1951-2), p. 89.
7. Needham, pp. 39-40.
8. While cataloguing the paper used to print the three editions of Piers *Plowman* issued by Robert Crowley in 1550, I eventually identified thirty-nine different watermark pairs; nine of the pairs had their design repeated – sometimes quite closely – in a second pair of moulds.
9. David Vander Meulen, 'The Identification of Paper Without Watermarks: The Example of Pope's *Dunciad*, *Studies in Bibliography*, 37 (1984), p. 60.
10. Bidwell, p. 73.
11. Stevenson, 'Watermarks', p. 68.
12. Needham, p. 31
13. Vander Meulen, p. 61.
14. One should not however expect absolute consistency; slight variation can result from differential rates of shrinkage or inaccurate measurement – even moving one's head slightly to one side or another can alter the apparent position of a chain by a half millimeter or more.
15. The reference system for naming watermarks was developed ad hoc for the project. The initial superscript indicates whether the watermark is centreed *on* (O) or *between* (B) chainlines; the second element identifies the basic design, following which I add particular distinguishing features like the initials 'PA' which appear on the wrist of this example; the final superscript 'a' or 'b' distinguishes the two twins that make up the watermark pair.

How Things Work: Teaching the Technologies of Literature

Matthew G. Kirschenbaum

I'm interested in how things work. Many of my colleagues will also own up to that: they're interested in how narrative works, or how culture works, or how poems or sentences work. The keyword in my first sentence, however, is 'things', I am (especially) interested in how *things* work ('made objects' to use the term favored by Henry Petroski in his book-length history of the pencil). Often in English departments, however, we're not much interested in made objects, in things. We're interested in language, ideas, and discourse, as embodied and expressed by 'texts'. This is, of course, a gross generalization, but it is a generalization broadly upheld in the public language we use to represent ourselves to the outside world. The mission statement of the department in which I teach, which I select only because it is typical, reads as follows: 'to give students a sense of the history and variety of literature written in English'; 'to introduce students to the debates about literature and language'; and 'to use the critical study of literature and language to help students think carefully and express themselves well'.[1] What this statement (and many others like it) fails to capture is much sense that language and literature are phenomena embodied by made objects, actual things.[2]

I believe it's important to know how things work, and more specifically (for us, as literary scholars) to know how textual things work. One of my favorite examples of what I sometimes call the technology of literature involves William Blake, routinely taught as a poet, but in his own lifetime a printer, engraver, and artist. Famous for declaring 'I must create a system or be enslaved by another man's,' Blake invented and perfected a technique known as relief-etching which allowed him to print and color what he termed 'illuminated books'. Relief-etching entails using brushes to draw and write (backwards) on a copper plate with an acid-resistant varnish, and then bathing the copper plate in acid to create a relief surface for printing (etching is typically an intaglio as opposed to a relief process, yielding a sunken rather than a raised printing surface).

To ink the raised lines of his relief-etched words and images, Blake pressed a dauber over the surface of the plate. If a line of verse ended before its neighbors, however, the dauber tended to deposit unwanted ink on the depressed areas of the plate immediately adjacent which then (because of paper sag in the press) tended to print. To alleviate this problem, Blake frequently added tiny figures, vegetative swirls, and flourishes to the right of a line of text, thereby extending the line to the approximate length of its neighbors and creating a uniform support for the dauber (see for example, copy D, Plate 4, of Blake's *The Marriage of Heaven and Hell*).[3] Thus we see a portion of the 'content' of the illuminated print influenced by the demands of its production through physical media.[4]

Numerous other texts also instruct us in the technologies of literature. When I teach T. S. Eliot's 'The Waste Land' I do so with the facsimile edition of the original manuscript drafts, emended by Eliot's own hand as well as that of Ezra Pound and Eliot's first wife, Vivian. Students learn to see the text as a social artifact, the product of a turbulent three-way collaboration that could have turned out in a variety of different ways, rather than as a singular act of spontaneous creative invention. Texts like Tom Philips's artist's book *A Humument* (a 'treated Victorian novel') or Jerome Rothenberg and Steven Clay's anthology *A Book of the Book* can achieve similar ends. When I teach novels, students research their publication and reception histories, an assignment I learned from Jerome McGann. These are not in and of themselves innovative ideas or techniques, and of course this approach to the material condition of texts is grounded in established fields like textual criticism and the history of the book. What I want to argue for here is the importance of this approach and these fields in a digital world.

To emphasize to students that books are technologies, and specifically that they are information technologies, no less so than the computer, I use a piece of internet humor which recasts the book as an acronymic BOOK and defamiliarizes it through a market-oriented presentation of its features. Here is an excerpt:

> BOOK is a revolutionary breakthrough in technology: no wires, no electric circuits, no batteries, nothing to be connected or switched on. It's so easy to use, even a child can operate it ... Compact and portable, it can be used anywhere – even sitting in an armchair by the fire, or on a plane – yet it is powerful enough to hold as much information as a CD-ROM disc ... BOOK may be taken up at any time and used merely by opening it ... The 'browse' feature allows you to move instantly to any sheet, and move forward or backward as you wish. Many come with an 'index' feature, which pinpoints the exact location of any selected information for instant retrieval. An optional 'BOOKmark' accessory allows you to open BOOK to the exact place you left it in a previous session – even if the BOOK has been closed.[5]

And so forth. The presumed humor of the piece derives from its application of a dot-com sales pitch to the book, that iconic artifact of the old knowledge economy. Importantly, though, nothing in the piece is untrue or even much exaggerated: you *can* browse a book by moving instantly from one place to another. That may seem obvious, but the implicit point of comparison is to devices that don't allow us that kind of lateral navigation: like a poorly designed Web site, for instance. Or a scroll.

The moment our students can begin to decouple a phrase like 'information technology' from its strict associations with gears and gizmos and circuits and microchips is the moment they begin to see that computers and books are not antagonists in some zero-sum cultural competition, but rather alternate solutions to the age-old problem of how to disseminate writing, images, and other inscriptive forms. And this is, arguably, one of the most important lessons literary studies has to teach at the present moment.

About a decade ago, Randall McLeod coined the term 'transformission' to refer to the ways by which texts (all texts, always) are transformed as they are transmitted. That something like transformission is endemic to the literary process will not be news to most readers, but aside from a handful of very famous instances (*King Lear* or *Hamlet* perhaps, or the multiple editions of *Leaves of Grass,* or the two different endings to *Great Expectations*) its minute particulars are rarely evident in the classroom. Most undergraduates and even some graduate students have no idea what textual editing is, or why there are so many different editions of Shakespeare's plays, or why the 'Note on the Text' at the front of the Penguin might matter, or that a 'critical edition' is something other than the assemblage of extras Norton provides – a kind of literary DVD. In short, most students have no idea where texts really come from, or even that that's a question that can (and should) be asked of all texts. Transformission, with its inflections of information theory, foregrounds precisely those questions, and the agenda they imply – an agenda rooted in technologies of media and mediation – is central to the concerns of contemporary literary studies.

Let me offer two examples of how this plays out in the classroom, one at the graduate level and one at the undergraduate level. The University of Kentucky, where I taught for two years as an assistant professor, holds the Peal Collection, which contains, among much else, letters (some of them unpublished) from major figures of British Romanticism: Coleridge, Wordsworth, Charles Lamb, Robert Southey, Maria Edgeworth, and the Shelleys. When I taught a graduate course entitled 'Electronic Texts and Images' students used the collection to gain a practical understanding of how various digital tools work, but also to cultivate an appreciation for what John Seely Brown and Paul Duguid call the 'social life of information'[6] – in this case, the social life of literary information as it is migrated across different media by a variety of scholars and professionals in a process recognizable as transformission.

All students were assigned two or three letters to take through each stage of the digitization process. Using the library's stand-mounted Kontron digital camera, they created high-resolution full-color images of both sides of each leaf, as well as the fronts and backs of the envelopes. They then set about transcribing the originals. This step utilized no digital technology, but was central to our discussions of transformission because of the debates that ensued: should we preserve in our transcriptions the original letters' lineation? Should we transcribe the postal codes? How best to order and sequence the sheets? In some cases, the writing went sideways up and down the page; should the transcription reflect this? Once transcriptions were in hand, students then used standardized document encoding schemes (SGML and XML) to add descriptive tags.

In all of this – and here is the key point – the students constantly made decisions about what counts as information. Is the lineation of the text information important enough, relevant enough, to be preserved? Or is that information expendable? What about postal marks on envelopes? If these are not transcribed, then they are not represented as machine-readable data in the electronic transcription (though they are visible in the document image). A literary scholar might find their omission acceptable, but what about the postal historian interested in the Royal Mail? Wouldn't they want the postal codes as machine-readable (searchable) data fields? Well, why not just do it all then? Transcribe everything, preserve lineation and all other documentary features? Because neither the scholar's time nor the library's resources nor the machine's memory nor the user's patience are infinite, so decisions and trade-offs are inevitable – if not here, then elsewhere in the process.

The end result of all this work was a digital archive hosted by the university library. Each student got a publication credit on his or her vita. The students also learned something about digital imaging and electronic textual editing (one of the primary goals of the course) and most importantly, something about how literary documents subsist in a world of information. Whether it is a diplomatic transcription in a scholarly edition, or a digital facsimile on a Web site, they will no longer be able to take texts for granted.

The second example of transformission at work in the classroom comes from my undergraduate teaching. My upper-level 'Computer and Text' course at the University of Maryland begins with a reading of Mary Shelley's *Franken-stein*, one of the greatest fables of artifice and technology we have. We discuss the major themes and critical controversies surrounding the text, but I also introduce students to the rudiments of textual criticism. I tell them about the first edition, published anonymously, and the way Mary Shelley rewrote certain portions of text by the time her name appeared on it in the third edition, including altering the relationship between Victor and Elizabeth to avoid the suggestion of incest. We read the textual note in our Penguin edition, and take note of the fact that the punctuation has been modernized. We also look at the title page, reproduced in facsimile to discuss what counts as 'data' – why was it important to the editor to include that reproduction? – and why is it that the whole of the novel isn't presented in facsimile form? We discuss the innumerable adaptations of this (particular) text: the abridgements, the comics, the films, etc. The point I strive to make is that transformission operates across *all* materials and media, and not only at the threshold between the printed word and the digital. Students begin to see electronic textuality not as a special case, a disruption in the otherwise static and stable sphere of the literary, but rather as yet another instantiation of an ongoing condition.[7]

We then use that text of *Frankenstein* as the vehicle by which we traverse a wide array of experimental digital landscapes, including Shelley Jackson's refashioning of the original tale as her hypertext novel *Patchwork Girl* and the text-based virtual reality milieu that is the *Geographies of Frankenstein* in the Romantic Circles MOO.[8] We might also play a round of IVANHOE: A Game of Interpretation (an electronic role-playing game devised by Jerome McGann and Johanna Drucker at the University of Virginia).[9] Students use HTML to 'visualize' a portion of the narrative for presentation on the World Wide Web, and, if time allows, XML to perform a descriptive analysis of a key section of Shelley's text. Our objective in constantly positioning and re-positioning *Frankenstein* within these textual and technical spaces is to explore (hands-on) a variety of new literary technologies while gaining an appreciation of the rich and diverse forms of textuality made manifest in existing and emerging electronic environments.[10]

Foregrounding textual transformission in these ways yields at least two dividends. First, students learn some fundamental lessons about written language and textuality that they can – by definition – bring to bear in any other class with a text in it. Second, through these hands-on methods, students become critical consumers of information; they learn not take an interface for granted, to ask why a Web page (or a printed page) was designed and presented in a particular way, and – perhaps most importantly – they learn how (and why) to compare multiple representations (often in multiple media) of the 'same' text and to appreciate the differences that distinguish them. These are the skills that form the basis for literacy in a post-print world.

Some may object that the kind of project my Kentucky class was engaged in – transcribing and digitizing letters for publication on the World Wide Web, making decisions about 'information' – is fine for textual or documentary editors, but not the stuff of literary studies. But as Geoffrey Nunberg has pointed out, the philology underlying our contemporary usage of the word 'information' is quite complex, arising from a dual conflation of the word's earlier meanings: first, what he describes as information's 'particularistic' sense – facts about the world – with the notion of the *Bildung*, with which it was historically consistent through the nineteenth century; and then, in the twentieth century, the introduction of a specialized definition of information in emerging scientific fields like signal processing and cybernetics (which posits information as an entity independent of meaning). Our current use of information (abstractions such as 'the Information Age') is an aggregation of these conflations.[11] The point is that information is not merely the sorting and sifting of facts and figures, but rather an epistemologically vital and critically rich aspect of knowledge production.

Understanding how things work is, I believe, one of the best ways finally to come to terms with the important changes now well underway in media and technology, and their impact on literary studies. By 'how things work', however, I don't just mean mastering the ins and outs of bits and bytes. I mean how texts work – how they work in and through and across time, media, and the old and new hardware and software that embodies them. And while humanities computing is not the only way to do this, I am convinced that if we don't do more to teach the technologies of literature the numbers of our majors will continue to dwindle, and things will play out more or less as they do in Robert Scholes' *The Rise and Fall of English*, which draws analogies to the once unthinkable demise of rhetoric as the flagship of the liberal arts.

Notes

1. This example is from the University of Maryland, College Park – the department in which I teach. Numerous others can be found by browsing from a site such as David L. Hoover's 'English Department Home Pages World Wide': http://www.nyu.edu/gsas/dept/english/links/engdpts.html (accessed 7 May 2006).
2. The exception inevitably occurs when one student raises his or her hand to say that they have a different edition from everyone else's, and please, what page can they find some particular passage on? This is, in fact, an unacknowledged question about the technology of literature.
3. Available online at: http://www.blakearchive.org/ (accessed 7 May 2006).
4. I am grateful to Professor Joseph Viscomi for introducing me to this example.
5. A complete copy can be found at: http://www.geocities.com/Athens/Olympus/4631/techjoke.htm. The original version is R. J. Heathorn's 'Learn with BOOK', *Punch* (May 9, 1962); reprinted in Philip J. Hills (ed.), *The Future of the Printed Word*, (Westport CT, Greenwood Press, 1980), pp. 171-2.
6. See http://www.glue.umd.edu/~mgk/courses/fall2000/570/ for the course Web site (accessed 7 May 2006).
7. Another way to perform this exercise is to ask students to bring to class a copy – any copy, from any source – of a famous poem, say Shelley's 'Ozymandius'. The copies are then compared for textual variants, as well as the work's material presentation; an anthology versus an online copy, for example.
8. See http://www.lcc.gatech.edu/~broglio/rc/frankenstein/ (accessed 7 May 2006). A MOO is a nested acronym, standing for MUD Object Oriented. MUD stands for Multi-User Domain. A MOO is essentially a chat room with both spaces and objects (and characters to interact with them).
9. See: http://www.virginia.edu/mediastudies/speclab/ivanhoe/ (accessed 7 May 2006).
10. See: http://www.glue.umd.edu/~mgk/courses/spring2002/467/ for the course Web site (accessed 7 May 2006).
11. Geoffrey Nunberg, 'Farewell to the Information Age', in Geoffrey Nunberg ed., *The Future of the Book* (Berkeley, University of California Press, 1996), pp. 108-115.

'Not to pick bad from bad, but by bad mend': What Undergraduates Learn from Bad Editions

Erick Kelemen

Textual criticism and scholarly editing traditionally have been topics reserved to graduate school curriculums, probably because they have been seen as the domain of the college professor who prepares the texts and not of the broadly educated reader who consumes them. But we err if we do so, since such instruction nurtures kinds of analysis and communication useful beyond the professions of scholars and teachers, skills desired as much outside the academic world as inside it. Specifically, textual criticism encourages in students new attitudes toward the text. It helps address a quasi-fundamentalist approach too common in our students, that textbooks are unmediated, uncorrupted by human hands, singular texts possessing singular truths as intended by the authors.

Though textual criticism is valuable enough to deserve a course unto itself, it can be easily incorporated in small or large assignments as a part of every literature course. At one end of the spectrum, one might teach the 'unediting' that Leah Marcus and others call for,[1] working backward through textual notes for a passage to reconstruct the witnesses and to interrogate editorial decisions. Such an assignment takes between ten and fifteen minutes of lecture to prepare the students, but in my experience the ensuing discussion practically runs itself. On one of the days devoted to *Othello* in a Shakespeare course, using *The Riverside Shakespeare*, I have students scan the textual notes to find the differences between Q1 (1622) and F1 (1623) in selected scenes, differences that are sometimes small but surprising.[2] I preface the exercise with definitions of 'quarto' and 'folio', a brief summary of the history of the text (mainly that both editions were printed after Shakespeare's death), and a quick look at the many abbreviations they are about to encounter. With a little coaching, students begin to decode the textual notes and can scan for longer passages where the editors find substantive differences between Q1 and F1. There are many in *Othello*, but I generally have students look through the notes for IV.ii, where they find Othello's speech:

Was this fair paper, this most goodly book,
Made to write 'whore' upon? What committed?
[Committed? O thou public commoner,
I should make very forges of my cheeks,
That would to cinders burn up modesty,
Did I but speak thy deeds. What committed?]
Heaven stops the nose at it and the moon winks;
The bawdy wind, that kisses all it meets,
Is hush'd within the hollow mine of earth
And will not hear't. What committed?
Impudent strumpet! (IV.ii.71-81)

When students reconstruct witnesses from the notes, they discover that the speech in their textbooks is a conflation, F1 providing the four lines (in brackets) absent from Q1, and Q1 providing the last line, which is not in F1. To help the class hear the differences, I have some students read aloud the reconstructed speeches as they might perform them. Students will usually want to account for the differences, which is a good place to give them the terms 'eye skip' and 'authorial emendation'. Usually some students will have had some experience in the theater or on a newspaper and will be able to discuss the collaborative natures of the theater and publishing as possible explanations. Fairly early on in the discussion at least one student will have asked some variant of the question, 'which version is right?' It's the kind of question that begs to be turned back to the class, so I rephrase it for them in a way that generates discussion to last the rest of the meeting: How does the meaning of the speech (and therefore the scene) change if we adopt different readings? I often phrase it as a performance-related question: what are the different effects a director might be able to get from the actors using one version instead of another? The exercise raises the theoretical questions about meaning that haunt us by foregrounding the centuries-long collaborative processes and recent editorial choices – the textual layers – that produced their textbooks. I find that unsettling students' textbooks in this way, raising their awareness of the editorial process, makes them more capable and more engaged critics. Of course, such an activity, on the other hand, requires a scholarly edition – that is to say, one with copious textual notes – and it requires a particular idea about all editions, on the other, namely that the editor might be wrong, or that there might be more than one good text, the very idea that gives impetus to the scholarly edition in the first place.

Normally we shun bad editions, but paying attention to another's errors can be as instructive as paying attention to one's own. Errors in a textbook can make this important cognitive leap to skepticism easier for students, as I was reminded when I taught Elizabeth Cary's *Tragedy of Mariam* in a literature survey, using the first edition of *The Longman Anthology of British Literature*.[3]

While it was a very good textbook overall, misprints in the play, such as 'love' for 'live', and misplaced stage directions frustrated my students when they first read it, and we all know the dangers attendant on frustration: we are lucky if some students complain that they don't understand the reading, for most will simply shut down and wait, yielding a particularly deadly discussion. Pointing out how and why their frustrations are justified usually will win back that second group of students, but it doesn't ease the frustration for anyone. This situation called for a new kind of participating in the text: students had to learn how to discover the errors and correct for them – without the aid either of a better edition or of textual notes to check the editorial work. This requires a kind of double reading – something that textual scholarship shares with grading student essays, as David Bartholomae describes the latter activity in his essay, 'The Study of Error'[4] – combining proofreading and close reading in a kind of 'error analysis', where errors are not 'noise' but meaningful data, evidence of an author or editor attempting to communicate but failing somehow. It requires having a theory of error in place when we begin reading, so that we can both isolate and reintegrate errors to keep them from unduly halting our progress through the text. But learning that the text was occasionally in error had a secondary effect for my students, since it led some to begin to read their textbooks against the grain, becoming budding poststructuralists. Rather than only develop greater competence to correct for misreadings as one corrects for slips of the tongue, students began to overcome their sense that the book appears from nowhere and that interpretation of the literary work begins only after the book is in print or comes ready made like a fortune cookie. This introduction to the rudiments of textual criticism was, in my view, a remarkably valuable step in the development of their critical faculties. My point is that textual criticism teaches an attitude toward the text that allows for even bad editions to be pedagogically useful.

But we can't rely on every textbook to be bad. So I have students themselves make them. It is an assignment that I call the collaborative edition, and it works best, in my experience, as a semester-long project, with the entire class working as a group over the course of eight weeks or so. Working from facsimiles – in my Shakespeare class, it's usually *The London Prodigal* (1605), a play attributed to Shakespeare on its title page and included in the third and fourth Folios[5] – students engage in each stage of editing the text, from transcription to layout. Most of this work is carried out outside of class, keeping in-class attention to the project limited to discussion, usually in ten-to-fifteen-minute bursts once a week or so. It is a long project, so many things can go wrong in the process, including students disappearing at key moments, which means both that the teacher's supervisory role is increased to a degree and that the assignment needs to be flexible enough to account for such problems. There are several natural stopping places in the process where students trade work, where their efforts can be evaluated, and where the class can pause to discuss the project in terms of the knowledge and skills they have learned so far.

In my classes, the assignment breaks down into as many as six graded and ungraded segments: transcribing, proofing, preparing the text, preparing the textual notes, preparing the content notes, and preparing the editor's preface. Before beginning the project, you'll find it a good idea to map out the whole process for the class, to tell them what the major educational goals are – learning about the process that results in their textbooks, for instance, or about a play that once was but no longer is considered to be by Shakespeare – and to prepare them with a sample and a one-page transcription exercise. Since this particular assignment uses an early printed edition, I also cover questions of orthography and spelling that are likely to come up, such as the difference between long *s*-es and *f*-s and the conventions about *u* and *v*, *i* and *j*. Depending on the size of the class, I usually have students transcribe two or three pages of the facsimile as homework. The next week's homework is to proofread another student's transcriptions; sometimes I require them to proofread two. I usually pause here for the first time to allow them to discuss the assignment, and I will collect proofread transcriptions and grade them for accuracy.

Once students have corrected their transcriptions, we combine them to make a single document and distribute it to the class. Then, in the third or fourth week of the assignment, with the diplomatic transcript before us, I engage the class in determining editorial procedures. These discussions are often so instructive in themselves as to be worth the price of admission alone, and sometimes there are contentions over ideas students once might have dismissed as trivia. Once, some students insisted on preserving all italics because they perceived more italic *I*'s when the prodigal speaks in *The London Prodigal*, which they thought might be a typographical reflection of his egotism. Other students objected that italic and roman types were sometimes nonsensically mixed, as in the words '*If*', '*Lancelot*' and '*Lady*' on C2ʳ alone. Students then begin to write the introduction that explains their editorial policies, a task which they often find difficult, partly because they have trouble justifying their often inconsistent decisions, partly because they must justify corporate actions with which they don't always agree. Once we have developed guidelines for editing the text, students emend and regularize (if they have chosen to do so) their assigned sections, writing textual notes about substantive changes. On occasion I have had students trade work at this point to check each other for adherence to editorial policy and to collaborate on tougher editorial decisions. In this version of the collaborative edition, there is only one witness, so the class does no collating, but in other iterations of the assignment, such as editing Chaucer's lyric poem 'Truth', I have had students work with as many as five witnesses. Each witness that must be collated makes the assignment that much harder, in my experience, so I would recommend keeping the number of witnesses inversely related to the lines of text being edited.

Preparing the content notes takes several weeks, and I usually have students work in small teams to determine what needs to be annotated and to find sources that will help them complete the notes. Deciding what content to annotate soon has them thinking more carefully about their readers than I find is normally the case. One student, who wanted to gloss half the words in his section, told me in my office hour that he'd prefer fewer notes himself but felt that some of his classmates really needed the help. While the students are writing explanatory notes outside of class, in class I have them determine what sort of layout they wish to have – where to put the notes they have been drafting, which practically necessitates a discussion of the ways notes can influence reading. When their notes are done, we assemble the final edition, which becomes the textbook for our last week of classes.

By the end of the process, the edition is truly terrible. It is uneven, full of errors, and difficult to read. But the class knows it is bad, and they begin to know why, and that's the goal. Knowing that it is a bad edition means several things. First of all, it means that they know the text very well, having read some portions of it more carefully than perhaps any other text in their careers. I am suggesting that the assignment teaches a kind of reader-discipline that may be more effective than close-reading exercises; it teaches them to be very careful readers. It means also that they can distinguish between a bad work (*The London Prodigal* is an interesting case, clearly not by Shakespeare, but probably not all that bad a play) and a bad edition. This distinction means that they are better at reading to appreciate and are more alive to nuances, which I think comes because they have begun to see editorial policy at work. Perhaps most importantly, it means that they have begun to see every literary work as a collaboration, which deepens their understanding about how interpretations and meanings are produced. In short, they are not only more careful, but more critical readers. Moreover, they have engaged in work that can often be more like the kinds of thinking and writing they will encounter as they enter the workforce.

Obviously, editing is a very different assignment than unediting. Students discover that it is one thing to question editorial choices but another thing altogether to make such choices. But the main realization I want them to come to in both assignments is that editing requires interpretation. They usually come to it on their own, and it arrives as a productive epistemic crisis, disrupting the fundamental ways they have been thinking about literature. Too many students come to college looking for notes to put in their notebooks, for the right answer, for the single meaning. Even those students who have left behind the banking model of education (as Paulo Freire calls it) [6] benefit from the radical destabilization of the text that such unediting produces. When I say that they are more capable and engaged readers, I mean that they are more skeptical critics, more attuned to the layers that comprise their textbooks, even when their textbooks do not reveal the layering process in the way that *The Riverside Shakespeare* does. I believe that this skepticism serves students well not only in deepening their appreciations of literature and other cultural productions but also in their attentions to the texts and tasks that come to them in their working lives, whether they become lawyers, librarians, bond raters, or software developers.

Notes

1. Leah S. Marcus, *Unediting the Renaissance: Shakespeare, Marlowe, Milton* (New York, Routledge, 1996).
2. William Shakespeare, *The Tragedy of Othello, the Moor of Venice*. In The *Riverside Shakespeare*. G. Blakemore Evans, et al. ed., 2nd edn., (Boston, Houghton Mifflin, 1997), pp. 1251-96.
3. David Damrosch, et al. ed., *The Longman Anthology of British Literature*, 2 vols. (New York, Longman, 1999).
4. David Bartholomae, 'The Study of Error', *College Composition and Communication* 31 (October 1980), pp. 253-69. Reprinted in *The Writing Teacher's Sourcebook*, 4th edn. Edward P. J. Corbett, Nancy Meyers, and Gary Tate (eds) (Oxford, Oxford University Press, 1999), pp. 258-72.
5. *The London Prodigal*. (Old English Drama, Students' Facsimile Edition, 1910)
6. Paulo Freire, Myra Bergman Ramos trans., *Pedagogy of the Oppressed* (New York, Seabury Press, 1973).

Book History and Reader-Response Theory: Teaching Shakespeare's *Romeo and Juliet* **and** *King Lear*

Tatjana Chorney

I have incorporated my work with seventeenth-century manuscripts, bibliographical studies and the phenomenology of reading into a year-long course covering eleven Shakespeare plays and his sonnets. The results were good; students enjoyed the activities and wrote final papers reflecting a more meaningful engagement with the texts. We brought book history and a pragmatic textual criticism to bear on two tragedies with complicated textual histories: *Romeo and Juliet* and *King Lear*.

The text of *Romeo and Juliet* exists in two Quartos, of 1597 and 1599, whose striking differences in content have led editors to construct, and critics to rely on, editions that amalgamate the two versions. Similarly, the 1608 *Shake-speare His Historie, of King Lear* differs significantly from the 1623 *The Tragedie of King Lear* published in the First Folio. Recent developments in book history and textual criticism have revitalized study of texts from the past. As a result, different versions of one dramatic text are no longer assigned designations 'bad', 'corrupt', or 'inauthentic', but are instead embraced as important and often equally valid parts of the social and theatrical history in which these texts were produced and performed. Thus, in 1997, the one-volume Norton Shakespeare, based on the Oxford edition, printed the two *King Lear* versions separately,[1] and Oxford 'World's Classics' did the same with the two Quartos of *Romeo and Juliet*, edited by Jill Levenson.[2] Students also have access to Levenson's online compilation of over 170 promptbooks providing performance records of each play from the seventeenth century to about 1980.[3]

In my course, I often use the contrasts between such editions to engage students in bibliographical and interpretive analysis of texts. For example, students can profitably analyze parts of *Romeo and Juliet* in two versions. The first Quarto, published in 1597, is entitled *AN EXCELLENT conceited Tragedie*

OF *Romeo and Iuliet*, while the second Quarto of 1599 bears the title *THE MOST EX-cellent and lamentable Tragedie, of Romeo and Iuliet*. Q2, traditionally considered the authoritative version, is considerably longer than Q1, the so-called 'bad Quarto'. Specifically, Q2 contains over 800 lines differing from the corresponding lines in Q1; several passages, particularly II.v, III.ii.57-60 and V.iii.12-21, are completely different.[4] In II.v, for example, Friar Laurence marries Romeo and Juliet in an episode significant both to plot and characterization. In Q2, the lines all three characters speak contribute to our understanding of the plot as foregrounding the association between love and death through the idea of excess. The diction foreshadows the events of the last act (the lovers' suicide). The rich emotional charge of this scene in Q2 is difficult to miss, both in its own right and in its relation to the play as a whole. Once students see the significance of the scene in Q2, they find the differences in Q1 striking. In Q1, dialogue is brief; Juliet expresses herself in stylized, brief sentences; the passages carrying emotional and structural meaning in Q2 are here absent, and replaced by a brief communication between the Friar and Romeo that in no way matches Q2's feverishness of thought.

We start by analyzing tone (the speakers' attitude toward their subject). Cautioned that tone in drama often depends on the actor's personality and delivery, and is therefore, a potentially variable attribute, students watch clips from Baz Luhrmann's 1996 film *Romeo + Juliet*, and discuss his treatment of this scene. Most students quickly notice that Claire Danes and Leonardo DiCaprio deliver a performance suggesting the passion and excess of Q2 coupled with an undertone of unselfconscious innocence, which, as many begin to see, may or may not be present in either textual version. The simultaneous awareness of the three 'versions', two textual and one interpretive (on film), enables students to perceive the process of interpretation as a creation of meaning in which they participate. The awareness helps them differentiate between what is 'there' in the text, and what is meaning extrinsic to the text; they see that one text can suggest many things, but these are not indefinite, as they are bound by the text's material contexts.

The questions we can explore after closely studying the differences between equivalent passages in the two versions are of larger thematic significance. How does our perception of Juliet's character change based on her words in Q1 and Q2? The same question can be applied productively to both Romeo's and Friar Laurence's characters. What is the relationship of image/diction/words to action? How do the titles of the two versions situate the play even before we read them? Could the 'conceited tragedie', as the play is referred to on the title page of Q1, be linked to the stylization, 'ceremony of speech', and the sort of conventional artifice we see in it? And finally, is this the same play in two different versions, or can we speak comfortably of two different plays?

Close attention to language necessarily involves attention to style, which in turn cannot be understood without reference to the reader's perception of and response to language. After being exposed to the differences between versions and the potential for difference in meaning, most students were struck by the dynamic of the relationship among text, reader and interpretation. They also perceived that the text is 'fluid' – not (as they had previously thought) an entity possessing a fixed identity and a single meaning accessible with one 'key' interpretation, usually something they expect the instructor to provide.

We adopted a similar approach to the two versions of *King Lear*. The 1608 Quarto version contains about 300 hundred lines that do not appear in the 1623 Folio version, and the Folio contains about a hundred lines not in the Quarto. The format of the Norton Shakespeare, which prints the two texts on facing pages, makes comparison of the two versions easier. The most notable differences include two scenes that appear only in the Quarto, for example, the so called 'mock trial' scene and IV.iii; the final speech of the play, delivered by Edgar in the Folio and by Albany in the Quarto; and a six-line difference in Lear's opening speech in I.i.[5]

The mock trial scene, for example, is bound to the themes of Lear's moral blindness, insight, or attainment of self-knowledge. As a result, it makes sense to ask students: what is the effect of the omission of this scene from the Folio, both on these themes and on Lear's character? Is there a consequent difference in the representation of Lear's madness in the two versions? How is madness represented in each version?

The two versions differ in an equally important scene, I.i, where we see Lear for the first time, and hear his intentions. Lear's speech in the Quarto is shorter by 6 lines than in the Folio. It omits his more descriptive reason for wishing to divide his kingdom so he can 'unburdened crawl toward death'; it omits his declaration, 'now, we will divest us both of rule/ Interest of territory, cares of state', and his justification for dividing the kingdom among his daughters so that 'we our largest bounty may extend / Where nature doth with merit challenge'. The questions arising from these differences are as follows: what is the effect of the omission or addition of these lines in Lear's opening speech? What does Lear seem to be saying in the first case and what in the second? How does the presence/absence of these words create the effects you are noticing? The omitted lines give some indication of Lear's understanding, or at least, attitude toward 'nature' at this early point, a concept that becomes increasingly relevant as the play progresses, especially in that this concept changes in the wiser Lear at the end.

The interpretations students arrive at through this approach are often different, but this difference affirms (to borrow a term from Hans Jauss) the texts' 'answering quality', their ability to 'mean' diversely to a body of readers and across great historical divides.[6] Students are encouraged to build credible arguments based on textual evidence because in large measure interpretation can be understood as a function of identity.[7] Norman Holland explains this claim in relation to William Faulkner's 'A Rose for Emily', where single terms potentially determine an interpretive context: 'since the text presents just the one word 'fathered', one cannot explain by means of the text alone why one reader would find that word heroic, another neutral and abstract, and a third sexual'.[8]

In addition to encouraging individual capacity for forming arguments, what this sort of inquiry easily leads into are pertinent generic questions based on the differences in the titles of the two versions. While the Folio prints the play under the unambiguous title, *The Tragedie of King Lear,* the title page of the Quarto refers to the play as a 'true' history, and seems to indicate Edgar's particular significance for the plot by assigning him a place in the long title: *M William Shak-speare: His True Cronicle Historie of the life and death of King Lear and his three Daughters. With the vnfortunate life of Edgar, sonne and heire to the Earle of Gloster, and his sullen and assumed humor of Tom of Bedlam.* Students can explore productively the relationship between history and tragedy in the Renaissance, as well as consider whether anything has changed in our perception of the two genres today.

The methodology underlying my questions is adapted from a number of influential reader-response theories in which interpretation is conceived of as a 'natural consequence of motivationally governed language experience'.[9] In one sense, this approach makes students aware of their own expectations raised by the text. What I ask them, in effect, is what expectations are raised by different versions of the text, and how are they related to the structure of the versions? Do the differences contribute to a sense that the finale of the play may be interpreted as 'closed' (an ending clearly marked by the resolution of all open questions or as 'open' (refusal to supply a neat ending)? Through these questions we link traditional, formalist explicative paradigms to Jauss' notions of expectations and literature as process. Literature is a process only in relation to the praxis of historical human beings, since the 'life of a work results not form its autonomous existence but rather from the reciprocal interactions of work and mankind'.[10] An emphasis on literature as interaction foregrounds the notion that reader expectations can be more productively thought of in relation to Jauss's 'horizon of expectations': each new text – or version of a text – evokes the horizon of expectations, or what Stanley Fish called 'competencies', acquired from other texts. Interpretation then results from the reader's ability to articulate those expectations with as much precision and detail as possible within the syntactic and semantic structures of the current text.

My methodology also relies on Roman Ingarden's idea that the literary work contains 'a series of places of indeterminacy' (spots of meaning not specifically determined by the text but supplied by the reader/audience), in the sense that it offers different 'schematic views' readers recognize and try to 'concretize' in

the attempt to understand its meaning.[11] The presence of these places of indeterminacy is embedded in the nature of language and the many denotative and
connotative fields of individual words that enter into equally numerous syn-
tactically-determined relationships which produce the 'answering' or 'mean-
ing-charged' quality of the text. These places of indeterminacy are even more
conspicuous in dramatic texts studied primarily as texts to be read, rather than
as blueprints for performance. In the classroom, picking up the geographic
metaphor implied in Ingarden's phrase, we discuss the endings of the two versions of *King Lear* literally as 'places of indeterminacy', since the arrangement
of text on the page is very different, and likely to produce a different emotional
effect: the 'geographical' tightness of lines of one version seemingly parallels the
characters' desire to end Lear's suffering in this world.

The pragmatic approach underscores that the interpretive agency of the
reader/viewer/editor constructs meaning. The acknowledgement of this notion
encourages involvement with the text because it empowers readers/students
who often see themselves merely as receivers of knowledge demonstrated and
transmitted by scholars and specialists. This pedagogical practice thus confronts
what Cary Nelson has called 'the collective professional illusion of objectivity'.[12]
Looking at different versions of the text and perceiving these differences clearly
encourages careful reading and reasoning, and brings to the forefront the editorial agency responsible for creating a 'third' text in performance. It introduces
students to editing, textual scholarship and bibliography, while exposing the
choice involved in the construction of the apparently immobile printed text.

The issues arising from this kind of engagement lie at the crux of the critical and interpretive enterprise, as they encourage thoughtful telescopic shifts
between the general/thematic and the particular/textual. The terms and methods traditionally used to discuss dramatic texts (theme, scene construction,
imagery, character development) serve as necessary vehicles for an integrative
instruction in critical thinking, reading, and analysis. This approach also allows
students to understand relationships among evidence, reasoning, and logic in
argumentation. They see through practice that 'all reasoning contains inferences
or interpretations by which we draw conclusions and give meaning to data',
and thus the need to 'infer only what that evidence implies'.[13] Also, they realize
that all reasoning happens from some point of view; this perception encourages
them to identify their point of view, to seek others, identify their strengths and
weaknesses, and to be fair in evaluating them. The method reveals to students
editorial involvement in the creation of what they often see as the 'monument'
of Shakespeare's plays, and thus breaks down some of the obstacles they feel
when confronted with a Renaissance text. Through this approach, they learn
that the plays at their inception and long after that were perceived as 'mobile
texts',[14] since at the time of performance several versions likely carried similar
authority. My practice thus engages the 'objectivity of the text', a notion Fish

declares 'an illusion, and moreover, a dangerous illusion, because it is so physically convincing. The illusion is one of self-sufficiency and completeness. A line of print or page of a book is so obviously *there* ... that it seems to be the sole repository of whatever value and meaning we associate with it'.[15]

The relationships between textual criticism and book history, and between reader-response theory and reading, are made more evident by recent indications that book history is shifting its attention from texts to readers, and the more explicit acknowledgment that texts cannot mean without those who read them. It has never been a better time to practice this form of integrative pedagogy. The so-called Late Print Age (following the rise of the hypermedia) ensures that the idea of the 'fluid' or 'unstable' text is no longer entirely new to our students whose daily activities, even outside the university, involve interaction with a moving screen. The changed nature of communication, data processing and management fostered by the new medium is predicated on 'disjuncture and discontinuity, fragmentation' and indeterminacy, resulting in great part from the ease with which electronic texts and images can be manipulated and modified.[16] Book history and textual study, when combined with reader-response theories, thus offer a beneficial synthesis of existing and emerging reading practices with discipline and course-specific aims, and produce a three-fold effect. They make students aware of the timelines of history in relation to authorship and audience, revealing that 'early drama texts look different, unstable and shifting' and that 'it is very doubtful whether, especially in the case of earlier plays, there ever existed any written "final form"'.[17] They foster one of the fundamental skills of the discipline of English – critical analysis. Finally, they reveal that although interpretations can be various, they ultimately have to rest on a solid basis in textual evidence.

Notes

1. Stephen Greenblatt, Walter Cohen, Jean E. Howard, and Katherine Eisaman Maus (eds), *The Norton Shakespeare, Based on the Oxford Edition,* (New York, Norton, 1997).
2. Jill L. Levenson (ed.), *The Oxford Shakespeare Romeo and Juliet,* (Oxford, Oxford University Press, 2000).
3. Jill L. Levenson, *Romeo and Juliet Prompt-Book Databases*, Centre for Renaissance and Reformation Studies: http://www.crrs.ca/publications/electronic/romeo.htm. (Accessed 7 May 2006.)
4. Levenson, *Oxford Shakespeare*, p. 111.
5. Cf. Gary Taylor and Michael Warren (eds), *The Division of Kingdoms: Shakespeare's Two Versions of King Lear* (Oxford, Oxford University Press, 1983), reprinted 2000, which details many differences between the two versions.
6. Hans Robert Jauss, Timothy Bahti trans., *Toward an Aesthetic of Reception,* (Minneapolis, University of Minnesota Press, 1982), p. 69.
7. Norman Holland, 'Unity Identity Text Self', in Jane Tompkins (ed.), *Reader-Response Criticism: From Formalism to Post-Structuralism* (Baltimore, The John Hopkins University Press, 1980), pp. 118-33.
8. Holland, p. 123.

9. David Bleich, *Subjective Criticism* (Baltimore, John Hopkins University Press, 1978), p. 139. In addition to the theorists I cite, see for example, Guglielmo Cavallo and Roger Chartier ed., *A History of Reading in the West* (Amherst, University of Massachusetts Press, 1999).

10. Jauss, p. 15.

11. Roman Ingarden, Ruth Ann Crowley and Kenneth R. Olsen trans., *The Cognition of the Literary Work of Art* (Chicago, Northwestern University Press, 1973), pp. 50-3.

12. Cary Nelson, 'Reading Criticism', *PMLA*, 91 (1976), p. 813.

13. These premises are adapted from Richard Paul and Linda Elder, *Critical Thinking: Concepts and Tools* (The Foundation for Critical Thinking, 2001).

14. Levenson, p. 103.

15. Stanley Fish, 'Literature in the Reader: Affective Stylistics', *New Literary History*, 2:1 (1970), p. 123: pp. 62,140.

16. Ronald Deibert, *Parchment, Printing and Hypermedia: Communication in World Order Transformation* (New York, Columbia University Press, 1997), pp. 179-80.

17. Levenson, p. 103.

Teaching Textual Criticism: Students as Book Detectives and Scholarly Editors

Ann R. Hawkins

In her fine essay on teaching book history to MLS students in this volume, Dierdre Stam opens with this sentiment: 'I had been teaching book history surreptitiously for years before I was lucky enough to teach it openly ... So secret was my pursuit that even I was barely aware of it' (p. 72). Like Stam, it's hard for me to identify a particular moment when I started teaching the skills of textual criticism. I seem to have always been approaching texts in these ways, from the first time I taught the two versions of Sir Thomas Wyatt's 'They flee from me' from volume one of the *Norton Anthology*. That activity – a great one for helping students see the value of individual words in creating meaning – was also (though I didn't call it that) an exercise in collation, with students identifying the differences between the versions. I still use that activity, but I now introduce students to field-specific terms. As a class we determine our 'copy-text' based on information I give them about the origins (and uses) of the different versions, and they provide their results in an actual collation formula.

I can say, however, that in the past several years, my pedagogy has become more and more directed toward teaching with textual criticism. I teach the skills involved in textual criticism because – at every level – they translate immediately into both practical research skills (the ability to use reference works to find answers) and theoretical understanding (the ability to answer such questions as who is my audience, what kinds of annotations will they need, what is the nature of my text, why is it so unstable over time, etc). In this essay I outline what I now do in many of my classes, why, and what benefits I see for students – whether sophomores in a general education courses or graduate students learning research methods.

On the sophomore level, I teach several genre-based courses such as 'Introduction to Poetry.' Since the primary audience for these courses are traditional college students majoring in something other than English, my goals focus on skills they can take with them: reading attentively and critically, using evidence appropriately and fully, knowing how to use library resources to find answers to historical, cultural and intellectual questions. Many of my students find reading attentively difficult, in part because they do not do things that good readers do. In particular, they perceive their books as more valuable than they are in their million copy print runs, and that conviction – combined with years of teachers threatening punishment if they mark in the class texts – makes them strongly opposed to writing in their *own* books. To help students understand that marking in books is a time-honored reading activity, I developed a series of assignments that placed their experiences as readers in a historical context. In class, we examine marginalia in old and rare books (in some cases using online examples) and looked at textbooks with interleaved pages of notes. Students respond to this activity by writing informally and reflectively on why readers have written in texts. Next, students read Mortimer Adler's 'How to Mark a Book,' propose a system of marking for their own uses, then mark texts as a course requirement. To this point, students are just learning about how generations of readers have interacted with their books, but the next step asks them to think like editors.

Having written in their books and thought carefully about the goals of such writing, students then go a step further. Students move from writing marginal notes for themselves, to annotating a text for their classmates. Whether using a long work divided among the class members or a group of short texts assigned individually, this activity works best if students prepare a report in advance, then articulate their findings to the class when their text (or section of it) is under discussion. These are not formal presentations but rather the student-annotator acts as a resource to the class discussion, explaining unfamiliar terms, words, and references. To do so effectively, the student-annotator needs to consider carefully the kinds of information their classmates might need and anticipate their questions with adequate research. Students do this with varying levels of success. In fact, students who work hard often put less-diligent students to task, asking questions those students ought to have anticipated. This activity decenters textual authority nicely: students don't turn for answers to the teacher (unless their classmate fails them), and students learn how to find answers for themselves. Students who have been lax in researching adequately are often taken to task by their classmates and are asked to justify their choices ('why this, but not that?'). This typically leads to discussions about the nature of editions, about the approaches that different editors take to texts, about the trustworthiness of annotations and editions, and about how to use both effectively. This discussion is essential for students who largely trust the internet to give them accurate information.

To provide their research in a more formal venue than our informal reports, students turned in annotation reports: these look just like a page of references from the back of a novel, so it's easy for students both to find models and to see the value of their work in a professional context. Reports provide page number (from their textbook), the line of the term on that page, a lemma, and their annotation. Unlike annotations in books, however, students have to cite their research within each annotation and provide a works cited page. Since in doing research, students will turn first to internet search engines, I allow that strategy explicitly. However, I stipulate that all information they find using the internet must be verified by an authoritative print source. Using the internet allows students to establish the general intellectual terrain of the detail (history, farming, cookery, biography, etc.). They then go to the library with a clear sense of purpose for the kinds of sources they need to consult. All reports are due on the same day regardless of the day of the individual presentation.

In my upper-division course for junior English majors – a survey of nineteenth-century literature – students annotate as well. But here annotation helps teach texts that are typically inaccessible, such as satires or occasional verse. For example, with Byron's satiric *English Bards and Scotch Reviewers*, annotation lets students (gleefully) discover the jokes behind all the 'names' in the poem. As in the lower-division courses, students are responsible to their classmates to explain all references in their section of text in an informal presentation. But at this level, we theorize their experience more, explicitly calling their activity 'textual editing.' As editors, students must provide information to make their 'edition' useful to a variety of reader orientations – a term and concept I adapt from Peter Shillingsburg's discussion of *editorial* orientations from *Scholarly Editing in a Computer Age.*[1] Adapted, Shillingburg's categories – documentary, aesthetic, authorial (adapted to biographical), sociological (adapted to cultural), and bibliographic – help students think about the considerations that 'real' editors have to take into account in choosing and writing their annotations.

In the junior-level class students also collate variants: with my guidance they choose a text from their anthology and investigate its stability over 10 published versions. When the class gets to their poem, students report on the status of the text, where the major/minor variants appear, and where they think the version in our book came from. This assignment benefits from our textbook's deplorable lack of copyright or source information. Using the textbook copy as their copy-text, they assign names to their source-texts, and use those abbreviations when indicating variants. Written reports include a list of variants (using standard formula), all copies of the text (with variants highlighted) and cover memo, reflecting on their experience as an editor collating variants. Students are amazed to find that texts can be very different from one version to the next (though they acknowledge that teachers have told them so).

At the senior-level, in a major authors class, students use published sources (like collected letters and journals) and facsimiles of contemporary reviews (frequently from Donald Reiman's *Romantics Reviewed* series) to write a textual history, which includes composition, publication, and contemporary reception. Students use as their models introductions to scholarly editions; we look to see the kinds of sources that editors use for their evidence, the kinds of claims that editors make from that evidence, and we assess how convincing their decisions are.

The graduate research methods courses integrates all of these activities with other basic scholarly skills. Early in the semester, we read Robert Hume's 'Aims and Uses of "Textual Studies"' which criticizes any theoretical or critical approach that doesn't take into account 'genesis', 'production', 'dissemination' and 'reception'.[2] In that intellectual context, students transcribe primary documents (letters, journals, and manuscripts of literary texts) from our rare books collection, and annotate those documents. They use the MLA's 'Questions for Vettors of Scholarly Editions' to examine several scholarly electronic editions, such as those affiliated with Jerome McGann's nines.org.[3] Understanding how their editions are evaluated, they then use their transcriptions and annotations to create a small electronic edition coded in TEI.

Graduate students also choose a text on which to write a textual history (though the graduate students overview the full reception of the text, not just contemporary reviews); and as part of that assignment, they use published editions to collate variants for a section of their chosen text.

At all levels, students typically respond to these activities with real pleasure, often finding this kind of research a kind of literary detective work. In fact, most comment that doing research is more fun than 'yet another' interpretive essay, an activity they distrust as *always* disadvantaging them in the face of the teacher's greater knowledge. Learning the skills of textual criticism, then, gives students the ability to be the 'authority' in the classroom and better equip students to understand what their teachers mean when they ask them to use 'authoritative' texts.[4]

Notes

1. Peter L. Shillingsburg, *Scholarly Editing in the Computer Age: Theory and Practice*, 3rd edn. (Ann Arbor, University of Michigan Press, 1999), pp. 17-27.
2. Robert D. Hume. 'Aims and Uses of "Textual Studies"' *Papers of the Bibliographical Society of America*, 99:2 (June 2005), pp. 197-230.
3. Committee on Scholarly Editions. Modern Language Assocation. 'Guidelines for Editors of Scholarly Editions, with Guiding Questions for Vettors, a Glossary, and an Annotated Bibliography.' September 17. 2003: http://www.iath.virginia.edu/~jmu2m/cse/ (accessed 7 May 2006); Nines, a networked interface for nineteenth-century scholarship: http://nines.org/contributors/associations.html (accessed 7 May 2006).
4. Assignment descriptions for the assignments are available at our companion website.

Afterword

Daniel Traister

What to say to a reader who has plowed through two dozen or so richly instructive and provocative essays after that journey has been completed? Anyone who teaches the history of books and printing, bibliography and methods of research, textual scholarship, or other related subjects, should find ample materials here to assist in planning classes devoted solely to such subjects or which treat them as subfields in broad courses. They will work for instructors in a college or university English, history, or history of art department, a library school, or a state or regional center for book arts, and for instructors in undergraduate or graduate classes, certificate programs, or continuing education. Covering an immense amount of the bookish waterfront, they are full of ideas, often extremely good ones. Their writers have thought usefully and carefully about many of the pedagogical issues and possibilities that classes in these related fields pose.

Nonetheless, in what follows I would like to speak not about the strengths of these essays – does any reader who has got this far in the volume need to be told about them again? – but rather to try to extend the conversation these essays provoke. That conversation, it seems, must concern not only pedagogical techniques but also the nature and purposes of the field these essays address.

One obvious issue that needs additional discussion and thought emerges from the insistence, reiterated throughout these essays, on the primacy of the material object, even though their writers also carefully tell their readers that they would never negate the merits of theorized (or 'abstract,' as one writer calls them) aspects of book studies. My orientation to this subject similarly begins with the materiality of the objects I acquire. I often pay a lot of institutional money to get them, one 'material' aspect of the book I must worry about constantly. I also assist in caring for the many material objects by which my colleagues and I are surrounded. But my orientation *begins* with the materiality of these objects. It does not *end* with their material nature – or their material cost. In the kind of institution for which I work, it cannot. I have to consider how the objects we acquire might be *used*: that is, in thinking about purchases or gifts or transfers, my colleagues and I need to ask what the intellectual, programmatic, pedagogical, and research *purposes* of the materials in question might be. Documentation of the history of books and printing will rarely justify a purchase. ('Rarely': not 'never'). There had usually better be something else.

Striking some sense of appropriate balance between the material and the 'abstract,' the theoretical, is extremely difficult. Few even of those who give it lip service actually seek to strike it; and what would 'balance' look like? Yet, however difficult a balanced relationship between the material and the theoretical might be to envisage, an *over*emphasis on the material will, in many academic contexts, have a chilling affect on future development of this field. If book history courses, on their own or in other contexts, become too tightly tied to type, presses, printing exercises, papermaking, binding exercises, and similar activities, then book history, after the initial thrill has worn off, will be in real danger of attaining the academic respectability of finger painting. It will be a kind of shop class – all right for Vo-Tech students (in American academic jargon) but not for the kind of courses in collecting and connoisseurship pioneered by Chauncey Brewster Tinker at Yale and George Parker Winship at Harvard, or the history courses taught by Robert Darnton at Princeton and Elizabeth L. Eisenstein at Michigan, or the literature courses taught by Peter Stallybrass at Penn and Evelyn Tribble at Temple and Otago.

Such academic snottiness may not be a good thing, but it is nonetheless the kind of real thing that practitioners of book history located in the academy need to consider carefully – and politically, with a weather eye on the ethos that prevails in their home institutions. My own institution forms the context of biases from within which I speak. But long observation, at several institutions, of the relative institutional esteem of art history vs. fine arts, of English literature vs. writing (or even creative writing), or – more troublesome still, for in this example the balance is clearly shifting – of Arts and Sciences vs. Business or Engineering, convinces me that my experience reflects a reality far more common than not.

Technological determinism, which many book historians adopt as part of the materialist air we breathe, poses related issues. When, for instance, the growth of literacy is related primarily to technological advances in the printing press, but other factors are ignored, I sense a problem. Of course, changes in the technology of printing and of papermaking are important. So too, however, are developments in mass public education. Studies of France, Germany, Russia, the United Kingdom, and the United States, among others, have long demonstrated that, in the nineteenth century and on into the twentieth, mass public education was not simply a publicly-funded response to the need of book- and newspaper-printers, now able to print more, to increase the markets for their increased numbers of products. It was seen, and rightly, as serving other important social and economic needs in industrializing societies. Literacy was (from some points of view, unfortunately and dangerously) a necessary foundation for altogether other purposes. This is a point more easily recognized, perhaps, when expanded literacy and the press are studied in relation to the progress of the Protestant Reformation than when the object of study is a much later historical period. A related although slightly different question occurs to someone whose training is literary, not historical: can one, *should* one, teach nineteenth-century developments in printing technology without attending, at least a bit, to Balzac, to Hardy, to Gissing? (We already know, with respect to the Reformation, that to omit not only printers but also Luther, Erasmus, and Tyndale, would be mistaken. Is it not just as mistaken to omit Rabelais or Jonson?)

Some of the most interesting recent studies in the fields broadly construed as book history impress me by how greatly *non*-'material' and *non*-technological factors influence all of them. Four monographs – chosen at random, from those on my desk as I prepared this essay, and presented in chronological order of their topics – exemplify this point.

André Du Ryer, the first person known to have translated the entire Koran directly from the Arabic into a European vernacular, published *L'alcoran de Mahomet* in Paris (1647). The Englishman Robert of Ketton had been among those who produced a Latin translation in Toledo around the year 1145. Although several manuscript translations were produced, his became the basis of Andrea Arrivabene's Italian version of the Koran (Venice, 1547) and, later, of Salomon Schweigger's German version (Nürnberg, 1616). Du Ryer took a fresh look at the Arabic text, reflecting new developments in European 'Orientalist' studies. As I write about these texts, it is unnecessary to point out the contemporary importance – which extends far beyond the worlds of printing historians – of studies of Christian-Islamic interrelationships past and present. From some perspectives, it must be noted (whether or not one agrees – and *without* suggesting *any* other parallel between these texts other than the importance of knowing something about them at first hand!), this subject is as significant as that studied by the printing historians James J. Barnes and Patience P. Barnes in *Hitler's* Mein Kampf *in Britain and America: A Publishing History, 1930-39.* [1] That book also asked how knowledge of an important text circulated, or failed to circulate, among people who would be making life-and-death decisions based on their knowledge and understanding of what that text contained. Clearly these are more than book history questions. But they *are* book history questions too. Alastair Hamilton and Francis Richard's *André Du Ryer and Oriental Studies in Seventeenth-Century France* exemplifies how they can be answered with an eye on developments in language study, travel, the history of libraries, and the production and dissemination of manuscripts and printed books.[2] The means by which books such as the Koran or *Mein Kampf* get written, printed (or copied), published, distributed, and received are technological *and* cultural, social. The materiality of the production process, and of the object, does not by itself account for its ability to circulate to the audiences that need to know about it.

A massive study by a retired civil servant (at the Bank of England), William St Clair's *The Reading Nation in the Romantic Period* is informed by an acute consciousness of the details of quotidian life (the material basis of book history).[3] How those details can matter is suggested, for me, by an exercise suggested by several essays in this volume: reading by candlelight. Of course, this is a useful experience for the young, although over the years I have found myself reading by candlelight surprisingly often, whenever the power goes off – as it does during thunderstorms perhaps once or twice a year where I live – and I don't see any special problem with this form of illumination. St Clair corrects my dull misapprehension at the drop of a sentence: '*Frankenstein* by firelight is a different reading experience from *Frankenstein* in a university library'.[4] Now *that* is 'technological determinism' with a vengeance. But it is not simply technological in its insightful combination of technology with a specific literary effect. With an eye both on the 'consequences' of reading and the 'materiality of print,' the details of how and where books got into readers' hands, and stories about what readers do with the stuff they read, St Clair extends the ways in which his readers think about the expansion of the printing industry and of literacy during the nineteenth century. He also provides an enormous amount of sheer data, not only in his text but also in appendices that, *inter alia*, record prices, print runs, and the genres of printed materials, describe libraries and reading societies, and summarize an impressive amount of Shakespearian printing history through the nineteenth century.

A biographical study of a printer and printing historian that looks at the life, the business, the books, and the esthetic and intellectual product of its subject in ways that cross disciplinary bounds is Irene Tichenor's *No Art Without Craft: The Life of Theodore Low De Vinne*.[5] Tichenor looks with equal ease at credit relationships and architecture while keeping her eye clearly on her subject's contribution to intellectual history. One can no longer study the history of the history of books and printing without knowing of De Vinne and his relation to nineteenth-century American social and commercial life. Tichenor's book is immersed in details about craft and means of production, the materials, and the physical remains, of De Vinne's output. Rooted in De Vinne's physical books, and itself designed with a bibliographic audience in mind, *No Art Without Craft* extends its branches over a much larger area.

Wanting anything that could be considered elegance of design, James F. English's *The Economy of Prestige: Prizes, Awards, and the Circulation of Cultural Value* brilliantly – and amusingly – studies one important mechanism through which books get to readers, and then may find themselves part of the canon of stuff that readers continue to read.[6] By examining the culture and the effects of prizes (Nobels, Pulitzers, National Book Awards, National Book Critics Circle Awards, Bookers, Oranges, Goncourts, and so forth; film awards also come in for consideration here), English describes the ways in which, in their hundreds and thousands, they affect the choices that bookstores, reviewers, readers, and teachers make about what to promote, read, and teach. He does not ignore the material – some of the photographs he prints of what actual prizes look like are almost literally unbelievable. So are some of the stories he tells. (Does anyone really think judges *read* the books they judge? English provides quotations to confirm the very darkest of suspicions.) English begins with facts – here are the prizes; here is how they are awarded; this is what they look like. His concern is the significance of these facts for issues that matter not only to book historians but also to students of literature, cultural practice, and contemporary life.

None of these books ignores the material base from which book history and its pedagogies must begin. But if each starts there, none rests there, either. Each takes its subject in directions – intellectual and educational history; readership and distribution; commercial life; publicity and canonization processes – that make book history a subject able to elicit academic status and standing. Such status and standing, of course, may not be the only end one can strive for. But in the academic world – in which books like these and essays like those contained in this volume get written, and in which courses such as those this volume is intended to assist get taught – it is not an end easy to ignore.

Student familiarity with the material objects and processes by which books come into existence – books themselves; presses; type; illustration and binding techniques, and so forth – matters. But so does the intellectual and societal context out of which these objects and processes emerge or for which they have been produced – or the context in which they are under discussion, their 'matter' or 'subject matter.' If the embrace of the material object and its universe of 'fact,' materiality, even *hints* that it is also a way to reject theorized modes of discourse, still dominant in humanities and social science faculties throughout the academic world, then materialistically-oriented book history will be in trouble. Such rejection or deferral of the theoretical will also be a means, possibly unintended but not ineffective for that reason, of limiting the sorts of explorations book historians can undertake, the sorts of knowledge book historians can produce. Point of view, 'subject position', does make a difference. People looking at the objects of book history from the perspective of a history of technology or a musicology program will see, will 'foreground', different issues. For some purposes, the material *is* the 'context' and the context (or content) *is* the 'matter.'

Years ago, Robert Darnton asked a question that has not, I think, yet been answered satisfactorily. *What is the history of books?* Can we expect it to be the same thing for people who study medieval plainsong, or papermaking in North Africa in the tenth century, or literacy and industrialization in south America, or the textual tradition of Torquato Tasso, or technological innovation in the American northeast during the nineteenth century, or the illustrations of the *Hypnerotomachia Poliphili* or *The Yellow Book*, or bookbinding practices in Humanist Florence or colonial Philadelphia, or the dissemination of the poetry of Guillaume de Machaut in fifteenth-century Europe, or of Zionism in eastern Europe before World War I? I do not think so.

A field that is (genuinely!) interdisciplinary not only lacks an address – where does one *find* the book historians at one's own institution? – it also offers opportunities. These might include jointly-taught classes. Why not unite in one classroom the different voices and distinct perspectives of a historian and a literature instructor looking at how revolutionary ideas spread in France before the Revolution? of religious and book historians looking at transmission of Buddhist texts in China through the T'ang dynasty? of a humanist and a technological historian looking at developments in novel writing and distribution and the growth of printing and transportation technology in mid-twentieth century America? of an art historian and an economist looking at the Dutch print trade in the seventeenth century? Perhaps such cross-disciplinary courses and conversations will assist our efforts to understand better than we now do the nature of the field in which we labor.

Perhaps they will even assist us in reaching some definition of this field that satisfactorily answers Darnton's question. Or perhaps these and other efforts will help us think about other questions. Does anyone even want the history of books to *be* a 'field', in fact, to *have* an address? For many years, bibliography and textual scholarship were cheerful 'handmaidens' to a variety of disciplines. Lacking disciplinary status of their own, they served the interests and needs of students of literature, music, philosophy, art history, codicology, and the history of science. Book history has come to subsume those earlier handmaiden fields. As yet, however, no one seems certain whether it remains a handmaiden or aspires to 'field' status in its own right – an academic address.

The essays in this volume offer useful hints, useful tools, to assist people teaching those courses that now exist. But they assume – necessarily – that there is a field out there whose pedagogy they assist. What there is, however, is not yet a field but rather a miscellaneous mélange of more or less vaguely related courses. To pedagogy in this still unsettled field, these essays clearly contribute most usefully. But another, perhaps equally major, service they can provide might be provocation of one or more of their readers to ask why they speak to so many different, and not always easily reconcilable, classroom and intellectual concerns. Speaking as they do to an as yet unsettled present, these essays, this volume, suggest the need for future consideration and discussion that builds on what has here been assumed.

Notes

1. James J. Barnes and Patience P. Barnes, *Hitler's* Mein Kampf *in Britain and America: A Publishing History, 1930-39* (Cambridge, Cambridge University Press, 1980).
2. Alastair Hamilton and Francis Richard, *André Du Ryer and Oriental Studies in Seventeenth-Century France*, Studies in the Arcadian Library, no. 1 (Geneva and Oxford, Oxford University Press, 2004).
3. William St Clair, *The Reading Nation in the Romantic Period* (Cambridge, Cambridge University Press, 2004).
4. Ibid, p. 394.
5. Irene Tichenor, *No Art Without Craft: The Life of Theodore Low De Vinne* (Boston, David R. Godine, 2005).
6. James F. English, *The Economy of Prestige: Prizes, Awards, and the Circulation of Cultural Value* (Cambridge, MA: Harvard University Press, 2005).

Resources

The following list of resources is highly selective, culled from the recommendations of the writers in this book for what they have used and found useful in class. Other resources are listed on our companion website: http://www.pickeringchatto.com/bookhistory.htm.

Organizations

American Printing History Association, http://www.printinghistory.org/
Association for Documentary Editing, http://etext.lib.virginia.edu/ade/
Bibliographical Society of America, http://www.bibsocamer.org/
Bibliographical Society (London), http://www.bibsoc.org.uk/
Bibliographical Society of the University of Virginia, http://etext.lib.virginia.edu/bsuva/
European Society for Textual Scholarship, http://www.textualscholarship.org/ests/
Society for Textual Scholarship, http://www.textual.org/
Society for the History of Authorship, Reading and Publishing, http://sharpweb.org
    SHARP's website offers an extensive list of online research resources, scholarly societies, online exhibits, teaching resources, etc.

Training Programs for Faculty

Rare Book School, founded in 1983, offers one-week courses across the US in the history of books and printing and related topics. http://www.virginia.edu/oldbooks
Texas A&M's Cushing Memorial Library hosts a one-week workshop each May in the History of Books and Printing Book History, providing hands-on experience with type casting and setting, binding, paper making, running a common press, etc. http://library.tamu.edu/cushing/bookhistory/
The Institut d'Histoire du Livre at Lyons organizes seminars and conferences in support of book history research. http://ihl.enssib.fr/index_eng.htm
The University of London's Centre for Manuscript and Print Studies offers one-day courses and an intensive one-week summer school in book history

and related topics. http://www2.sas.ac.uk/ies/cmps/Events/Courses/SummerSchool/index.htm

For other educational programs, see RBS's list of 'related institutes around the world', http://www.virginia.edu/oldbooks/2006/related/

Electronic Discussion Lists

BookArts-L focuses on the book arts, but can be useful for projects, modern-day examples, supplies, etc. http://palimpsest.stanford.edu/byform/mailing-lists/bookarts/

Exlibris specializes in rare book and manuscript librarianship, including special collections and related issues. http://palimpsest.stanford.edu/byform/mailing-lists/exlibris/

Humanist Discussion Group focuses on issues surrounding 'humanities computing and the digital humanities'. http://www.princeton.edu/humanist

Lis-libhist, the discussion list of the Library and Information History Group, examines the history of libraries and librarianship. http://www.cilip.org.uk/groups/lhg/mailing.html

SEDIT-L is the Scholarly Editing Forum of the Association for Documentary Editing. https://listserv.umd.edu/archives/sedit-l.html

SHARP-L records conversations related to the history of print culture. http://sharpweb.org/sharp-l.html

Bibliographic Indexes online

Book History Online, http://www0.kb.nl/bho/
British Book Trade Index, http://www.bbti.bham.ac.uk

Scholarly Journals online

Studies in Bibliography, http://etext.lib.virginia.edu/bsuva/sb/
Papers of the Bibliographical Society of America, http://www.bibsocamer.org/Papers/default.htm

Helpful websites for class or class preparation

Terry Belanger, 'Descriptive Bibliography', http://www.bibsocamer.org/bibdef.htm

The Book Guys, web archive of programs broadcast on US National Public Radio, http://www.bookguys.com/archives.htm

Book History Chronology, part of the Book Information website, http://www.
xs4all.nl/~knops/timetab.html

Richard W. Clement, 'Glossary of terms for pre-industrial book history', http://
www.kansas.edu/~bookhist/glossary.html

Richard Clement, 'Medieval and Renaissance Book Production – Manuscript
Books',
http://www.kansas.edu/~bookhist/medbook1.html

English Renaissance in Context (ERIC) provides online tutorials on textual
issues surrounding early modern texts.
http://dewey.library.upenn.edu/sceti/furness/eric/> - online

HoBo offers a useful 'snapshot' of the field as a whole. http://www.english.
ox.ac.uk/hobo/

Selected Digital Collections

100 Highlights from the Koninklijke Bibliotheek digitizes images of the 'most
beautiful and most interesting' books and manuscripts in its collection
http://www.kb.nl/kb/100hoogte/hh-en.html

English Emblem Book Project, Penn State University Libraries, http://emblem.
libraries.psu.edu/

The *Gutenberg Bible* – digitized – is available at three sites:
- British Library, London, http://www.bl.uk/treasures/gutenberg/
homepage.html
- Goettingen State and University Library, Germany, http://www.guten-
bergdigital.de/gudi/start.htm
- Harry Ransom Center, University of Texas, http://www.hrc.utexas.
edu/exhibitions/permanent/gutenberg/

Literary Manuscript Analysis (*LIMA*) includes links to online watermark archives
like Gravell and Briquet. http://www2.warwick.ac.uk/fac/arts/ren/publica-
tions/lima/

Schoenberg Center for Electronic Text and Image (*SCETI*) offers 'virtual facsimiles of rare books and manuscripts in the Penn Library's collections'.
http://dewey.lib.upenn.edu/sceti/

Shakespeare in Quarto, British Library, London, http://www.bl.uk/treasures/
shakespeare/homepage.html

Useful Audio-Visuals

RBS prints a catalog of its Video/DVD holdings, which includes contact and
ordering information for all holdings. $10.

Anatomy of a Book: I: Format in the Hand Press Period (1991), 30 minutes. DVD includes *The Making of a Renaissance Book* (1969) 30 minutes. From RBS. $60.

Basic Reproduction Processes in the Graphic Arts." (1963; 16mm color film), 25 minutes. Distributed by Graphic Arts Films Inc, Box 176. Glenville Station, Greenwich CT 06830.

Farewell Etaoin Shrdlu: An Age-Old Printing Process Gives Way to Modern Technology (1980; originally color 16mm film), 30 minutes. Written, produced and directed by David Loeb Weiss; narrated by Carl Schlesinger. DVD distributed by Carl Schlesinger, 39 Myrtle St, Rutherford, NJ 07070; 201-935-5504. $53.

From Punch to Printing Type: The Art and Craft of Hand Punchcutting and Typefounding, with Stan Nelson (1985), 45 minutes. DVD includes *How to Operate a Book, with Gary Frost* (1986), 30 minutes. From RBS. $60.

Infinite Secrets: The Genius of Archimedes, [the recovery of the Archimedes palimpsest], 60 minutes. VHS/DVD distributed by WGBH Video, P.O. Box 2284, South Burlington, VT 05407; 888-255-9231; http://shop.wgbh.org. $20.

Making of a Renaissance Book (1969), 30 minutes. Produced by Dana Atchley. VHS/DVD includes *Anatomy of a Book* as described above. From RBS. $60.

Out of the Ashes: Recovering the Lost Library of Herculaneum. VHS/DVD distributed by Brigham Young University; 800-962-8061; http://creativeworks.byu.edu/catalog/index.php; $20/25.

Papermaking. Five programs of various lengths on VHS/DVD, documenting Western and Japanese-style papermaking. Produced and distributed by University of Iowa Center for the Book. The Western II and the Japanese III tapes cover the routines the Center for Paper Research uses in making papers for rare book and art conservation. http://www.uiowa.edu/~ctrbook/store/videos.html. Five-program set, $250; individual programs, $60.

The Parchment Makers: An Ancient Art in Present-Day Ethiopia. VHS distributed by Hope College, International Education, 112 East 12th Street, Holland, MI 49423; 616-395-7605. $20

A World Inscribed: The Illuminated Manuscript (1996), 24 minutes. Written, produced, and directed by Kathleen McDonough. VHS/DVD distributed by Films for the Humanities and Science, 12 Perrine Road, Monmouth Junction, NJ 06852; 800-257-5126, http://www.films.com. ISBN: 1-4213-1661-7. $90.

Supplies

Facsimile Chainline Paper for teaching the principles of bibliographical format. Sheets of 11" x 15" paper with schematic deckles, chainlines, tranchefiles, a watermark and a countermark printed on both sides of each sheet. From RBS. 25 sheets, $10; 100 sheets, $25; Ream of 500 sheets, $100.

Facsimiles of Bibliographical Format. A set of six facsimile sheets showing various bibliographical formats (2º, 4º, 8º, 8º in half-sheet imposition, 12º in 12s, 12º in 6s). Each set includes eighteen format sheets (three copies of each of the six facsimiles), ten sheets of facsimile chainline paper (see description above) and the Format DVD workbook. From RBS. $35.

Facsimile early printed books in signatures (without boards). Colonial Williamsburg Printer's Shop, P. O. Box 1776, Williamsburg, VA 23187-1776; 757-229-1000; Priced by title, $8-$18.

Paper Specimens Set. University of Iowa Center for the Book. Center for the Paper Research and Production Facility. Oakdale Campus. Iowa City, IA 52242; 319-335-4410; handmade-paper@uiowa.edu; http://www.uiowa.edu/~ctrbook/store/handmadepaper.html

Historical Bookbinding Model Set for Teaching. Ten model books from various cultures and periods. Iowa Book Works (Gary Frost) http://iowabookworks.bookways.com/ or http://iowabookworks.bookways.com/stories/storyReader$41. $3000.

Other Equipment

Collator

The Comet, Contact Carter Hailey, Assistant Professor of English, Tucker Hall, The College of William and Mary, Williamsburg, VA 23187.

Lights

Zelco Micro Fluorescent Lanterns. Available from various vendors, e.g. Kitchen & Home Gadgets, http://store.yahoo.com/dotcoms/zemiflla10.html. $25.

Magnifiers

a. 10x Peak loupes

B & H Photo, 420 Ninth Avenue, New York, NY 10001; 800-606-6969; http://www.bhphotovideo.com, Item no. PK203210 (B&H Catalog # PE2032). $10.

b. 60x pocket microscopes

RBS recommends the Radio Shack MM-100, 60-100x Illuminated Microscope, catalog number 63-1313. $10.

Carson Optical MicroMax MM-100, 60-100x lighted Microscope, http://www.carson-optical.com/scopes.html. $15.

c. ProScope

Scalar 10-50-100x ProScope digital microscope, http://www.theproscope.com/ or http://www.scalarscopes.com/usbsupport/. $100.

Index